My Favourite People and Me
1978–1988

My Favourite
People and Me
1978–1988

ALAN DAVIES

MICHAEL JOSEPH

Published by the Penguin Group

Penguin Books Ltd, 80 Strand, London WC2R 0RL, England

Penguin Group (USA) Inc., 375 Hudson Street, New York, New York 10014, USA

Penguin Group (Canada), 90 Eglinton Avenue East, Suite 700, Toronto, Ontario, Canada M4P 2Y3
(a division of Pearson Penguin Canada Inc.)

Penguin Ireland, 25 St Stephen's Green, Dublin 2, Ireland (a division of Penguin Books Ltd)

Penguin Group (Australia), 250 Camberwell Road, Camberwell, Victoria 3124, Australia
(a division of Pearson Australia Group Pty Ltd)

Penguin Books India Pvt Ltd, 11 Community Centre, Panchsheel Park, New Delhi – 110 017, India

Penguin Group (NZ), 67 Apollo Drive, Rosedale, North Shore 0632, New Zealand
(a division of Pearson New Zealand Ltd)

Penguin Books (South Africa) (Pty) Ltd, 24 Sturdee Avenue, Rosebank, Johannesburg 2196, South Africa

Penguin Books Ltd, Registered Offices: 80 Strand, London WC2R 0RL, England

www.penguin.com

First published 2009

2

Copyright © Alan Davies, 2009

The moral right of the author has been asserted

Set in 13.5/16 pt Monotype Garamond
Typeset by Rowland Phototypesetting Ltd, Bury St Edmunds, Suffolk
Printed in Great Britain by Clays Ltd, St Ives plc

A CIP catalogue record for this book is available from the British Library

ISBN: 978–0–718–15487–5

This edition produced for The Book People Ltd, Hall Wood Avenue, Haydock, St Helens WA11 9UL

www.greenpenguin.co.uk

Contents

Introduction

Growing up, every year brings new people with attributes to admire or ideas to inspire. Remembering those times and looking back over the heroes and villains of my own younger life led me to consider why I thought the world of such and such a person when now I don't give them a second thought. Which of them were just passing through my world, while I was passing through a phase, and which of them had an influence that was lasting, for better or worse? Soon I started to arrive at a list of my favourite people, not all obviously heroic, just personal icons.

The process of evolving from an unknown figure, through the admirer's first awareness, to icon status can be a rapid one, particularly if the person attributing that status is young, impressionable, and pink with naïvety. Before sharing my list I considered researching historical, political, cultural and sporting events to beef up the collection of heroes, to strive for a wider significance. A couple of things undermined the value of detailed research, in my mind.

One was the realization that the significance, to me, of one of the most important events of 1981, the attempted assassination of US president Ronald Reagan, was the recollection of my dad's indifference when I called out to him in the kitchen:

'Reagan's been shot!'

I repeated the shock news and when he came in to look at the television, he said:

'Oh, I thought you meant Regan in *The Sweeney*.'

Of course, John Thaw's character in *The Sweeney* was pronounced R*ee*gan, whereas the president went for Raygun. The point is that anyone's memory of significant events is so couched in the where and when of their own life that there seemed no way of establishing the true influences on me by trawling through old newspapers and history websites. World events connect with individual lives un-expectedly and the connections that matter to me are those that are lodged in my mind still.

1978 was really the year when I started venturing out more, without adults, with other eleven-, twelve- and thirteen-year-olds. The year in which the accumulation of personal heroes accelerated.

1988 was the year I graduated from university to pursue the possibility that stand-up comedy could be an alternative to finding a job where I'd have to do what I was told, some-thing I was struggling with at the time. Stand-up would also afford me the chance to continue mimicking heroes well into adulthood and, in fact, might allow the postponement of adulthood altogether.

The second thing that happened that deflated my interest in research was an early attempt at just that. The first port of call for researching anything, now and for the foreseeable future, is the infernal interweb, accessed, more often than not, by the mind control device that is Google. I typed 1982 into my Google box and was predictably offered the assistance of the eagerly unreliable and peculiarly selective Wikipedia site. I scrolled down to August 1982 and these were the only six entries:

August 4 – The United Nations Security Council votes to
censure Israel because its troops are still in Lebanon.

August 7 – Italian Prime Minister Giovanni Spadolini resigns.

August 12 – Mexico announces it is unable to pay its large foreign debt, triggering a debt crisis that quickly spread throughout Latin America.

August 13 – In Hong Kong, health warnings on cigarette packets are made statutory.

August 17 – The first compact discs (CDs) are released to the public in Germany.

August 20 – Lebanese Civil War: A multinational force lands in Beirut to oversee the PLO withdrawal from Lebanon. French troops arrive August 21, US Marines August 25.

I'm not suggesting that the break-up of The Jam should have been noted as a world event twenty-six years later but, for me, August 1982 meant going to one of their farewell gigs at Wembley Arena before searching through Camden Market to find a bootleg tape of the gig. I've lost the tape but I still have the poster.

I considered that to be the most important event of August 1982, until there was a knock on my front door only minutes after writing the above paragraph. A package had arrived for me, containing *The Guinness Book of British Hit Singles and Albums* that I'd ordered the day before. I had been looking for my old copy, to check that some song or other had fallen between 1978 and 1988, only to discover that it not only fell apart in my hands, but had been published in 1978.

The new book shows that The Jam charted with *Beat Surrender*, their farewell single, in December 1982. Another search led me to www.thejam.org.uk which shows the farewell gigs also to have been in December 1982. It actually shows only one at Wembley when I know (or I think I do) that four extra dates were added.

So, I decided on a new policy: fact-checking, a safety net for my addled memory. Rushing back to Wikipedia, in case I had doubted it unadvisedly, I checked entries for December 1982. Unless you're a regular at Times Beach, Missouri, they are largely forgettable, apart from Marty Feldman dying in Mexico. Oh, and Greenham Common, but more of that later:

December 2 – British comedian and writer Marty Feldman dies in Mexico.

December 3 – A final soil sample is taken from the site of Times Beach, Missouri. It is found to contain 300 times the safe level of dioxin.

December 7 – The first US execution by lethal injection is carried out in Texas.

December 12 – Women's peace protest at Greenham Common: 30,000 women hold hands and form a human chain around the 14.5 km (9 mi) perimeter fence.

December 23 – The United States Environmental Protection Agency recommends the evacuation of Times Beach, Missouri due to dangerous levels of dioxin contamination.

December 26 – *Time Magazine*'s Man of the Year is given for the first time to a non-human, the computer.

Scrolling down the page brings you to my favourite entry for 1982. It's the only one in a section for the year marked 'Ongoing' and reads simply:

Cold War.

Some things need to be established before picking through the people who inspired and influenced, initially in my teenage years, and then through four years at university, with all the malnourished frowning with episodes of ideal-istic ambition (and constipation) that I endured there. I'll rephrase that: the four years of playing pool in the pub (and constipation) that I enjoyed there.

I was born on 6 March 1966 and my star sign is Pisces. Which must mean nothing, surely, as horoscopes are an escapist fantasy, except that I really like fish, I eat it all the time, pollock, haddock, mackerel, all sorts, and I'm Pisces. Unrelated? Surely not.

My top 10 fish

1. Tuna, but we shouldn't eat that because they're dying out. The same goes for
2. Anchovies.
3. Salmon, but, watch out, are they farmed and if so are they getting out, mixing with the wild salmon, and then producing young who can't remember the way upriver to the spawning grounds? Think on.
4. Cod, because, am I right, they use it for taramasalata? Cod roe? Anyway, it's lovely with chips but it's been overfished, so think on.

5. Haddock. Get a piece from Steve Hatt on the Essex Rd in Islington, or your local fishmonger, whichever is nearest. Then go to the herb rack in your grocery store where they might have a little jar with 'fish' on it. It's a mixture of herbs but primarily dill. Sprinkle liberally on your haddock and grill it for 10–15 minutes. Lush, lush, lush.
6. Trout. Often have that in Italian restaurants. They're good with capers, your Italians. That is to say the capers go on the fish, not on the Italian.
7. Sardines. On toast or with potatoes. Lovely.
8. Monkfish. I didn't realize, they only use the tail. Meaty and thick. Ugliest fish you'll ever see. Poor sod, just looks a mess.
9. Rock. Get this from the chippy. Bit chewier and more flavour.
10. Swordfish. Growing up I imagined swordfish as lethal. They looked so fearsome in pictures, as if they could saw your arm off, but actually they're quite nice for tea, it turns out.

My top 10 fish from the early '70s
(by way of comparison)

1. Fish fingers. Cod ones.
2. Fish from the chip shop. Don't know what it was but very likely cod.
3. Boil in the bag cod with parsley sauce.
4. Plaice with chips and peas.
5. Haddock with chips and peas.

6. Prawn cocktail.
7. Tbc.
8. No data.
9. Tba.
10. Goldfish, in a clear bag from the fair but you don't eat them. Also, you don't necessarily flush them when they float on the top of the water. They might not be dead. Sadly we didn't know that in our house in the '70s and several went down the lavatory who may have been alive.

Loughton is in Epping Forest, which straddles the border between Essex and Greater London. At different times both Boadicea (that's the '70s spelling) and Dick Turpin used the forest to hide out in but nowadays it's on the Central Line. That's the long red one that goes across the middle of the tube map for those of you who have been to London. For those of you who haven't been to London: What are you *doing*? Get your *act* together. Is someone *reading* this to you?

Although London isn't to everyone's taste. I met a woman from Preston once who told me, in a broad Lancashire accent, that the trouble with London is:

'It hasn't got any good shops. There isn't really a High Street as such.'

I've no idea where she'd been, she said London but maybe she'd disembarked at Euston, thought Tie Rack and WH Smith a poor show, and gone home. She can't have, though, because she also said:

'There was one place that were good, now what were it called . . .? Oh yes, TGI Fridays! Have you been?'

I hadn't, even though I like stripes.

'You should go, it's brilliant.'

In 1992 I did a stand-up gig in Preston and The Temptations were playing in the same building. The Temptations! I love them and they were playing the Guildhall, Preston, even though at least two of them were dead. I snuck in next to the mixing desk and watched 1,500 Lancastrians, on their feet, singing that they were doing fine on cloud nine. Joyous.

I was going to say Loughton was boring but that seems harsh. Soporific is fair though; so is quiet, and boring.

My mum had died of leukaemia in 1972 so I lived with my dad, elder brother and younger sister. I seemed to drive the family mental. Every day I looked into the eyes of at least one exasperated relative. The mantra in our house was:

'What are we going to do with you?'

They were The Exasperated. Which would be a good film title perhaps. It brings to mind *The Departed*. Bagsy Mark Wahlberg to play me. Sadly, Adam Woodyatt was more me (that's Ian Beale from *EastEnders*, so you're clear).

I went to Staples Road County Primary, which I liked, particularly because of the surrogate parenting of our twenty-three-year-old teacher, Mrs Thorogood, but in 1976 I started at Bancroft's School in Woodford Green, which was *either*:

a) an old-fashioned English institution that drummed stuffy, outdated pre-war values into pupils suffocating in modish, post-war nylon shirts

or

b) a Minor Public School with an exceptional exam record and reasonably good personal hygiene in the staff room.

It was both actually, so less ambiguity there than I intimated. No ambiguity about the prefects though. They were tossers.

By 1978 I was cycling everywhere and wanting to go out a lot more, which I was allowed to do a bit, as I was nearly twelve and starting to grow up. This book covers that growing up from 1978 to 1988. It is intended to be a nostalgic trawl with a little anecdotal back-up. An attempt to remember who and what I liked as a boy/youth/idiot and to work out why.

There are also some pictures.

1978

Barry Sheene

In 1978 I collected stickers assiduously, doggedly, obsessively and privately, in a fog of seeking and accumulating. There was a sticker book called *Motorcycle 78* and another called *Football 78* and filling the appropriate space with the appropriate image was satisfying but no cheap thrill. I was also afflicted with a potent, potentially upsetting, not to mention pricey, emotional attachment to Arsenal Football Club that had taken root early in the decade and by 1978 ought to have been a source of concern for those who ought to have been concerned. By then though I was an eleven-year-old pathological liar and kleptomaniac so why would anyone be concerned?

In 1978 I had joined the Barry Sheene Appreciation Society, the Starsky & Hutch Fan Club and the Arsenal Supporters Club. I was an enthusiastic joiner. I loved having membership cards. I wanted to belong to something, to feel part of a group, a collective. Perhaps, in part, this was tribal boy stuff, looking for societies and clubs and gangs. For me though, these were solitary activities. *My* things that *I* liked. I didn't join to meet people. Deeply ingrained in my siblings and me throughout our growing up was a fear of new people and the perils associated with them, principally of conversation, of having to listen or contribute to it, for a time rarely specified, often with no end in sight. This was a reason to be fearful and we became expert solo players. To this day I have no interest in hooking my games console to the internet. I'll play alone, thank you. Fortunately when you're eleven, so long as it's not too late, or *too far away,* you can go out by yourself and ride your bike by yourself and in doing so you can become Barry Sheene, by yourself.

Barry Sheene raced motorbikes, by himself. He was World Champion, by himself. He was cocky and cool and he'd been smashed to pieces a couple of times in horrific 170 mph accidents so he was held together by screws. He was also good-looking in a dimply, tousled, grinning, disobedient sort of way which appeared to me to be the best way to be good-looking and something to aspire to.

Hurtling down our front drive (sloping speckled Tarmac) and out on to Spring Grove, I could career into Mr Newby's front drive (flat crazy-paving) next door before heading back again, which constituted a lap. It was a decent-sized lap as we lived in big houses with big gardens in leafy suburban Loughton, out on the edge of North-east London.

Despite the London proximity, the Central Line station and the 01 phone number, people were generally proudly and resolutely Essex. Chingford, where I was born and spent the first couple of years, was now London E4, though most of its residents would have nothing to do with their new urban postcode. Many of their grandparents had moved out to Chingford for their health, to get away from the smog and grime of London, and the last thing they wanted was for the dirty old town to catch them up.

The poor next-door Newbys. Eventually they must have had a quiet word with my dad about the endless Grand Prix-length repetitious solo bike riding of his second son. Whether they were really bothered about the cycling or the enthusiastic Murray Walker-style commentary that accompanied it is hard to say. They may just have thought I was obsessively lapping the two drives for a very long time and that I was heading for social misfitness (I was) with few friends (none to speak of) and I could do with varying my activities (I would if someone would *buy me a skateboard*).

Well, that's all very well for you to say, Newbys, with your functional relationships and family jaunts up the Matterhorn and suchlike but some of us are going mad with Sheeneitis as there's little else to do at the moment. I'll stop when *Grange Hill* comes on, OK? I have a crush on Tricia Yates, and Tucker Jenkins has enough of Barry Sheene about him to enjoy.

The Newbys were actually very tolerant in the face of repeated incursions into their property, with footballs and cricket balls finding their way over their fence, several slats of which were bashed and cracked. They rarely complained about my scrumping (their crunchy red apples which were nicer than those on any of our three trees. I didn't call it scrumping then, I called it nicking and I thought I was good at it and moved unseen). The most exciting time, though, was when I set off their burglar alarm, with a boomerang that did not so much come back as go next door.

Barry Sheene was, in fact, a double World Champion, in 1976 and 1977, and a national hero. We had a car racing champion in 1976 too, James Hunt, but he was a posh'un and it perhaps said something about you, which of them you preferred. Hunt was a racing driver, which was apparently cool and something to wish to be, without appealing to me, but then it was also a commonly held belief that all boys wanted to be train drivers, which was not true. I didn't. Why drive something that has to go on someone else's tracks? Especially as the drivers could no longer hang perilously from an open-sided cab like Casey Jones while they were a-steamin'an'a-rollin'.

Hunt had a funny peculiar round-shouldered gait when he competed on *Superstars*, which counted against him. He was also a bit ill-tempered in competition and sounded posh. It was not cool to be well-spoken, like my dad. It was cool to sound working class and a bit cockney, like Barry Sheene. Nowadays, the peculiar mixed-race, hip-hop inspired *patois* of Britain's youth causes mirth and exasperation in equal measure when adopted by adolescents in the bespoke kitchens of Southern England. Similarly, in the '70s, it drove parents mad that their kids wanted to sound like the Artful Dodger and not Oliver.

Sheene also had a beautiful blonde better half called Stephanie (routinely described as a glamour model) who could be seen in photographs looking too good-looking for Pan's People, which is saying *a lot*. Pan's People dancing on *Top of the Pops* was the closest thing to erotica anyone in Loughton could experience. Unless they caught the 20a bus to the Green Man roundabout where the Green Man pub advertised 'Sunday Lunch 'n' Strippers' on a giant blackboard by the road.

Sheene's fame went beyond fans of bikes or even sports. He'd gone household. He featured on the first record I ever bought. The Barron Knights had their own brand of musical spoof. On a record called 'Live in Trouble (Part 1)', they did a version of Brotherhood of Man's 'Angelo', about Ann and Jo, which had the lines:

> *Long ago, outside a chip shop in Walthamstow,*
> *Was a young rocker called Greasy Joe.*
> *He put on his helmet and said, 'Let's go.'*
> *He was keen,*
> *Off up the High Street like Barry Sheene,*
> *Doing his best to look very mean,*
> *Till he met Anne on her new machine.*

This was hilarious to me. Though for years I maintained that 'Wig Wam Bam' by Sweet was the first record I ever bought, the truth was that it was bought for me, rather than by me, aged seven. No, the first time I went in to Pop Inn on Loughton High Road with my own pocket money, it was to buy a Barron Knights record. As a hoarder, I still treasure it. It's a remarkable memorial of what passed for entertainment in the '70s.

Sheene always had a fag on, which I hadn't noticed at ten but had down as cool at eleven. Smoking was ace and I couldn't wait to get started. Outside Loughton tube station was a fag machine. Just sitting there on the pavement. It should have said 'fags for kids' on it. Smoking was difficult. It took commitment and effort. This was primarily because it was rank. It smelt like football grounds while tasting like shoes but I was determined to have my dream look. The cool smoker. This was a sure fire way to impress my peers too, which I was rarely able to do throughout my school-days.

It worked too. The coolest kids in my year *were impressed by my smoking.* That they were work-shy vandals whose principal aim at school was to flob (spit) higher and further than anyone else was unimportant. They were the rebellious, cocky, couldn't-care-less kids and I aspired to their periphery. We had one thing in common: we hated the school and everything in it. Now we had a second thing in common. Fags.

Coming by fags was difficult but I had the 'fags for kids' option which no one else appeared to know about. Fags were great but inhaling was grim and took a while to master. It put me off smoking and I didn't really get the hang of it until 1980 whereupon I smoked for twenty-seven years, with occasional breaks of anything from a week to a year while I attempted to give up. I'm not blaming Barry Sheene or other hero-smokers for my subsequent addiction; after all we always had Mr Baker the PE teacher barking away at us that each cigarette was five minutes off your life. That sounds bad until you point out that each episode of *EastEnders* is thirty minutes off your life. None of us did though, principally because *EastEnders* didn't start until 1985. Still, you definitely had to want to smoke and I did.

To be Barry Sheene meant being immersed in motorcycle racing from birth. Sheene says in his 1976 autobiography (*The Story So Far* – the title said so much) that the day he was born his father phoned a friend to say: 'I've just been presented with the winner of the 1970 TT.' As it was, Barry Sheene never liked racing on the Isle of Man as, ironically for a man with an astonishing history of breakages and metal reinforcement, he felt it was much too dangerous and only rewarded those racers most familiar with the thirty-eight-mile road circuit.

We went as a family to the Isle of Man in the mid-'70s to watch the TT. Motor sport was always an enthusiasm of my dad's. He had a previous life as an amateur rally enthusiast who competed in many events as a navigator (principal requirements: meticulous route planning and an ability to fold maps in the dark). These appeared to have been his most exciting days and he still has a cabinet full of odd little trophies from rallying. Consequently, we would always have motor sport on TV if there was any being shown and I still remember the excitement when Formula One was first shown in colour, thereby enabling the viewer, at last, to identify the cars.

Motorbikes flying round the streets, hills and mountains of the Isle of Man are terrifically exciting for a boy already in possession of his own race circuit at home. Despite the noise- and adrenaline-fuelled excitement, when we weren't watching the racing I had my nose in Anna Sewell's decidedly non-macho *Black Beauty,* which remained my favourite book until about 1983.

On one occasion we were standing near some racing sidecars. Low-slung powerful machines on which the rider virtually lies face down, with a platform attached to the side that some crazed *volunteer* would roll around on to help cornering. Barmy. A young boy was fiddling with one of the bikes. He looked dirty and mechanicky but was, in reality, about ten. I watched him and he tampered seriously with some moving part for my benefit, looking cool. He then stood up, asked me to mind the machine, and went off. My dad found me (I had a gift for getting lost) and I said I had to stay and look after the bike. He tutted and walked away, with me following, protesting pointlessly. He didn't believe that any racer would leave their prized machine in the hands of a strange nine-year-old. Shows how much he knew.

I felt bad about letting that kid down. It was the closest I ever came to some kind of 'in' with the racing fraternity. But I was hooked; I loved the noise, the speed and the glamour. Despite a crush on Stacy Dorning from the TV series that lasted a decade, I was leaving *Black Beauty* behind; I wanted to be like Barry Sheene.

David Starsky

I also wanted to be like Starsky out of *Starsky & Hutch*. *Starsky & Hutch* was an American cop show set in Los Angeles about two thirty-something detectives who smiled and bantered their way through episodes while effortlessly catching crooks in '70s' three-piece brown suits. This was shown on Saturday nights on BBC1.

The BBC always ran an American cop show on Saturday nights prior to *Match of the Day* and by the time *Starsky & Hutch* came on in the late '70s, I was allowed to stay up and watch. For years there had been shows about serious tough solo cops like Cannon and Kojak but Starsky and Hutch were different. They made policing seem fun as they raced around in a noisy red Ford Torino with a white stripe down the side. This was the best car ever and it was Starsky's. He was the bouncy, funny, dark-haired one who had burgers and shakes on top of the dashboard at all times, particularly prior to a chase. Hutch had a knackered old car which Starsky always rebuked him over. Hutch also liked health food and chastized Starsky over his diet. Ooh, they were a right pair.

Hutch was more contemplative, less mischievous, than Starsky who was forever being insubordinate to their boss, the captain at the precinct, who was unfailingly furious with them both. He was a round angry black man played by the late Bernie Hamilton, who was eighty when he died, which makes the show seem a very long time ago.

The other main character was Huggy Bear, who knew

what 'the word on the street' was and without whom the boys would never have caught anyone. Antonio Fargas had a relaxed comic screen presence and a memorable character name that somehow survived his non-resemblance to a bear and his no-hugs acting. He was, by the way, not a pimp, as portrayed in the catastrophic film version of the TV show which, infuriatingly for devotees, changed the characters around and made Starsky the serious one. What rot. He was a maverick and so he should always be

I was devoted to Starsky and Hutch and I knew everything there was to know about them through the Starsky & Hutch Fan Club. What personal details would anyone want to obscure from the viewers? Everything that mattered was clearly going to be in the fan club literature. I knew, for example, that in reality it was tall, blond and handsome David Soul, who played Detective Ken Hutchinson, who actually liked burgers and Paul Michael Glaser, who played Dave Starsky, who was the health foodie in real life. Isn't that ironic? I *remember that*. I *did not* look that up.

There was an occasional official mini A5-size magazine and unofficial (whatever that means ...) magazine/poster publications were very popular then too. A normal-looking magazine would open out into a huge poster with sixteen pages of articles and photographs on the back. One of those devoted to your favourite TV show or band was worth spending your pocket money on. I had two Starsky and Hutch posters. 25p each. My dad couldn't understand the extravagance. On one occasion he absolutely thrilled me by pulling a Starsky and Hutch magazine from his briefcase when he came home from work. Later that same evening he wrote down the cost of it (30p) in his daily cash book. Money was the most important thing in the world.

For me, TV was the most important thing in the world.

We weren't a literary house, an artistic house or a musical house. We were a TV house. It was never off. When me and my brother and sister sat down to have our tea, our TV on wheels was pulled up to the table as if it was a fourth sibling. This meant we didn't have to talk. It meant *Grange Hill*, *Boss Cat*, *Wacky Races*, and *Rentaghost* over our fish fingers.

One evening I was sitting on my own watching *Coronation Street* (one of the best sitcoms on telly in the late '70s) when Vera Duckworth tucked her fag in her mouth, thereby freeing her hands, so she could Blu-Tac a poster of Starsky and Hutch on her wall, with a few amusing suggestive remarks to her watching friend. The penny dropped that *ladies* had Starsky and Hutch on the wall, ladies like Vera Duckworth. I recall feeling that Vera and I should not have the same posters.

I didn't fancy Starsky and Hutch, did I? I joined the fan club. I had shop-lifted an *I'm a Starsky & Hutch fan* sticker for my school briefcase (yes, a briefcase. My dad bought it for me. On the first day it only had a recorder in it. I covered it in Mr Men stickers from packets of Ricicles and in time it was replaced with the obligatory Adidas bag). No, I wasn't in love with Starsky and Hutch, well, not madly. I idolized them, certainly. They were funny and laid-back as well as tough and good-looking. These were all attributes that seemed immensely desirable. So much so that I began to imitate Starsky. I'm hopeful that this behaviour went unnoticed by my peers. It involved a slight swagger, a rolling gait to affect casual self-assurance, something no twelve-year-old has (self-assurance that is; there are many gaits on show among boys expanding, hormonally and otherwise, into puberty).

I carried a toy revolver stuffed down my back into the waistband of my school trousers. That was where Starsky kept his gun. Hutch went for the shoulder holster but Starsky just shoved his gun down the crack of his bum. What if it went off when he sat down? He could shoot his nuts off. Or maybe one of them anyway, unless they were squashed together, and he did wear tight jeans, made tighter still by the gun expanding the waistband.

I only had a cap gun, which rarely had caps in anyway, since caps were something that I found difficult to make last, so my nuts were safe. Indeed, they may not have dropped yet; my genitals had been making slow progress, which our family doctor put down to junior Y-fronts. I was able to hold my dad responsible as he bought the pants in our house and his were massive after all. I didn't say anything, too embarrassing.

I never pulled the gun out at school, or wore it if we had PE and I'd have to get changed. It just sat there secretly and allowed me to fantasize about being a cool American. America was an obsession for everyone who liked telly, since Americans were never off the telly, in cop shows, films, cartoons and sitcoms. They had a seductive, hypnotic effect on England that perhaps lingered from the GI invasion of the early '40s and grew as cinema and then television took hold. Everything they did was so much more informal, loose, their conversation an appealing mix of colloquialism and grammatical shortcuts that washed through stuffy old English. They didn't say: 'Do you know, I think I'll have a glass of water?' They said: 'I guess I'll be a-partaking in a little ol' drink of somethin' right now an' hell if water ain't such a dreadful notion.'

Even more than us kids, our parents were smitten with American film stars and were forever saying things like 'Here's lookin' at you, kid', 'Get off your horse and drink your milk' or 'You dirty rat' in strange mutilated RP accents unrecognizable as either English or American. America was cool and we all wanted to go there.

American guys were good hero fodder too. In England we did have *The New Avengers*, enjoyable for the startling beauty of Joanna Lumley as Purdey, racing about in a yellow TR7. We also had *The Professionals* throwing disillusioned 'birds' out of Capris, unable to explain why, as they went off on a secret mission with the butler from *Upstairs, Downstairs*. Then there was *Blake's 7*, *Dr Who*, who was a weirdo, Dr Weirdo in fact, or *The Sweeney*, but that seemed like a lot of whisky and cigarettes even for a budding smoker, plus they were on late on a school night.

In fact it was a depiction of American school life that really delighted England in 1978. I went to see *Grease* five times. I've never been to see a film in the cinema more than once before or since. Some would have you believe that punk and new wave were the big thing that year but, out in suburbia and all over the country, people were mad for Olivia Newton-John and John Travolta. Some time later the American *Mad* magazine, which ran strip cartoon spoofs of films, ran a *Grease* strip which culminated in Olivia Newton-John's Sandy character deciding that, in order to get her man, she would become a 'SLUT!' with the tagline: 'What a great message for the youth of America!'

We were oblivious to the negative imagery. She looked great in her skin-tight strides. We lapped up *Grease* and everything American (the Australian actress included). Terry Wogan talked about *Dallas* so much to his 400 million listeners that you had to watch the show to enjoy his radio show. So we did. There were Westerns on every weekend and American cartoons like *Scooby-Doo*, *Dastardly and Muttley in Their Flying Machines* and *The Flintstones*. All of it seemed cooler, less constrained and restrained and no one wanted to go to their own hideous school when the fantasy world of Rydell High was there at the Woodford ABC.

At that time songs went to number one in the charts for two to three weeks if they were lucky. You did well if you had a number two or three. In fact anything in the top ten was a big hit. 'The One That You Want' was at number one for nine weeks. Unheard of. They followed that up with 'Summer Nights' for seven weeks. A total of getting on for four months at the top of the charts. Virtually every other song in the film charted too. It was cultural carpet bombing.

Boys wanted to be T-Birds and girls Pink Ladies even though, collectively, they were as thick as a cart of planks. Within a year I was thirteen and may have denied ever seeing *Grease* at all but for a little while I couldn't get enough of it.

The first time I went was with some friends from school. As we jostled on to the bus, I pressed the ticket button on the driver's machine. It was on the passenger's side as you stood in front of him and he used to reach over with his fingers and strike it a glancing blow. I put my 10p down and hit the button. He gave me my ticket and my 10p back and threw me off the bus. Obviously none of my mates would wait with me for the next one so I turned up at the cinema on my own. At the end of the film, when the lights came up, I realized I'd been sitting just a few rows away from my mates. I walked out with them but didn't say much. I thought Danny Zuko and Kenickie were the coolest people in the world and I was posturing, acting tough, in an effort to mimic them. Ironic really, given how effeminate John Travolta was in the film. One of my mates said, 'What's wrong with you?' and that was the end of that.

We also went to see *Grease* as a family. I was confused by the scene where Rizzo is concerned she has skipped a period. It seemed important in the context of the film but why would she care about missing a period? She was the coolest, toughest chick in the school; she surely missed lessons all the time? I whispered to my dad:

'Does that mean she's missed a lesson?' I could tell he didn't like the question, even though it was dark.

'No, that was a very rude joke indeed.'

Joke? Rude joke? What did he mean? I could see my brother on the other side of him wearing a patronizing smirk and the rage bubbled up in me a little. If he wasn't to have one up on me I'd have to bluff:

'Oh yes, yes. I knew that.'

'No you didn't,' he muttered.

Periods. Damn. What are they? I think I worked it out on about the fifth viewing. But I never spotted the rude joke.

I liked Travolta but there was something a little squeaky-creepy about him. I was more of a Kenickie man myself. In the same way I preferred Han Solo to Luke Skywalker or the Artful Dodger to Oliver. I was never going to be the squeaky clean hero in the 'what are we going to do with you?' world I grew up in, so I never went for the hero, I always liked the jokey one, with a short-term view and possibly too-small underpants.

I liked Starsky and I carried on liking him even by the third series when the leading actors took a stand on reducing the violence in the show. This had some consequences when a person was shot. After shooting someone, Starsky would slump against a wall while Hutch ran up and said: 'Are you OK?' Starsky would mumble some kind of assent while trying to shake off his feelings and get on with The Job. Hutch would slap him comfortingly on the shoulder and check he was not in need of a proper cuddle, before leaving him to have 'a moment'.

This emotional content would irritate my dad and my brother, as the bleeding heart, wet-blanket stars flopped around the screen when there were perfectly good anonymous victims to track down and waste (as they always said in those days, rather than the ubiquitous 'clip' of the new millennium).

I didn't mind the 'taking a moment' scenes; after all, over on my sister's favourite show, *Charlie's Angels*, a similar outbreak of resistance to the glamourizing of violence had led to the Angels having a full sob-off every time they wasted/clipped a villain. I never liked Starsky because of his killing prowess, I liked him for his *personality* and that's where I parted company with Vera Duckworth too.

Pat Jennings

Much of my early '70s had been spent running around the garden playing football, often with my brother. The rest of the time, when not reading Enid Blyton books, I watched television, which provided most of my favourite people. Some sporting heroes, though, I had seen in the flesh since my dad was keen on sport. We used to go to White Hart Lane to see 'The Spurs', as he called them, because that was his team. Quite often we saw their reserve games, as there were fewer people and you could get kids in for free if you could carry them through the turnstile. Inside, the seats were wooden and didn't flip back up after you'd sat in them so, after games, I would walk up and down the rows putting seats back in place for as long as my dad could stand to wait.

Playing in goal for Tottenham Hotspur in the '70s was a big Northern Irishman who could leap out and take crosses one-handed. He had astonishing reflexes, an ice-cool temperament and the ability to stop goal-bound shots with any part of his anatomy, his legs as often as his hands. He was unassuming and heroic but in the main he had massive shovel-like paws, remarkable things, like an unevolved larger primate, and Spurs fans never tired of telling you he was THE BEST GOALKEEPER IN THE WORLD.

As I became more of an Arsenal fan, the pressure exerted by my brother's campaign at school, to deny my being related to him, forced me to re-evaluate my relationship with The Spurs. The campaign was unsubtle but effective. Kids from my brother's year would point at me and ask him: 'Is he your brother?' and he'd say: 'No.' My opinion was sought but he just told them I was lying if I said yes. I wish I'd got my own 'no' in first, just to throw him. The truth came out of course but he kept up the pressure by ignoring me. This was wearing and I began to take against Tottenham in response.

I decided then that Jennings wasn't the best, that Peter Shilton was. Except he wasn't because he let one in under his body and England didn't qualify for the '74 World Cup and as for Ray Clemence, he never had to make any saves since Liverpool were too good and Gordon Banks didn't play any more because of his car crash and losing an eye and Dino Zoff was Italian and, drat, maybe Jennings *was* the best.

Without him Spurs would certainly have been relegated to Division Two in 1976 when he was voted the Players' Player of the Year. The following year even he couldn't keep them up and they, remarkably, decided he had to be moved on. For a bargain transfer fee of £40,000 he moved to Arsenal, where he played for eight more years and over 300 games. More importantly, Arsenal had the best goalie in the world and Spurs fans couldn't deny it.

Fortunately, for me, I had already eschewed Tottenham Hotspur in favour of Arsenal before I ever went to White Hart Lane. This was the single best idea I had in the first forty years of my life. There is no single moment that could have gone so badly wrong as the moment, in 1971, when I chose Arsenal. What a terrifyingly close near-slip into a pit of bitterness and despair, of false dawns, anger and con-tinual, second-best disappointment. To have never had the joys of Arsenal heroes like Liam Brady and David Rocastle. It was them or Glenn Hoddle. Even though he was from Essex and I knew where his house was (Harlow) and once looked over his wall (he wasn't in) it makes me anxious to think I even considered Spurs. That was a Great Escape of mythological proportions, a turn-to-stone, don't-look-back-or-someone's-a-pillar-of-salt moment. For Spurs are truly, shamefully, terrible and Arsenal are the custodians of human decency in a world of lies.

I had decided on an Arsenal shirt, given the choice by my mum in 1971. I was keen to have a shirt but equally keen not to have the same one as my brother. Actually, it may have been that *he* wanted me in a different-coloured shirt, which is ironic given he's a lifelong Spurs fan like my dad. Thankfully, he said: 'Why don't you have an Arsenal shirt? They're top of the league.'

Not exactly recruiting for Spurs there but perhaps he had no idea of the rivalry. Arsenal were League Champions in 1971, which must have registered with him, even though he was only seven. I was shown the shirt and I liked it. I still have it. I was asked what number I wanted on the back. Did I want number 9 for John Radford because he gets all the goals? No, I wanted to know who the captain was. It was Frank McLintock, who wore number 5. My mum sewed it on to the back of the shirt and a club badge with a cannon on to the front. The badge faded to pink while the shirt itself stayed red and the number 5 fell off years ago but the shirt is something I'd consider rescuing in a fire. I remember odd little things about my mum but that shirt-choosing moment, for me, was her finest hour.

After that I'd be taken to the occasional game at Highbury, the home of Arsenal. The first being a 1–0 defeat by Stoke in August 1971. I spent much of the game kneeling on my seat facing the wrong way staring at a fat man with a large, livid purple birthmark on his face. It was a revulsion-fascination for me. I'm surprised he didn't tell me to stop staring. I'd never seen so many people but I remember liking it, especially the smell, which I couldn't identify (it was cigarettes, thousands of them).

After that most of my trips to Highbury came in early March as my birthday treat. I still remember a game v Sheffield United three days before my sixth birthday in 1972. Arsenal won 3–2 and it was fantastically exciting. There was even a goal as we were getting up to leave early and beat the traffic. Charlie George scored twice but I don't remember that, I only really remember Alan Woodward of Sheffield United because he had grey hair, which made him stand out, and he was called Alan, which meant he was good, obviously.

Towards the end of the 1977–78 season I had the urge to go more often. Arsenal had the makings of a good team, with Jennings the senior man amongst six Irishmen. I read in the match programme that the Irish boys loved to play tapes of The Dubliners on the team bus for a sing-a-long. It was only in later years that I realized what a living hell that must have been for the four Englishman and one Scot who made up the rest of the side. Terry Neill, the manager, was Irish as well, so what could they do?

I was old enough now that my dad wouldn't have to trek in with me, provided my brother could be persuaded to go. He really hated Arsenal so it was a little surprising that he agreed but then I had been to White Hart Lane many times, so it was fair. Maybe he wanted a glimpse of the superhero in goal. I managed to get to three or four games with my unsmiling sibling. Arsenal won them all, which only made him grumpier, and they scored pots of goals. Previously, when we were going to Highbury in the '70s, they were as likely to lose as to win but now they were on fire and they reached the FA Cup semi-final v Orient, who were the nearest club to us in Loughton, doomed to be everyone's second-best team.

I felt part of things, having seen Arsenal's 4–1 fifth round win over Walsall. They beat Orient 3–0 at Stamford Bridge with a goal from a budding hero, Graham Rix, and two bagged by Malcolm 'Supermac' Macdonald, which were both deflected into the net by Orient players with the original shots heading for Fulham Broadway rather than the goal. Supermac was as straight-faced as he had been after another goal I saw him score at Highbury, when he claimed a hat-trick in a 4–0 win v West Bromwich Albion even though their left back, Derek Statham, claimed he'd booted one of them into his own net. Admirable in a way, embarrassing in another. Supermac's autobiography was called *Never Afraid to Miss.* I once saw a picture of him in an Arsenal programme, boarding the coach to go to a game, and he was wearing a pale-blue pinstripe three-piece suit. He looked the confident type. He was bandy-legged but fast, like a hog in the undergrowth, he was buccaneering, he was super!

On the day of the semi-final we were at White Hart Lane to see Spurs 1 Bolton 0 in front of 52,000 in the old second division. At the end of the 1977–78 season, Spurs won promotion narrowly in third place and the win over eventual champions Bolton Wanderers was key. There was euphoria at White Hart Lane. I remember hearing the Arsenal result and having to check that that meant they were through to Wembley. The FA Cup Final was the biggest game of the year and Arsenal were going to be there. My team, that I went to see at Highbury, what bragging rights at school. My dad was distinctly unsmiling when he confirmed the news with a hint of displeasure at Arsenal's success, though it may have been displeasure at my grinning twelve-year-old chops twittering on about the Cup Final.

The FA Cup Final build-up was extensive, with daily articles as well as colour pull-out-and-keep supplements in the London evening papers which I pulled out and kept. A house in our road was completely decked out in Arsenal flags and banners, which was an odd sight in suburban Loughton. Television coverage on the day started around noon. I had no idea that the whole country would instinctively back any team against a London club and that most of London also wanted Arsenal to lose. They were about to make everyone very happy.

Jennings, Rice, Nelson, Price, O'Leary, Young, Brady, Sunderland, Macdonald, Stapleton, Hudson, sub Rix (sadly I didn't have to look that up) was the Arsenal team, fifth in the first division, against Ipswich from the bottom half of the table. I imagined that the clubs all sat round tables in a long room according to who was first, second, third etc right down to the likes of Ipswich down in eighteenth or something.

It was a massacre. Ipswich poured forward. All week, Bobby Robson, their manager, had been talking up their injury problems but in the end it was Arsenal's stars who were lame. Macdonald and Brady should not have played by their own subsequent admission. It was hard on Rix to be on the bench when he'd played all season and he was lively when he came on for Brady but the feeling was that the Irishman's lack of fitness had slowed the heartbeat of the team to near-flatline. Bobby Robson took a lot of credit for deploying David Geddis on the right wing to peg back Sammy Nelson and take the initiative away from Arsenal's inventive left flank. Ipswich hit the bar and then John Wark nearly broke the post twice with thumping shots.

Jennings kept them at bay as best he could, pulling off one astounding save from a header by George Burley, but eventually Roger Osbourne scored and then collapsed in shock. It was the biggest moment possible for a player in those days. The winner in the Cup Final. 'Osbourne, one nil!' said David Coleman on the BBC. The final whistle had me welling up. My dad looked at me: 'It was one nil but it could have been four,' he said. That put my bottom lip out. There followed a good stomp upstairs to my room, with my acrylic hat and nylon scarf thrown down with such force it was lucky they didn't ignite. Then came crying face down on my bed.

I'm not sure what I was doing on any specific day in 1978 other than on that Cup Final day when Arsenal lost and I was in my room all evening. I could try to make it seem romantic: 'He wept alone, shunning consolation, practised in solitary misery, he ached into the night, the first FA Cup Final day he hadn't enjoyed,' but it was more: 'He was crying in his room and wouldn't come out *for ages.*'

I didn't go back to Highbury until after Christmas following that defeat. It's hard to say why it hurt so much. Perhaps it was because there was no one else I knew going through this *torment.* My sister may have sympathized if given the chance but then again I was hard to sympathize with, and she had no interest in sport other than a devotion to Chris Evert. One year she was taken to Wimbledon and saw Little Miss Cool up close: 'As close as I am to you!' she said later. 'So what?' I said. 'I've been that close to Liam Brady.' I hadn't but it wasn't the lie that caused the whole family to roll their eyes. It was the entirely predictable rain-on-your-parade contrariness of Mr What-are-we-going-to-do-with-you?

I was sometimes accused of spite but not always fairly. At infants' school soon after my mum had died, I was in a spat of some kind, waiting on the stairs to go into Mrs Baker's class. Mrs 'I've got eyes in the back of my head' Baker claimed to have witnessed the whole thing: 'Just because your mother's died, Alan, there's no need to be spiteful.'

Bit of a shock that. I didn't think the rest of the class knew about my mum, I hadn't yet told anyone. I didn't want to lose friends, I was having enough difficulty making any in the first place, and now there were unaddressed bereavement issues. Perhaps the class had been forewarned about my situation. I didn't ask anyone and no one said anything. It would have been nice to be able to say: 'She's not dead actually,' but even I couldn't manage a fib that size.

It was a lonely Saturday evening holed up in my room after the Cup Final. I was sure most of the people I knew were actually pleased Arsenal lost. Oh yes, no flies on me back in '78. Living vicariously through a football club, even one as successful as Arsenal, will lead to many downs. It's best not to attach emotions to the club that are actually created by something else. 'What are you really angry about?' is always a good question. It's rarely the football results.

I should have gone down the road to the house decked out in Arsenal flags for my tea. They'd have taken me in and said all the right things, I'm sure. Or, they may have been totally barmy. The grass is always greener and all that.

Wolfie Smith

When you're eleven years old, it's possible to enjoy tales of a South London revolutionary who idolizes Che Guevara and leads the Tooting Popular Front without having any idea about who or what the following are:

a) a revolutionary   b) Che Guevara   c) Tooting.

Wolfie Smith wore a beret and a Che Guevara T-shirt. He and his motley friends were an inept band of would-be revolutionaries called, by Wolfie, the Tooting Popular Front. That sounded funny to me, as it was supposed to, even though the concept of a Popular Front was one more thing lost on me. The notion of a people's struggle, of a band of comrades finding the collective will to effect real change through a pooling of effort, ideas and resources, was something rarely discussed at home, at school, or anywhere as far as I knew.

The ever-reliable Wikipedia lists the following Popular Fronts (so it's possible that some of them may have existed . . .):

Azerbaijan Popular Front Party
Belarusian People's Front
Frente Popular (Philippines)
Popular Democratic Front (Italy, 1948)
Popular Front (Chile)
Popular Front (France)

Popular Front (Mauritania)
Popular Front (Senegal)
Popular Front (Spain)
Popular Front of India
Popular Front for the Liberation of Bahrain
Popular Front for the Liberation of Oman
Popular Front for the Liberation of Palestine

and they're only the ones from non-communist countries ...

Citizen Smith was a sitcom written by John Sullivan for the BBC. Sullivan had worked in the props department for years but always wanted to make an unlikely leap across to scriptwriting, which he managed to do with a little help from Ronnie Barker, who took some of his sketches for *The Two Ronnies*. After *Citizen Smith* Sullivan created *Only Fools and Horses*, as popular a television show as there has ever been in England. He also wrote *Just Good Friends* and more recently the *Fools and Horses* spin-off, *Green Green Grass of Home*. He is now well past thirty years as a writer of popular comedy. I've loved watching his shows for all of that time.

I didn't know about scriptwriting when I was eleven, or acting, I just liked the people and the world they lived in. I didn't really understand what Wolfie was on about when he conducted, virtually weekly, emergency Annual General Meetings of the Tooting Popular Front in the Vigilante, the local pub run by villain Harry Fenning, who was hilarious and menacing in equal measure, much like Grouty in *Porridge*.

It was the mischief and energy of Wolfie Smith that I enjoyed. He was childlike and cheeky and perhaps at eleven and twelve childlike and cheeky were attainable characteristics. Wolfie wasn't macho and tough but those types always seemed one-dimensional and dismally humourless. I never aspired to be the man with no name who walks into town and shoots everyone who gets on his nerves. Some girls claim that a good sense of humour is what they look for in a man. I've always wondered why they have the monopoly on the humour hunt. A good sense of humour is exactly what I look for in a man too. My love of jokes, sitcoms and silly folk generally flourished throughout the '70s. From *Tom and Jerry* to *Paddington* and *Crackerjack*, then from *Sykes* and *Morecambe and Wise* to *It Ain't Half Hot Mum* and *The Dick Emery Show*, from *Dad's Army* to *The Two Ronnies* and *Dave Allen at Large*, from *Porridge, Rising Damp* and *Open All Hours* to *The Good Life, Fawlty Towers* and *Are You Being Served?* Humour was the most important thing for me in front of the telly. I really liked funny people. I didn't mind what they said, so long as they said it in a funny way. Hence my great affection for Robert Robinson on *Ask the Family* and, in recent years, William Hague. There's nothing like a silly voice.

This was something the family did together. All families it seemed. Sitting and laughing at Windsor Davies and his 'lovely boys' or Molly Sugden and her 'pussy', John Inman being 'free', Granville ffffetching his cloth, Private Fraser being 'doomed' or Dick Emery's 'you are awful, but I like you', which everyone in Britain must have said at one point or another in the '70s.

Catchphrase comedy is derided by some as easy but it just looks that way. It's thoughtless to assume that any audience rolling in the aisles or tuning in by the tens of millions is being entertained by actors who find it effortless or writers who are lazy. The skill and timing of a generation of comic turns was gratefully received via the box in the corner of the room. The performers themselves must go nearly mad with people in the street every day shouting: 'He's from Barcelona' or 'Miss Jones, Miss Jones' at them, but the laughs were wonderful.

On top of all these sitcom stars there was the organized chaos of *The Generation Game* as well as a steady diet of Syd James, Hattie Jacques and Kenneth Williams in the *Carry On* films that the BBC ran and reran. The pleasure brought to me by all those people is inestimable. Were this a popular science book I'd quantify it by saying, 'My pleasure could have covered an area the size of Wales.' Everything always seems to be an area the size of Wales.

I laughed a lot growing up, to the point where I'd often be bought joke books for birthday presents as if I had a humour affliction. I may have been giggling hysterically out of anxiety half the time. To me a funny person was a good person. A warm, kind smiley person. I had no idea of the tantrums and tiaras of showbiz, never mind the rum and rent boys end of things beloved of BBC4 dramatists. It seemed that anyone who made people laugh for a living must be happier than the average bear.

Older actors reminisce happily about working days at the BBC rehearsal studios in Acton, with different casts from different sitcoms all convening in the canteen at lunchtime. BBC shows now often rehearse in a church hall under Hammersmith flyover since the BBC's own rehearsal rooms became too expensive for BBC shows to hire. There are no lunchtime canteen conventions for the actors, just some queuing in a sandwich shop on the Fulham Palace Road. If the BBC didn't exist today no one would invent it in its current form. But then the same is true of Christmas. And Manchester United.

So many of my favourite sitcoms featured ensembles of characters who interacted as if they were in a family.

Everyone was there every week and there was no escaping their associates.

Usually there were generational differences in the cast too, so people took parental or child roles. Ronnie Barker and Richard Beckinsale, as Fletch and Godber in *Porridge*, were perhaps the best father and son double act of them all.

Often the senior parental figures are distinguished by class from their subordinates, a rich seam to mine for English comedy writers. In *Are You Being Served?*, the older floor manager, posh Captain Peacock, ran things like an exasperated father who is no longer in love with his snobby 'wife', Mrs Slocombe. The pair of them tried to manage the unruly Mr Lucas and Miss Brahms while John Inman's Mr Humphreys skipped about like the irrepressible black sheep. Then there was the old granddad figure behind the counter.

It seems to be a model for a good sitcom. Create a dysfunctional group who adopt familial roles, don't, whatever you do, try and create an actual family unless you have a comic genius like Bill Cosby or Roseanne Barr at the helm holding it together or they are animated like *The Simpsons*, with grown-ups playing the kids.

It's possible I enjoyed those ensemble family shows like *Are You Being Served?*, *Hi-de-hi*, *Dad's Army* and *It Ain't Half Hot Mum* so much because it looked like it would be fun to be in those gangs. They never fell out irreparably, they couldn't, they all had to be in the next episode. Family comedies work well when they've created enough variety in the behaviour of the characters for one of them to appeal to each member of an actual family. With the exception of *Outnumbered* (where the child actors are not, as far as possible, required to learn any line) it is best not to have children in a sitcom because children are not funny on telly, unless they are either talking to Michael Barrymore or falling off a trampoline on *You've Been Framed*.

By the age of twelve though, these family sitcoms were becoming less and less involving as I became more independent. How do you become independent when you spend very little time outside the house? Shut up in your bedroom is how, or occasionally by picking a TV show to watch that no one else wants to watch. In 1977–78 I became hooked on a WW1 Royal Flying Corps drama on the BBC called *Wings*. No one else in the family wanted to watch it and so I wasn't able to until it happened to be my birthday and they were forced to concede. I watched it while they all feigned boredom. Or they may actually have been bored. It was brilliant, if you ask me.

In our house *Citizen Smith* became my show. Other people in the family may have watched it, I don't remember, but I loved it right from the opening credits, with the whistling of 'The Red Flag' (I didn't know what the song was or what it represented) played over shots of Wolfie walking the streets of Tooting, grinning at passers by, kicking a can along, marching out of Tooting Broadway tube station, before shouting, 'Power to the people' at the top of his voice with a half-smile on his face as if he was imagining being at the head of a vast rally, a feted revolutionary hero.

I had no idea, either, that Britain was struggling economically in the late '70s, that long-haired work-shy busking layabouts like Wolfie caused middle England's blood to boil. Middle England was represented by Wolfie's girlfriend's dad, Peter Vaughan (who also played Grouty in *Porridge*), a man enraged by the 'yeti' as he called Wolfie. Enraged that is, when he wasn't laughing at him, as in the episode where Wolfie stands for the Tooting Popular Front in a bye-election and only receives six votes.

John Sullivan also created Del Boy, another bright aspirational spark surrounded by dimwits, in *Only Fools and Horses* but, while he was hilarious, there was only one character in sitcom land that I revered and that was Wolfie.

There were similarities with Starsky but Wolfie lacked Starsky's courage and athleticism while Starsky lacked Wolfie's vanity and ego. By 1978 I'd never met a man who I wanted to be like, so heroes came straight off the telly. It didn't occur to me that Paul Michael Glaser and Robert Lindsay were charismatic actors using their talents to bring scripted dialogue to life. If I wanted to be like them, the best thing was to actually copy them. Being an actor never crossed my mind when being a cop or a revolutionary seemed so much fun.

1979

Margaret Thatcher

Sometimes a favourite person can retain that status for life, yours not theirs; at other times someone can come from nowhere to be the most important person in your world for just a few days.

On 3 May, the Conservatives, led by Margaret Thatcher, won the 1979 general election. I didn't find out the result until the next day and I immediately phoned my dad at work to give him the good news.

I'm not sure why I was at home that day. Either the Easter holidays had stretched into May or I'd been feigning earache again. Dad had ear trouble as a boy, so when I had an earache it was an almost foolproof way to miss school. He nearly always believed me if I said my ears were hurting (sometimes they actually were) and he would put drops and cotton wool in my ear. In every other area of my life, it was much harder for him to believe me, as I was working hard on my fibbing. Previously I'd been a hopeless fibber. When I was four, having peed my pants in Mrs Gomer's class while she was reading us a story, I was found some dry clothes by the headmistress. When my mum arrived to pick me up she asked:

'Where did you get those shorts?'

I said: 'They're my PE shorts.'

She said: 'You haven't got any PE shorts.'

I made a mental note to improve my fibbing and by thirteen I was pretty good.

It was no fib, though, when I phoned dad's office to tell

him the election result. It was unusual to phone him at work but this was evidently *very important*. He'd be delighted not just that they'd won but that I'd taken the trouble to break the news. I was put through:

'We've won!' I said.

There was barely any reaction, he seemed to know the result already (how?) and appeared to be a little bit busy actually.

I suppose the news didn't qualify as the emergency you'd expect when one of your children rings you at work out of the blue. I had hoped he'd be delighted, with both the message and, particularly, the messenger. I was as keen to please as most boys are with their fathers, hanging on every word and bending behaviour constantly in the hunt for praise, which could never be enough. Perhaps it's all the more important when there is just the one parent to keep happy. Diminishing positive feedback for me at this time may have been due to an irritating tendency on my part to be thirteen. There were occasions when I delighted him, such as when I was silent and/or in another room.

I knew we wanted the Conservatives to win since I had checked: 'Who do you want to win the election?' I said and he'd said: 'The Conservatives,' with more than a hint of 'Who else?' in his voice. Previously I'd had no idea who could win or what anyone stood for, or what standing for something entailed, but from that moment, I knew who I supported. It was clear that there was a right and wrong:

Conservatives = right
Labour = wrong/absurd

Parenting is a difficult task. The people most confident in their parenting skills are generally those without children.

How many could find the time to explain, so a thirteen-year-old could understand, what was happening in the general election? To lay out whose interests were best served by which candidates, what the possible outcomes may be and to provide a rudimentary guide to party policy and ideology (ideology! Those were the days). Far easier to break it all down into a simple subliminal mantra:

Conservatives = common sense
Labour = nonsense

A dictatorship of 'the sensible' was his preference, with sensible as an absolute not a variable.

On Saturday nights on BBC1, with an audience of millions, the impressionist Mike Yarwood could be seen mimicking the Labour prime minister, Jim Callaghan: 'Now I'm going to be perfectly blunt,' he would say and the audience roared with laughter, as we all did at home. Dad often did an impression of Yarwood doing Callaghan, '*Blunt*' was said bluntly while sticking out your chin. Yarwood also did the Labour chancellor, Denis Healey: '*You silly billy*,' he would say. Healey had never actually said 'silly billy', but later adopted it, as Yarwood had made it popular on his behalf.

Many southerners found northern accents intrinsically amusing and some saw them as a reliable indicator of thinly concealed stupidity. All Mike Yarwood, a Lancastrian, had to do was sound northern and he was halfway to making the south laugh. This was a good idea, since it was in the south that BBC contracts were dished out. As Callaghan and Healey were both Yorkshiremen he was doubtless keeping his friends in Lancashire happy too.

I was picking up a few indicators that dad didn't just find

the jokes and silly voices funny, he really couldn't stand the Labour Party. I had no idea why and didn't ask. What would I ask anyway? It wasn't long before then that I thought of a party as somewhere you passed parcels.

It's easy to like things your parents like but not so easy to dislike the things they don't like, particularly if you're not sure why they don't like them. It's not in a child's nature to dislike the new, other than new greens at teatime. Children are inherently trusting with people, they are prepared to like other children instinctively. Prejudice is not genetic. Although children will swap 'best' friends over night, it is the capacity to continually make new friends and to find common ground that is plainly innate. A distressing sight for adults is the child who cannot socialize. It appears both abnormal and irreparable. Only a damaged child could not make friends easily and damage done so early seems a curse on a young life.

Despite struggling to comprehend or share a dislike of the lampooned Labour leadership (in fact, Healey seemed nicely avuncular even as he was being ridiculed by Yarwood), I was nonetheless determined to like the Conservatives and not Labour.

There was a sense that Labour were somehow unpatriotic that was influential. The big word of the '70s that I heard continually but didn't understand was 'strike'. Judging by television news reports, a strike seemed to consist of lots of men, usually from the north (of Watford), angrily refusing to go to work and consequently wrecking England. The people who did the striking were in unions and these were bad. People on strike were greedy, selfish and bone idle. There was that and something called 'British Leyland', which was evidently a disaster.

British Leyland, the nationalized car company, was, it

turns out, a disaster. We had a variety of British-made cars growing up, a white Mk 1 Ford Cortina with groovy round rear lights, a big Morris that my mum hated driving because of its size (one time the passenger door opened by itself, as if the ghost of a stunt man had flung himself out). A Morris Traveller that Mum reversed into a ditch outside Staples Road School. I sat inside the car while lots of men pushed it out of the forest and back on to the road.

By 1979 we had a hideous Austin Princess; it was as ugly as a trodden beer can and the same excremental brown that Coventry City were using for an away kit. Could British Leyland survive, making ugly brown cars, with engines that had a reputation for not starting when you wanted them to, and stopping when you didn't want them to, built by a strike-happy workforce?

No, they couldn't.

Not to worry though. Maggie Thatcher was at hand and she was going to save Britain. She had posters put up everywhere, with the slogan 'Labour isn't Working' and a photo of a dole queue on it. Much emphasis was placed on putting the great back in to Great Britain, waving the Union Jack and implying that Labour and its supporters were less British Socialists and more Russian Communists.

In a 1978 interview for Granada TV's *World in Action* Thatcher had commented that:

'. . . people are really rather afraid that this country might be rather swamped by people with a different culture.'

Her approval ratings went up, suggesting that people *were* really rather afraid. These political conflicts were lost on children. They were powered by the fears of adults.

Children aren't generally 'really rather afraid' of other cultures, certainly not in Loughton at that time, when there were no other cultures. The only black people we saw were the little ones looked after by Mrs Curry who lived nearby. What sort of fostering programme she was involved with I don't know but she always had different little black kids with her. Perhaps they were refugees from Uganda, who knows? After Mum died I remember being looked after by Mrs Curry sometimes but even then I didn't meet any black kids.

I didn't meet a foreigner until 1971 when Dr Grunberger took my tonsils out. I've no idea where he was from but I suspect he'd been interned during the Second World War. He said my tonsils were going to go in the dustbin. I had to stay overnight in the hospital.

Early in the morning I was put on a trolley, taken into a room and gassed. When I woke up a big nurse was making me eat cornflakes. They were hard and jagged like a neckful of razors but she was unsympathetic and couldn't go until I ate them. It wouldn't happen now, fortified breakfast cereal? So twentieth century. My mum picked me up from the hospital and laughed in a slightly teary way when she saw I couldn't lift my little bag.

That nurse was the first black person I ever spoke to and the only one until 1976, when I spent a year in the same class as the only black kid at the school, noisy Derek, who later unexpectedly became Derek B, the rapper.

Near to my old school, on Woodford Green, stands a statue of Winston Churchill, who had been MP for the old constituency of Wanstead and Woodford. We often drove past the statue and my dad, who was just six when the war broke out and who became enamoured of Churchill's inspiring leadership as it progressed, would smile and say: 'Good old Winnie.' It was clear to me as a child that this was THE GREATEST MAN WHO EVER LIVED.

Maggie Thatcher was trying to channel Churchill by arousing a 'pull in your belts, grow your own veg and melt down your gates for nuclear subs' blitz spirit. This in a Britain that she maintained was going downhill after the notorious strike-ridden '78–'79 'winter of discontent'. Her no-nonsense scary school matron approach appealed to enough voters (three out of ten is enough, when four out of ten don't vote) and she was installed with a mandate to go after the unions, give tax cuts to high earners and indulge in populist fervent nationalism for the fearful.

People were afraid, Maggie Thatcher knew that. She was going to encourage them to believe in happier times gone by, which could return again, inducing nostalgia with war-time imagery and invoking the spirit of Good Old Winnie. The woman who had once voted for the return of birching in schools grabbed Britain by the scruff of the neck, put it over her knee, and beat it until it snapped in two. If you were lucky you ended up in the half where the money was. We were lucky . . . ish.

Debbie Harry

On *Top of the Pops,* just as I was turning twelve, appeared the stop-you-on-the-spot most captivating woman I'd ever seen. Debbie Harry, the peroxided eponymous heroine of Blondie, first wafted, skipped and smiled around the living room singing 'Denis (Denee)' in 1978. It was the New York band's first hit in Britain (number two, I remember) and afterwards many boys were never the same again. For me, if there was one person linking the boy of the late '70s with the adolescent of the early '80s, it was her.

Many men claim a monastic devotion to onanism. It's a common error, made in the hope that pronouncements of achievement in masturbation, chiefly concerned with frequency, will cement an enviable reputation for virility, in the certain belief that women will be attracted to a relentless tosser. In truth it doesn't appeal, the image of enthused self-abuse. Besides, I was average, nothing special at all and a bit of a late starter (13 August 1979).

Not long prior to that, I had known that I liked girls but it was their faces and the way they said things that was attractive as opposed to their limbs and protrusions. I fancied TV's Marti Caine and before her I had *loved* Jan Hunt off of *Crackerjack.* When another boy's letter was read out to Jan on *Crackerjack*, a letter in which the boy signed off by saying 'I love you, Jan', there was much aah-ing in the studio and Jan said she loved him too. The thing is, I suspect he really did love Jan, and she perhaps didn't really love him. To declare your love, for your message to reach the person, and then for them to go 'aah' in front of everyone (and with those '70s viewing figures it virtually was everyone), that can break a man, even at eight years old.

Trying to please my dad, by accepting the chance to go to secondary school a year early, meant that many of the boys in my year were as much as eighteen months older than me. The Mr Men stickers on my briefcase had drawn sarcastic comments and I felt the age gap from the first day. By 1979 I had been there for two and a half years and I was a follower and copier. This was hard going at times but better to follow the herd than stick out as the baby. On a school trip to Sorrento in Italy, to visit Vesuvius and Pompeii, I discovered how big a difference a year and a half can be.

Pompeii was just baking hot but Vesuvius was good. We all had to walk across a large flat expanse of sulphur crust. There were fenced off areas where the crust had given way and a bubbling volcanic broth was visible. We were under strict instructions (not strict enough) to walk in pairs, as a concentration of weight could see us as croutons in the black soup. A boy called O'Keefe, who had such big wide shoes some called him duck-feet, gleefully started to jump up and down. Several of us joined in. We wanted it to crack. Perhaps we thought we could leap aside if it collapsed. Our Italian guide turned and screamed at us with real fear in her eyes and we desisted.

In the evenings our time was our own. We discovered a bar on the beach that could be reached via a tunnel carved through the cliffside. This place had two things going for it:

1. None of our teachers had found it;
2. The staff were happy to serve bottled beer to fourteen-year-olds.

This was the first place I was ever drunk. We played table football with local kids and taught them how to swear in English. They then called us wankers all night which started to get on our nerves. 'No, *we're* not wankers, *you* are wankers,' we said.

We had to walk back up through the cliff to find our hotel. It was pitch black in the tunnel but I had a small portable 'combat radio' which had a light built in to it. This was a child's toy that I had taken to a beach bar. It was made in camouflage colours with absurd pseudo-military features, such as a button you could press that emitted a bleep. Intended for morse code transmissions (that could reach as far as the person standing next to you), it only served to nearly trigger a fit in an epileptic fifth former.

Another night someone had borrowed my radio so they could walk up through the tunnel in the dark. Later, stranded alone in absolute blackness, I was rescued by an Italian kid striking a match and lighting up the opening of the tunnel. I was too young to be staggering home from bars in the dark.

On our last night we drank lots of the foul beer and, when I returned to the room, which four of us were sharing, I found it was spinning. I knelt over the toilet for ages but was not sick. Each time I went to lie down the room would pitch and sway. If I closed my eyes it spun so violently I felt as if I'd fall off the bed. The next morning we had to wait for hours in Naples airport, which was a sweltering building site with no chairs. Perfect for a first hangover.

The four of us in that hotel room lay in bed at night talking about stuff that was a little advanced for me. This lot were practised onanists, or at least Gary at the far end was. As we lay there in the dark he would talk us through a strange synchronized masturbation ritual. He fiddled away whilst describing what he was doing and inquiring of his peers how they were progressing. Answers were generally informal, then monosyllabic and serious until, after a while, they became less frequent and any sounds were primal in nature. I was at the end against the wall furthest from Gary. The boy next to him moaned and strained slightly and Gary asked him if he had finished. He confirmed that he had indeed ejaculated and was advised to 'let it dry off'. I had never ejaculated and this 'drying off' process sounded a bit revolting. Soon afterwards the boy in the bed next to me announced his climax. I also intimated that I was done (I wasn't). Gary's shuddering endgame was alarming.

Thankfully the bedroom light stayed off and there was no post-mortem of the ejaculate. No height and distance comparisons and no biscuit introduced into the event as I had heard of in other institutions. I went to sleep unaware that a lasting impression had been made on me.

Returning home, I was delighted to be back in my own bedroom, with Debbie Harry staring down at me from the wall slumped on her knees in a zebra print leotard, ring-eyed and pouting. She was far from the picture of health epitomized by Farrah Fawcett from *Charlie's Angels* or Victoria Principal from *Dallas* who were both snipped from the *TV Times* and Blu-Tacked in place. In fact, Debbie had a little heroin chic about her, approximately ten years before there was heroin chic. But I liked her. Much more than the millions of other boys worldwide who would have done anything she asked except stop looking at her.

On top of all that X-factor sex-factor stuff, Blondie's music, in particular *Parallel Lines*, was distinctive, catchy and as edgy as big-selling popular music dared to be. I still have that album on cassette and the later *AutoAmerican* on vinyl.

I had unwrapped a small portable record player the

previous Christmas (or birthday). My constant use of the family record player in the living room had been wearing a bit thin, especially as I only had two compilation LPs to choose from, *Action Replay* and *Midnight Hustle*. I recommend them. In order to record on to a cassette I had to put my tape recorder up against the mono speaker when the charts were on the radio and then press play and record. From that moment everyone had to be totally silent or vacate the living room.

The new record player changed my life for the better and I saved up my pennies to buy my first album, *Regatta de Blanc* by The Police. Within a fortnight a friend had borrowed it for taping and when he returned it no one was in so he left it in the porch. My dad found it and I expected him to be annoyed at the expense but he bought my story that I'd saved up for it.

In truth I was nicking any coin I could lay my hands on by now and pilfering notes from the handbag of the lovely woman, Jenny, who was employed by my dad to be at home each evening when we came home from school. She made our tea and cajoled us into homework before sitting with us until my dad came home. Eventually, I confessed to my dad that I'd been stealing from her, when more and more unexplainable items began to appear ('I'd have bought you a stopwatch if you'd asked for one', 'No you wouldn't', 'Yes I would'). He told me that Jenny's husband had left her because of the money going missing from her handbag.

Thirty years later, Jenny's son e-mailed out of the blue and sent me some pictures that he'd come across after Jenny had passed away. We corresponded and he told me that I hadn't, in fact, broken up her marriage, which was a relief to hear. I was very fond of her and she had been a wonderful surrogate mother, particularly to me and my sister.

The Police were my favourite band by the end of 1979 (the year Blondie had number ones with 'Heart of Glass' and 'Sunday Girl' and The Police had number ones with 'Message in a Bottle' and 'Walking on the Moon') but no one could replace Debbie Harry as the top pop icon of her era. Sting was pretty but not that pretty.

1979 was remarkable for freaks and oddballs having hits. No one remotely fanciable. The Boomtown Rats were number one for four weeks with 'I Don't Like Mondays', which I bought without knowing that it was about a sixteen-year-old girl in San Diego shooting several children in a playground because she didn't like Mondays. Then there was Tubeway Army fronted by Gary Numan with 'Are Friends Electric?' That was a great song but he was no role model for me, I never had bleach and guyliner urges. 'Pop Musik' by M was as popular as a song could be without being number one. In January Ian Dury had a number one with 'Hit Me with Your Rhythm Stick'. I bought it in a record shop on Tottenham High Road walking back to the car with my dad after another Spurs game. The Clash released 'London Calling' but it made no impression on me; I had Amii Stewart, Sister Sledge and 'Le Freak' by Chic on my mini-turntable.

Top of the Pops was essential viewing but in 1979 I considered boycotting it if they kept putting Gloria Gaynor on singing 'I Will Survive'. Me and my sister found adult expressions of emotion ludicrous and, for years, had been turning away from the TV when couples kissed.

At thirteen I was yet to discover music outside the charts. I was a devotee of *Smash Hits* and that was as far as I was going to look, so I had to put up with songs charting that I found unlistenable.

There was an affecting combination of innocence and

47

sexual confidence about Debbie Harry, a childish sense of play in her fronting of the band. She sang in a high, childlike, voice too. But she was entirely adult and in her mid-thirties, which explains her relaxed demeanour, since she wasn't playing at what she thought might be sexy, as a young star might, she was actually sexy. If she winked at you it would leave you briefly paralysed. In 1980 Blondie had three singles in the UK ('Atomic', 'Call Me' and 'The Tide is High') and all of them went to number one. Then they went a bit weird, the music was good but not *as* good and in 1982 they split and Debbie was gone. All I had left was a couple of albums, a couple of singles, a calendar and the heroin-chic poster.

Liam Brady

On 23 December 1978 Arsenal played Spurs at White Hart Lane in the first game between the two clubs since Spurs were relegated in May '77. In the second half Liam Brady robbed Peter Taylor of possession on the left-hand edge of the Spurs' penalty area. Looking up, he swung his left foot across the back of the ball, hitting it with the outside of his boot. The ball leapt up, past the defender obscuring Brady's view of the goal, and took off in the direction of the terracing near the corner flag on the right-hand side of the pitch. No sooner was it travelling than it started to move in the air, pulling against its natural line, arcing high past the Spurs keeper. It still looked like it was going wide with a few yards to go before swerving hard left under the bar and smashing in to the net in front of the Arsenal fans.

John Motson was commentating for the BBC:

'Look at that!' he screamed. 'Oh look at that!'

When Brady finished his follow-through he had swivelled through 180 degrees and was looking back over his shoulder to see the ball go in. He then jigged, arms wide, towards the delirious Arsenal fans with a broad grin on his face while Graham Rix yanked on his shirt to try and catch him. Arsenal beat Spurs 5–0. I wore a badge on the inside of my school blazer with the date and the score on it for months afterwards.

That single moment propelled me back through the gates at Highbury a week later for the first time in nine months. Arsenal beat Birmingham 3–1 and Pat Rice scored, which was very rare. Pat became widely known as Patrice after so many years working as Arsene Wenger's assistant. I hadn't been to any games since Ipswich beat Arsenal in the '78 FA Cup Final but now Arsenal had a confirmed superstar in their midst and I wanted to see him. He'd always been good but now he was moving on to another level and was considered to be the best midfielder in the country. This was agony for Spurs fans, who considered the foppish under-achiever Hoddle to be the best.

The joy of Brady was his unathletic gait. He loped rather than ran, round-shouldered and persistent. He wasn't a powerhouse, he was slight and pale with tufty hair and bony knees, but he was beyond exceptional with the ball. Almost impossible to dispossess, with a shifting centre of balance and a speed of thought that set him apart from anyone else, he was the player everyone in the team looked for whenever Arsenal had the ball. He could drive it across the pitch, or loft it, or chip it, he had the full set of golf clubs to choose from, any height, pace or distance you want, with hook or fade and the ability to stop it dead, run it on or even spin it back. Older Arsenal fans compared him to Alex James (not the goat's cheese maker out of Blur but a Scottish inside forward) who played for Arsenal in their earliest heydays in the '30s. Forty years' worth of players had run out on to that pitch and only now was there someone worthy of comparison to James.

For the first few weeks of '79 I still had to be chaperoned to Highbury by my older brother, who agreed to come though he apparently hated the whole experience. In January Arsenal were playing Nottingham Forest, who were the champions of England. Late in the first half, John Robertson scored for Forest and they led 1–0. My brother celebrated their goal. Quietly, of course, so as not to draw the attention of Arsenal fans in the tightly packed terrace, but I distinctly heard him say, 'Yes!' when the goal went in. It's bad enough that he had to come with me but now he was supporting the away team, after all those years I had at White Hart Lane amusing myself while he cheered on Spurs with my dad. It all turned out all right. Arsenal won 2–1. There were 52,000 people packed in, the biggest crowd I'd ever been crushed by. A few weeks later I turned thirteen and I was allowed out on my own, at last, free.

I loved going. I loved the journey into my own time and space, on the 20 bus, past school without stopping, to Walthamstow Central for the Victoria line, and I loved Highbury, more than anywhere I'd ever been. Unfortunately, I've been all over the shop now and Highbury's probably still my top spot. You should look around though, would be my advice, you may find somewhere better than your favourite childhood haunts (you won't actually, nowhere will ever mean as much).

I went there all the time. Not only on match days. Sometimes I went to the club shop. This consisted of a room near the top end of Avenell Road. Inside was a counter with a stern old man behind it who didn't have much time for kids who just wanted to hang around in the shop. He assumed, I suppose, that kids who hang around in the shop might try and nick stuff. He did not assume – why would he? – that some of the boys who hung around in the shop did so because travelling there took nearly an hour and a half door-to-door by public transport from Essex. Any less than ten minutes peering over the counter would mean it was hardly worth the effort. Of course, as a raging kleptomaniac, I would have tried to nick stuff but it was all behind the counter with this narky old sod with a scarred forehead guarding it.

The narky old sod turned out to be Jack Kelsey, one of the greatest goalkeepers in Arsenal's history. A winner of a league championship medal in 1953, he played for Wales against Brazil, including the seventeen-year-old Pele, in the 1958 World Cup Finals. The Brazilians called him 'the cat with magnetic claws'.

In 1959, during a Cup tie for Arsenal, he broke his left arm but carried on playing, on the left wing. Kelsey was a tough, really tough, custodian of the Arsenal goal.

From Jack Kelsey I would buy, for example, an Arsenal comb. In a red leather comb holder. I used to carry a comb because sometimes on telly you'd see a cool American dude whipping a comb out of his back pocket and quickly tidying his hair. This would usually happen when a girl was approaching. This made him more attractive to the girl. At least the cool dude characters thought so and often the scriptwriter went along with it (especially where the Fonz in *Happy Days* was concerned). Generally though, preeners only make themselves more attractive to themselves, which is a narcissistic downward spiral best avoided.

I combed my hair often. Sometimes I would part it in the centre and then run the comb horizontally from the forehead to the crown. This would make my hair lift up in a kind of fluffy sub-Kid Jensen look. This was obviously a mistake on my part but I was twelve and didn't know any better. The centre-parted 'hairstyle' drew only two reactions. One from a kid at school who said: 'What have you done to your hair?' The other was from my brother. Having watched my lengthy preening ritual, he kicked me in the leg.

I managed to get Brady's autograph, ironically, at half-time during a Spurs v Man City game at White Hart Lane. He was sitting in the stands with Jimmy Holmes, a Spurs player who played with him for the Republic of Ireland. As soon as the half-time whistle went I was straight over to him. 'Chippy?' I said and he looked round a bit surprised. Chippy was his nickname, apparently coined because he likes chips. Nowadays he wouldn't be allowed chips at the Arsenal training ground and his nickname would be 'lightly grilled chicken'. He signed my programme and I left him alone. First rule of autograph hunting: don't linger, get in and get out. The autographer does not want to chat to you, you are twelve, he wants to chat to his friend. He signed a few more and then he stopped signing. I was close enough to be first in. How lucky.

Twenty-five years later I managed to get Thierry Henry to sign my programme at White Hart Lane the day Arsenal won the league title there (for the second time). I told Henry he was 'a legend', he said, 'Thank you' and I remembered the first rule, get out, he doesn't want to talk to you, you are thirty-eight, if you were twelve it might be tolerable but thirty-eight? Shut up and walk away. Well, dance away, Arsenal have won the league and everyone's dancing, except the Spurs stewards, who look livid.

It was around 2004 that I was asked to take part in a Comic Relief charity football match, preparation for which would involve an indoor training session at Highbury, run by Liam Brady. I agreed immediately. Arriving on the day, I was told that Liam, who is in charge of Arsenal's youth academy, wasn't going to take a training session and instead wanted us to play an eight-a-side game against Arsenal's under-fifteens. My heart sank. I was nowhere near up to playing against kids like that when I was fifteen, or ever in fact.

We went on to the indoor Astroturf pitch and, as if by magic, Liam Brady appeared. He was going to take us through a warm-up. He had us run across the pitch six times. I was out in front, running and smiling and getting noticed by Liam. After the sixth crossing we stopped to catch our breath. Immediately Liam said:

'OK, good, now again, *eight* times. Let's go!'

After three I was struggling, by five I was at the back of the pack where I stayed, not smiling. Liam called out: 'You flattered to deceive earlier, Alan.' I tried to return his smile but my grimace wouldn't shift and now of course Liam *had* noticed me and cut me to the quick.

The game started. Brady himself played at the back. At one point I ran over to close him down when he was in possession. He stopped dead and looked at me. He then lifted his left foot up so it was in mid-air over the ball. I stared at it. It seemed no one else was on the pitch. He began moving his foot from side to side and immediately my head was moving too, as I watched his foot, like a dog following its master as he moves a biscuit around in front of him. I snapped out of it and lunged for the ball. He whipped it away smartly and passed it to one of his trainees. They moved so fast. We were 6–0 down in a matter of minutes and I'd been personally toyed with by Chippy Brady. It was great.

Brady's finest hour for Arsenal came in the 1979 FA Cup Final against Manchester United at Wembley. A year after the Ipswich disaster the Arsenal team had reportedly pledged amongst themselves to go back to the final and win the cup. I was glued to the television as I had been in '78 only this time the house was empty. The whole family had decamped to deepest Essex to a family party. How could anyone hold a family party on Cup Final day? No one in our family ever held parties. I was excused from going. I would have been a terrible guest.

I had a scarf on and two rosettes stuck on the telly trolley.

Arsenal were in yellow, which some Arsenal fans considered lucky as they'd won the cup in 1971 in yellow. They had also worn yellow against Ipswich so that was a straw clutched.

Supermac couldn't play and Brian Talbot who Arsenal had bought from Ipswich came in. Graham Rix also started. Pat Jennings was his usual immense presence in goal and Patrice was captain. Most importantly Brady was playing and he was fully operational, only twenty-three but already the Players' Player of the Year.

Early on Brady dribbled across the pitch, eluding tackles ('Sweet skills from Brady,' said John Motson). He fed Stapleton who played in Price and his cross was bashed in by a combination of Talbot and Alan Sunderland. One nil. I jumped around the room. Then Brady ghosted past two defenders to the bye-line and chipped the ball on to the head of Stapleton for 2–0. He'd crossed it with his right foot, he never used his right foot. I could go and try to copy that since I never used my left.

The goal had echoes of two others scored in the cup run. In the fourth round v Notts County my dad came with me to Highbury. We saw Brady beat four players along the bye-line before playing the ball into the net off Talbot's backside. Then, away to Nottingham Forest, he drifted over a free kick that Stapleton managed to head over Shilton for the winner.

In the second half the game was uneventful but I was only interested in the outcome. I didn't know the difference between a good game and a poor one. I had no idea of tactics. I just wanted to win. With five minutes left it was still 2–0. Pat Jennings had hardly been busied all game. Then United scored and I became concerned. Immediately they equalized and I collapsed to the floor, tears shooting horizontally out of my face.

'NOOOO,' I wailed. 'No, no, no!' slapping the carpet, blubbing, managing to find two syllables in 'N-o . . .'

The game restarted and it looked like extra time would follow. Brady picked the ball up in midfield, moved past an opponent and forced himself into United's half. Holding off a second challenge, his socks round his ankles, he drew another defender towards him before passing gently to Rix outside him. The ball, as ever from Brady, rolled perfectly, so Rix didn't have to break stride. He lifted a cross deep in to the United area and Sunderland slid it in.

'Yes!' I screamed. 'Yes! Yes!' I was crying again now. 'YEESSS, YES, YES, HA HA HA Y-E-S.'

I was on my knees, touching the screen. The ref ended the game. Arsenal had won 3–2. I was emotional for ages.

My family returned in the evening. My brother said nothing. My dad and my sister told me they'd had the game on at the party and that they'd been cheering Arsenal, that someone else there wanted United to win and that they'd been supporting my team, which I was pleased to hear. They knew I'd have a meltdown if Arsenal had lost but Brady had pushed the team home and was a hero to a generation of fans. He was the best player in the country and he was ours for ever!

Valerie Harper

There was a feeling amongst my peers that, culturally, American was best. We'd been swamped by their popular entertainment and body-rotting soft drinks. We revered their fast food. When the friend who borrowed my Police album told me the band was English, I expressed surprise. He said, 'I know, they're so good you'd think they were American.' British sitcoms on TV were losing their appeal. They suddenly felt dated, rooted as they often were in a theatrical style of writing and performance. There were exceptions, *Yes, Minister* in particular, but generally I felt I was growing out of my old favourites. They were being usurped by a batch of original and more contemporary American sitcoms that BBC2 were finding a home for in the early evening. Shows like *M·A·S·H*, *Taxi* and *Rhoda*, with Valerie Harper.

In 1979 *Quadrophenia* was released and a gang of half a dozen fourteen- and fifteen-year-old boys boarded a 20 bus in Loughton to go to the Woodford ABC to see it. A thirteen-year-old tagged along. This was a hugely exciting excursion to see the much-anticipated mods and rockers film. A British film set in the '60s about kids running riot, about freedom and youth, with great music. We piled off the bus and headed into the foyer trying to look eighteen as it was an X certificate. The tallest boy went in front as we stood behind trying to look like a gang as opposed to a gaggle. 'Seven for *Quadrophenia*,' he said, wearing a serious expression, as we all did. Seriousness denoted maturity, kids smile at strangers, adults don't. The woman in the kiosk didn't flinch, didn't take her hands out of her lap, and looked at him:

'You're not old enough.'

'Yes we are.'

'How old are you then?'

'Eighteen.'

She smiled at this.

'No you're not.'

'I am but the rest aren't.'

'None of you are.'

He gave up. This was hopeless. If one had got in he could have opened the fire escape for the rest but it wasn't happening.

'We'll go somewhere else then,' a few of us said, in defiance.

'Yeah, we'll go to Gant's Hill.'

'OK then,' she said.

We didn't go to the Gant's Hill Odeon (where, oddly, we'd been to see *Star Wars* the year before on a *school trip)*. It was quite far away and we knew we wouldn't get in. I wasn't held responsible as the youngest; none of us had even tried to get in to an X before. It was an absurd certificate for that film even by old standards. There is a scene where Jimmy (Phil Daniels) has sex with Steph (Leslie Ash) in an alley but you don't see any flesh below the neck. We all became smitten with Leslie Ash, after we had eventually seen the film the following year; even though her character was cruel and self-centred, she was fit. We didn't say fit though; I don't remember what we said. If you liked a girl you fancied her, that was about it.

Finding our own entertainment was not easy. It had to be of no interest to parents. I was well on my way in this regard, struggling as I was to share my dad's weekend passion for Max Bygraves sing-along albums or Bing sodding Crosby. I was going to have to find my own favourites since my brother had been ignoring me since 1976 and my younger sister was, in my eyes, too young and sisterish. I imagined her as five years old until about 1987, when she turned nineteen.

Previously, family TV shows like *The Good Life* had been the norm at home. Picture the scene: one television only, no VCR, or hard drive recording, no watching illegal downloads on your phone on the bus. You had to be in at the right time and you had to watch Tom, Barbara, Margot and Jerry with your family. Fortunately, they find it funny too, so you're all happy for thirty blissful minutes of Penelope Keith. It won't be until you're thirteen that the desire to dislike anything they like and to like something they don't know about, thereby forging an emerging identity and sense of self, will become increasingly overwhelming.

There were comedy shows available that appealed to young adults and as I was on my way to being one of those, I watched them. Shows we did not watch as a family included *Not the Nine O'Clock News* and *The Kenny Everett Video Show*.

Kenny Everett's eccentric nonsense dressing-up show was consistently hilarious, with a cast of characters undreamt of by other comedians. He also featured the Hot Gossip dance troupe, with a nice line in fishnets, buckles and splayed-legged choreography. They made Pan's People look like Brownies and rapidly accelerated the hormonal development of a generation. They were also intimidating, in an S&M way, which is why Pan's People are more fondly remembered. Hot Gossip were dirty, frankly, and only the confident could have dealt with them. That the confident included Andrew

Lloyd-Webber, who married one of them in Sarah Brightman, was so shocking as to be mentionable only in a whisper.

Not the Nine O'Clock News was a revelation and became essential viewing for teenagers. Rowan Atkinson was an odd-looking comic wonder. A silly voice, a silly face and a silly walk, the full set, all in one bizarre package. He was hard to watch as he contorted his face into odd and ugly shapes for our amusement but he was unique and very funny.

Meanwhile, the bridge from the old style sitcoms to a more adult take on life was being provided by those American comedy shows. Unfettered as they were by a tradition of seaside postcard innuendo, they depicted adults in adult relationships with adult aspirations and adult disputes.

It would be unfair to suggest that no British sitcoms dealt with characters with a complex and credible emotional life. Carla Lane's *Butterflies* with Wendy Craig as Ria fantasizing about an affair, despite a good if unexpressive husband at home, was very popular.

Equally, the American shows were as prone to sanitized home environments and unbelievable characterizations. The Fonz in *Happy Days* was as daft as they come. How did he become so popular? It was unbelievable that he would snap his fingers and girls would flock around him, or that he was a tough guy who could win fights gymnastically while combing his hair. Why did he practically live in a diner populated by high school kids? He was as plausible as Spiderman. His function was as some kind of neo-cult leader who operated as an idol for young people (both in the show and watching at home) who were more intelligent, kinder and better dressed. It was an odd but warm and funny rose-tinted view of late '50s, early '60s Milwaukee. Mr and Mrs Cunningham were *über*-parents any kid would love to have, it never rained, and there was no burgeoning civil rights movement since there were no black people (other than those boxing on the TV). Perhaps they had their own jazz-diner on the other side of reality.

Happy Days was a kids' show really. Whereas the Korean War comedy *M·A·S·H* featured a different side of the '50s, as well as showing where one or two of those black people had got to.

M·A·S·H was for grown-ups. Surgeons up to their elbows in entrails should have been harrowing viewing but since they were wise-cracking in the tradition of the Marx Brothers while they were working, the same jokes they used to get through a shift served to take the viewers' minds off the carnage too. The gags came so thick and fast it was possible to watch an operating theatre and laugh. Then every so often they'd take a principled stand and draw out some pathos about humanity, inhumanity, or the finer points of distilling alcohol in a war zone.

Alan Alda was the main man in the fine *M·A·S·H* ensemble and his fast-joking, barely serious, skirt-chasing medic was right up my dad's street. He loved Alan Alda so much I thought he wanted to be him. I liked Alda because he was called Alan. (I was named after midget movie heart-throb Alan Ladd. After Mum had died, Dad would always mock Alan Ladd, by shouting: 'He's standing on a box!' whenever he came on the telly. He may have shouted that in the cinema when my mum was alive. Let's hope so.)

Taxi was on earlier in the evening so my dad missed it since he was on his way home from work. This was another ensemble show with a solid emotional heart and hysterical supporting nutcases, a staple form of American sitcom and rarely bettered than here. Alex and Elaine were the central characters whose divorces, disappointments and despondency would regularly be put aside to help their fellow taxi drivers. The two leads were perfect conduits for an audience who wanted good-looking funny people to watch, provided they were struggling a little. A cast of youthful optimists and wizened no-hopers tried to see the glass half-full while Danny de Vito's tyrannical dispatcher Louis barked at them from within his cage. When Louis first left the dispatcher's cage, to physically confront someone, and in doing so revealed himself to be only five feet tall and the cage to be actually raised up, it made for one of the funniest television moments I can ever remember. No one, in England at least, had any idea he was so short. The cage put him up at a regular height and he was so loud and bombastic he seemed, well, not to be little. Backed up by Christopher Lloyd playing a '6os LSD-casualty and Andy Kaufman's squeaky Eastern European mechanic, Latka, there was a comic strength in depth that left no line unplundered for laughs and no close-up opportunity passed up by comic players of the highest calibre. *Taxi* was one of my favourite shows but there was no one in there I wanted actually in my life.

Rhoda was another New York-set sitcom with a good-looking thirty-something whose life had gone wrong and who was now trying to muddle through after a divorce. She was actually married in an early episode but, by the time the show was up and running in the UK and I was hooked, she had an ex-husband and spent much of her time dealing with the problems of her younger sister Brenda, played to droll and helpless perfection by Julie Kavner, known for twenty years or more now as the voice of Marge Simpson.

Valerie Harper played Rhoda and created a character that seemed to offer the potential for perfection as a wife or mother. I would have taken either. Plus she was *my* favourite. No one at home or at school talked about her, no one else watched the show. Only I liked Rhoda. She was beautiful, funny, kind and unhappy; she needed me. Without a mother it was inevitable that other women would be examined, consciously or otherwise, through the mum-shaped prism I stored in my head. This one was a fit.

Rhoda, be my mum!

Then, with an unseen hormonal shift having momentarily adjusted my view of the world, I'd take another look. Seeing Rhoda with burgeoning adolescence about to break like a perfect storm in my life, meant seeing Rhoda very differently.

Rhoda, be my girlfriend!

This is not Oedipal, it is hormonal. Rhoda wore her beauty casually, and her warmth and kindness came through. She was immensely appealing in every way. Just watching her deal with slothful Carlton the doorman over the apartment intercom could have amused me all day.

1980

Harry Redknapp

In 1978 I still couldn't get into any school sports teams, so Dad told me to tell them that I was young enough to play for the year below. It was clearly *very important* that I play for the school even though I was *not good enough*. I told the teacher who ran the first year's cricket team. He looked baffled. This was clearly unprecedented, possibly in the history of the school. All schools perhaps. He agreed to put me in the team if that's what I wanted. When I turned up, the other players said: 'What are you doing here?' I said: 'I'm young enough to play with you.' They assumed I was lying (why would I do that?), only relenting when they'd checked my date of birth in the school calendar.

The game started. They didn't let me bowl and I was made to bat at number 11. I scored one run. That was the sum total of my school sporting achievement (other than coming fourth in the 200 metres one year, when the race leaders all stopped because they mistakenly thought they'd crossed the finishing line). I did not receive a, peculiarly uncoveted, 'colours' tie.

Lacking the confidence for team sports, I preferred skateboarding but that was only good for the summer when I'd go to the Rom Skatepark in Hornchurch with school friends. I loved the Rom. We also went to Skate City by Tower Bridge and the converted cinema, Mad Dog Bowl, on the Old Kent Road, plus there was another indoor one out in West London I went to by myself, or you could skate on the South Bank. There were some fibreglass ramps in

Waltham Abbey I liked but the Rom was the best with a huge area and plenty of different bowls on which to stretch the grip of my red 65 mm Kryptonic wheels.

When the weather was bad, skateboarding was not possible, Kryptonics or not. Weekends, especially when Arsenal were playing away, were dull. I'd go down the road to watch football matches played on pitches by Loughton station. When my dad asked where I'd been, he decided to try and find a football team for me.

By the beginning of 1980 I was halfway through a season with Loughton Boys under-14s. They trained in a school gym on Wednesday evenings. I'd go to the training sessions but found it difficult to fit in. None of them went to my school and they'd been playing together since they were ten. I knew one kid, who lived in my road, and another who went to a nearby school who I used to see on the bus. He was a big, quite hard kid, called Russell, who I bonded with over cigarettes on the 20a. The rest of them weren't too friendly, taking their lead from the manager, who was the father of the left back (an odd-looking boy, not ugly but with an almost perfect cube for a head).

The same eleven played every week and only one substitute was allowed. Each week I asked who was going to be sub but was ignored. I went to watch them one Sunday. They lost 3–0 and didn't seem bothered. There were thirteen or fourteen boys going to training and I was the only one never given a game or used as sub. Unused as a sub would have been a start. One week, I heard a few of them talking about me behind my back before a game of five-a-side. Nothing like my usual meek self, I was annoyed and aggressive, drawing complaints such as 'he kicked me', which was the highlight of my season. The kid from up my road was quick and elusive and we won. After that I didn't get picked on again but I didn't get picked either. I may have been rubbish.

Searching for Loughton Boys on the net reveals that they are now Loughton FC and have a website with photos of their clubhouse. The 1979–80 under-14s are referred to as 'The Magic Squad' and feature on a page about their twenty-five-year anniversary reunion. There is a complete record of their many championships and cup finals from 1977 to 1983 (including one from 1980 that I had no idea about). The manager says they all became fine young men.

I'd been to primary school with one of the squad a few years before, but he knew some of the team and was friendlier with them. They called him Slim, which he wasn't. His surname was Glasscock, which led my friend Jeremy to comment that you can 'always see him coming'. That was not an issue at age nine. One time, while I was playing round at the Glasscocks', Mrs Glasscock said she was popping out and warned us not to play with her replica-gun cigarette lighter. So we did. We lit bits of paper before blowing them out and dropping them in to the fireplace. Unfortunately, I couldn't blow my bit out and it burned my thumb. This hurt. When she came back I couldn't let on why I was crying and said I'd cut it on the tap. But there was no cut on my finger and no blood and the tap wasn't even sharp. Slim said: 'Fancy crying over something like that'. Well, Slim, just so you know: I WAS COVERING FOR YOU.

Mr Glasscock was a bookmaker, which I took to mean he made books. When he wasn't making books he gave us all pennies to bet on the racing on telly. I knew who Lester Piggott and Willie Carson were so would bet on them. This impressed him but I only knew because the telly was never off in our house and *Grandstand* stayed on all day except when we turned over to watch wrestling on ITV. It was enjoyable at the Glasscocks' place, when you weren't ON FIRE.

When the summer of 1980 came round I'd given up on Loughton Boys but wanted to play football so Dad let me have a week on a Bobby Moore Soccer School run at Forest School in Woodford. There were 120 boys divided into groups by age ranging from fifteen down to ten. I was in the under-15s group, where there were one or two really good players. They had a keepy-uppy competiton and the boy that won reached 500 before all the coaches threw footballs at him.

The head coach was Harry Redknapp. He'd been a team mate of Bobby Moore's at West Ham and again in the late '70s at Seattle Sounders. Bobby was the big name who could attract boys to a school and then he got his mates in to run them.

Harry was a fantastic head coach. All the boys loved him. He smiled at everyone all the time and was continually encouraging any boy who came into view: 'Hello, son', 'All right?', 'Nice pass', 'Good effort', 'Well done', 'Great, brilliant', 'That's the way, eye on the ball', 'Good, very good!'

All day long.

Being praised by Harry felt fantastic. He made you want to play well to impress him and then he might say: 'That's the way, son, eye on the ball, watch him, he's got it, that one.' This was inflating, exciting, making you desperate for another touch in case he might praise you again.

The coaches, even Harry, weren't unstinting in their praise of boys, like the kid who could do 500 keepy-ups, who could actually play. If they were too cocky and in danger of wasting their talent they received mainly constructive criticism or had the mickey taken.

Bobby Moore had won the World Cup in 1966 but at

three months old, I missed that. He later played for Fulham in the 1975 FA Cup Final, the only time I could remember seeing him play on telly. He was revered and didn't look like other players. He looked like he was in a washing powder commercial. One day at the soccer school we were told Bobby was coming down to see us.

He wandered round exuding charisma, one of the most famous footballers in the world back in his native Essex, with 120 boys eager to follow in his footsteps. He came to our group and took a brief volleying session. He would lob the ball to you and you had to volley it back in to his chest. The first time, I mishit it into the ground. He lobbed it again, I mishit it again. 'Come on,' he said, unsmiling. I felt tense and was relieved to hit the third one at him. He caught it and moved on with a small sound of acknowledgement. Royalty have a lot of people to see, don't expect much you-time.

Two years later I snogged Bobby Moore's daughter, Roberta, in the toilet at a party and became hopelessly smitten with her. I had been snogging her mate but Roberta appeared and found us a loo to hide in. Her mate was outside the door: 'Roberta and Alan, I know you're in there.'

Roberta was the best-looking girl at the party. She was probably always the best-looking girl at the party. She was blonde and she was beautiful. This didn't usually happen to me. She gave me her number. When I rang, Bobby Moore answered the phone. I didn't mention the volleying incident.

I took the tube from Loughton to Knightsbridge (takes ages) to see Roberta at her Saturday job at the Scotch House. That day her photo was on the front of the *Daily Mirror*, looking like a model, with some 'look at Bobby's girl now' caption underneath. When I turned up, she was on a break but wouldn't come out of the staff room. Instead of the penny dropping, that night I went to a party she was going to be at, for further rejection by her Essex girl mates, who delivered the brush off: 'You're only interested in her because she's Bobby Moore's daughter.'

No, it was because she was well fit, actually, girls.

At the end of the soccer school there was a penalty prize competition. They wanted to narrow it down to two from each age group. In order to qualify for the final our group kept taking penalties until everyone had missed. It seemed obvious that the best kids would breeze through but maybe they felt that way too and lost concentration. They missed. Everyone missed. But mine kept going in! All the other kids, including the ones who had trained with West Ham and Colchester United, were going out. In the end it was just me and another kid. I hit my pen straight at the keeper but he let it through his legs. The other kid hit the post and looked gutted. He held his head in his hands. I went over and shook hands with a serious expression on my face. I was in the final!

We had to take ten penalties with all the other age groups providing goalkeepers. It was really loud, with scores of kids screaming 'MISS, MISS, MISS!' at you. There was one boy there called Ewing so, understandably, someone was always doing the theme from *Dallas,* which was distracting. Despite all these attempts to put me off, I found myself smiling. One of the coaches said I was very cool but this was an act, I wanted to look indifferent when I missed. But I didn't miss! They all went in. All TEN. I won! The only thing I've ever won at football. I was given a Bobby Moore Soccer School plastic ball signed by all the coaches. It was presented to me by Harry. What a fantastic feeling. The highlight of my year. My life up to then. It's still in my top ten moments now. Joy, bliss, pride.

I nearly didn't get the ball home. Returning to the changing rooms I could hear two of the best players muttering that they should have been in the penalty final. When I appeared they stopped talking about it and said well done but keepy-up kid grabbed my prize and started, guess what, keeping it up. It bounced away from him near to some broken glass from a light fitting someone had just smashed for fun and I thought it would burst. The look on my face must have been troubling because they relented. I've still got the ball, there's no air in it and all the signatures have faded away.

For the 1980–81 season my dad found me a place with Garnon Rangers under-15s in Epping. The same problem arose with kids being frosty because they all went to a different school and I had no de-frosting skills, but I knew one from the soccer school and his dad was the manager so, apart from having to address the fact that a couple of them were refusing to pass to me, it was fine.

The manager's selection policy was to give everyone a game, rotating the team and using his subs. He was a nice man but the boys wouldn't listen to him, as his kindness translated into weakness to them. He kept yelling at me in one game, to get upfield and then back and then up, it was exhausting. I turned and swore at him. The ref said, 'Watch your language, number 8.' After the game I went and said sorry. He said:

'Thank you, Alan. It takes a big man to apologize. Brian! *Don't* smoke in the changing room.'

It was fun playing for Garnon even though we only won two games all season. We lost in the cup against Basildon. They laughed when we ran out on to the pitch, *our* pitch. They were taking it in turns to go up front and try to score. None of them could match our centre half, Mus, who scored three own goals. I had a one on one with their keeper which I tried to curl round him but I hit him with it instead. I'm still disappointed about that. It finished 13–1.

I can remember all five of the goals I did score, including one into the top corner v Romford Royals, after which the kid who wouldn't pass to me, and had punched me in the shoulder for bringing it up during a game, was actually friendly.

The only problem I had after that was when we played a team with black players in it. Most teams in our league were all white. I remember the game for a couple of reasons: we won 4–3 (and I scored) but also because when we went round the field shaking hands with our opponents, as we always did at the end of a game, I found myself alone in their half of the pitch, the only player in our team who bothered to go and shake hands with their black goalie. I was the last one back in to what I expected to be a jubilant changing-room but it was a bit quiet and then someone said: 'Nigger-lover.' I didn't reply. No one did. The ones who weren't racist hadn't heard or didn't want the aggravation. I was new and didn't know the drill, though I was familiar with the sentiment.

John Lennon

John Lennon's picture wasn't on my wall at the start of 1980. Although everyone knew the most famous Beatles songs, 'She Loves You', 'Can't Buy Me Love', 'I Want to Hold Your Hand' and so on, because they were played on the radio throughout the '70s. The Beatles weren't discussed by me and my peers. They had, after all, split up when I was four.

At four the Beatles record I liked most was 'Yellow Submarine'. There remains nothing about 'Yellow Submarine' I dislike. It's still the only Beatles single in my collection, released in 1966, the year I was born (the *Guinness Book of Records* says it charted on 11 August, went to number one and was a double A side with 'Eleanor Rigby'), I heard it in my cot, in my high chair and in my mother's arms. At least I imagine I did.

I still have the original 45 appropriated (from the family's long since unplayed record collection) because it was My Favourite Song from the Year I was Born. As an adolescent I preferred the other side, the B in the double A, 'Eleanor Rigby'. 'All the lonely people, where do they all belong?' Quite. Nowadays, I like 'Yellow Submarine' again. Early senility.

Those pictures that were on my bedroom wall were of footballers; the wallpaper put up years earlier was covered in them, footballers and astronauts. Over those were my own pictures, several Arsenal players of course, surgically removed from *Shoot!* or the new upstart *Match* magazine, and pop stars and their lyrics taken from *Smash Hits*.

Each week *Shoot!* featured four or five full-page colour photographs of players that were suitable for sticking on your bedroom wall. These were the only colour pictures of footballers available anywhere. Most weeks your club would not feature so it was exciting when one of their players appeared. When they did he was straight on the wall, naturally.

Smash Hits was the first magazine to print the lyrics from chart singles. Everything from Abba to the Sex Pistols. Now, with the words stuck up on your wall, you could sing along with incomprehensible vocals, headphones on, sitting on the windowsill, legs dangling out, smoking a fag.

Through these bedroom wall montages, we teenagers could project an independent identity. No more Mr Men stickers, this is now *who I am*, forged in collaboration with *Top of the Pops, Shoot!* and *Smash Hits*. The reincarnations were swift at this point and someone on the wall one day could be gone that night but it was up there, displayed with a fervent belief that it *wasn't* how anyone *else* was. Not in that house, not in that suburban town, *not on earth*!

Absent from my wall, from my life, were any thinkers, writers or artists. My wall portrayed no love of science or astronomy, botany or paleontology, ornithology, or tech-nology of any kind. I was a philatelist for a while but that died down. Seen one first-day cover, seen them all. There was no Oscar Wilde on the shelves, or Dickens or D. H. Lawrence. No map of the solar system or cutaway of some extraordinary design by Isambard Kingdom Brunel. There was no classical music, and no Warhol or Hockney prints. In common with everyone I knew there was an appetite only for sport and popular culture.

We did have a magazine called *Look & Learn* delivered every Saturday, full of why the Egyptians did this, how the

Druids built that and when the Vikings pillaged the other, but it remained unread. If a copy of ITV's *Look-In* should turn up, it would be devoured and any picture of Stacey Dorning (who was now playing the grown-up daughter in a sitcom about a cartoonist I watched primarily for scenes involving the grown-up daughter) would be cut out and added to the montage.

The big ideas in life were absent and in the absence of big ideas, of thoughtfulness and understanding, there is a void in an adolescent and that void may become filled with small ideas, thoughtlessness and wilful misunderstanding. Only a boy in such a state of vacancy could be influenced, as so many were, by a periodical called the *National Front News*.

The voice of the NF was sold, among other places, at Brick Lane, where skinhead boys went to get their Dr Marten boots from Blackman's, right in the heart of an area occupied by immigrants for 400 years, from Huguenots to Eastern Europeans, Jews to Chinese and, in the late twentieth century, by Asian families promised a post-colonial fresh start in a Britain needing them.

The first copy of the *National Front News* I saw was at school, proudly exhibited by a classmate I used to go skateboarding with. Its front page headline said:

1.5 MILLION UNEMPLOYED
1.5 MILLION IMMIGRANTS

'It's true though, isn't it?' he said.

It was a clear idea, clearly expressed. For all we knew those figures were accurate. What connection there was between the two statistics, other than that provocatively drawn by the National Front, is debatable. That wasn't a debate we wanted to have though. We had the small idea we needed. Within a few years unemployment was running at four million. I don't know what figures the NF used then, to make their point that, for Britain to attain full employment, people without white skin should 'Go home'. It seemed unlikely that 2.5 million new immigrants had arrived in the meantime.

'Go home' was what we used to say to the owner of what was commonly referred to as 'The Paki Shop' just up the road from school (ironically he lived above the shop, so he was, in a sense, at home). Previously known as 'The Shop', as in: 'Are you going up The Shop?', this was a popular destination for kids from school at lunchtime and daily expeditions would set out to procure sweets by fair means or foul.

Now, preoccupied with our new ideas, we renamed it 'The Paki Shop' and expeditions would set out, not just for sweets, but to make the Asian proprietor's life a misery.

The proprietor could be antagonized. If you banged on his window while he tried to serve people, making faces and shouting, he would eventually begin to move out from behind his counter, giving you time to flee, before he ran out, making threats regarding the school and the police to gales of laughter and shouts of:

'Why don't you go home?'

At primary school we used to refer to black kids as Bournvilles or chocolate drops, not to their faces of course, as there weren't any to say it to, just amongst ourselves as we explored budding attitudes. At Bancroft's our portly nose-picking history teacher never failed to pass comment on Jewish kids who missed school on Jewish holidays. In a lesson about Henry VIII and the dissolution of the mon-asteries he asked any Catholics in the room to raise their hands. There were only two and we were already convinced that one of them was gay, or 'bent' as we would have it.

Poor bloke, now he was bent *and* a Catholic (what that entailed I was unsure but the teacher would only pick you out to cast some aspersion so it couldn't be good). The time that teacher really lost his rag was when one kid turned up with dyed green hair and punk gear on. Even though it was 'own clothes day' and he was 'allowed', he sent him home. The punk was not displeased.

As our peer group's experiment with racism developed so it ran into the inconsistencies all bigots have to face. The real reason that all non-whites have to be shown the way to go home is that, if any remain, there is the clear and present danger of white people accidentally befriending them, thereby undermining the whole philosophy.

There were only a few Asian kids at school and they had previously gone unremarked upon. We'd been sharing classrooms with them for four years but now, it seemed, they had to go home. The odd devil's advocate would pipe up:

'Do you want Hussein to go home then?'

'No, he's all right, it's the rest of them I can't stand.'

'The ones you haven't met?'

This inconsistency was a problem. Attitudes would have to harden. These Asian classmates would have to be told to go home too but none of them could be intimidated; they'd known us for ages. Things did eventually come to a head for me though. I was making friends with an Asian boy. It just happened. I don't know when it started.

His name was Mohammed, or Mo, and I liked him only partly because his dad had a newsagent's and he used to nick fags from there and share them (the children's fag machine at Loughton tube station didn't last for ever). We were becoming friends, sitting together in class, that sort of thing.

I'd never really been an enthusiastic participant in the baiting of 'The Paki Shop' and I'd never bought a *National*

Front News. I'd also started to notice that one or two of my peers were being unkind to Mo, who was slight, perennially smiling and vulnerable-looking.

Eventually there came a lunchtime when I had to make a choice between my friends and Mo. It was all unspoken, done with looks and body language. I went with Mo and had a fag. Usually we would go up to the Shell petrol station (known as 'The Garage' as in: 'Are you going up The Garage?'), where we'd smoke round the back of the car wash. The petrol station isn't there now; I presume it was eventually blown up by a school smoking expedition.

My peer group was becoming hard to stick with. There was a grim incident involving a boy a couple of years below us whose mum had been the art teacher at my primary school. She was nice, even to those of us with no art skills. Her son had apparently been seen kissing a boy at a party. Therefore he had to be found at lunchtime and harangued, abused and made to cry if possible. So off we went, eager young homophobes, in search of our first actual gay person.

We found the boy in the wide corridor that led to steps down to our locker room. Abuse started raining down on him but it wasn't the hilarious witch hunt that had been hoped for. He had some friends higher up the school including the older brother of one of my classmates. I held back, now in two minds. As the prey and his friends fled, one of them turned suddenly and spat at the cruellest of the tormentors. This was impressive. They were outnumbered and a couple of the chasers were quite hard by our standards but suddenly it was over. This boy had spat like a venomous snake, flinging his head back over his shoulder and releasing a shooting arc of resistance at the enemy.

The defenders were more noble and motivated than the spiteful attackers whose resolve to continue evaporated. It was a chastening moment. The proposed victim had been a nice kid at primary school. I didn't know if he was gay or not and now I didn't care.

In December 1980 I put the cover of the *NME* that commemorated John Lennon on my bedroom wall. Subsequently his music swamped everyone. Prior to his death he'd been recording for the first time in five years and people flocked to hear what he'd been creating, in the knowledge that this was it, there would be nothing more from Lennon.

The tone of his new music was peaceful, as if made by a man who'd found contentment and wanted to share it. It was all so at odds with a Britain increasingly divided economically, with racial problems, unemployment problems and an unpopular government. Perhaps that's why it sold by the truckfull.

More than twenty years later, I was asked to present a documentary about Lennon, for BBC2's *Great Britons* series. The British public had voted him as one of their top ten Britons of all time.

Listening to Beatles albums one after another makes you realize how influential they have been. At first they sound like every other band, until you remember they were first. Every other band sounds like them. Making the film was a moving experience, learning about Lennon losing his mum, his upbringing in a suburban house very similar to the one I was born in, his struggle to adapt to his changing circumstances, the vulnerability he finally seemed to have conquered in his thirties, having changed himself from the drinker, the 'hitter' he said he'd been in his first marriage. It seemed sadder still that he'd been inexplicably taken. A cruel slaughter of a husband and father.

We visited the Strawberry Fields children's home in Liverpool, which stands on the site of the Victorian mansion that served the same purpose in the past. As a boy John used to play in the fields with the kids there. I was shown a photo of the dark, gothic edifice. When I later stood by the shrine to John in New York's Central Park and looked up at the Dakota building where he'd lived with Yoko Ono, the similarity between the two buildings was startling. He could have lived anywhere in the world and he chose this brooding, similarly gothic, apartment building overlooking the fields of Central Park. His childhood loomed large, the boy who played with orphans, who felt unrelated to the world. His pain is there in his songs, in 'Help', and in 'Julia', about his mum, and it's there in his face.

He's the only pop star on my wall these days.

There are still footballers.

Graham Rix

Escaping to Highbury every other Saturday was the most pleasure I could find at this time. I went by myself and the event was planned for and awaited impatiently all week. Leaving the house I would assume the persona of my cocksure alter ego: AL of AFC.

Upstairs at the back of the 20 to Walthamstow Central I'd look for space on the back of a seat to scrawl:

AL of AFC woz ere 7-4-80

The date seemed important. I liked to know, were I to board the bus again, when I woz there.

AL of AFC was here 7-4-80

'Was here' could have suggested the work of a middle-class public schoolboy. Who wants notoriety as a posh scribbler? 'Woz ere' became the mockney appendage to my moniker. I had decided to be AL when I shoplifted some marker pens. What to mark with pen? The smooth shiny interior surfaces of the buses I was travelling on every week were ideal. What to write? Lots of fellow vandals wrote their nickname and their club's initials, x or y of THFC or WHU, so I copied.

Standing in the wide corridor above the stairs that led down to our locker room one of my classmates said, 'Why do you write AL of AFC everywhere? No one calls you Al.'

Mind your own business, I'm a loner, a maverick, you don't know me.

I didn't reply but approaching from behind us at that moment was my older cousin Richard.

'All right, Al?' he said, without breaking stride.

I never had any more trouble with being known as Al.

Richard had a good sense of humour. The way he said 'All right, Al?' was an example of his comic timing. Comic because he'd never called me Al before. No one had. That's what you want from your family. Back-up. I was grateful and impressed.

Over at Highbury, I saw dozens of Graham Rix's hundreds of games for Arsenal. Two things stick out.

On one occasion a hamburger bun bounced on to the pitch near Rixy. He picked it up and made as if to eat it before tossing it out of play with a grin. Everyone laughed and I had him down as a funny person.

Secondly, from behind the goal, I watched as Rixy, standing by the goalpost, retrieved the ball from the crowd before dropping it to his left foot in order to half-volley it to the corner flag. The ball rolled all along the ground, watched by thousands, and came to rest in the quadrant marked out for corner takers. This came in a brief break in play prior to an Arsenal corner. He'd caught the ball thrown by a fan, turned round and done something nigh on impossible, *first time*. Everyone who noticed cheered and he smiled at us.

There were also many spectacular Rix goals, including one direct from a corner v Manchester United, plenty of goals made for others, often with Spurs on the wrong end, his match-winning cross in the 1979 Cup Final and his England caps at the 1982 World Cup. He had much going for him as a footballer but his relationship with the crowd showcased his good humour. He was so popular, even his bubble perm worked for him.

Arsenal were in the European Cup Winners' Cup in

1979–80 and made progress before starting their defence of the FA Cup in January. With FA Cup replays (including four semi-final games against Liverpool) and European trips, the players had a lot on and so did the fans.

In April came the Cup Winners' Cup semi-final against Juventus, who included several of the players who would win the 1982 World Cup for Italy. Two days before the first leg of the Juventus tie, Arsenal had to play away to Spurs on Easter Monday. Spurs had refused a postponement.

I made the familiar trip to White Hart Lane for the game, finding the away end for the first time. Arsenal rested several players and included an eighteen-year-old, Paul Davis. They won 2–1. I joined in chants of 'Arsenal Reserves'.

Away games turned out to be more exciting than home games. Later that year I joined the Arsenal Travel Club and went by train to Liverpool. Sitting alone in a compartment, a fourteen-year-old with *Shoot!* and *Match* magazines in hand, waiting for fans to pile in was intimidating at first but they all asked before they read my magazines. Cheese rolls, loose in a bin liner, were brought round and thrown one at a time at the starving travellers.

We passed through places I'd only heard of. At Crewe, train spotters were mocked cruelly but hilariously. Then there was an exchange of abuse with a trainload of Wolves fans heading to some other ground. On the outskirts of Liverpool, the track rises up over the type of red brick back-to-back terraced houses the like of which I'd only previously seen on the opening credits of *Coronation Street*.

On leaving the train we were herded out for the escorted three-mile walk up to the famous Anfield, home of Liverpool FC, league champions four times in the previous five years.

On the way there, one of our number was slammed

into a bus shelter by two policemen. It turned out we were 'coch-nees' and weren't too welcome. The accents everywhere were impenetrable and had I not seen *The Liver Birds* I'd never have managed to understand the programme seller.

Approaching an away ground involved cunning and subterfuge. Concealing your scarf so you can't be spotted as enemy personnel, feigning confidence in which way you are going as you walk, avoiding eye contact with anyone in case they ask you the time in order to identify your accent and then belt you. All that and the danger of being chased around unfamiliar streets afterwards gives rise to heightened emotions impossible to generate elsewhere.

It was emphatically worthwhile. Anfield was big, loud and packed, the mass of the crowd constantly shifting, swaying or surging forwards. Souness scored for Liverpool, causing a din, but Alan Sunderland unexpectedly equalized and it finished 1–1.

Returning to the station was slow and cold but the euphoria of our goal shortened the time. Three months later I went back to Liverpool for a cup tie with Everton and their ground was even more impressive, with a top tier suspended high between two steel and glass side walls. Another deafening arena. This time Arsenal's 2–0 defeat made getting home less threatening.

Leaving Spurs' ground after Arsenal 'reserves' had triumphed meant affecting neutrality, or attempting a defeated expression – even though the adrenaline was still tingling through me – all the way down Tottenham High Road, with the ecstasy of the win straining to get out, betraying itself in the occasional skip when crossing side roads.

There was always trouble at Spurs games. Standing in the corner of the North Bank at Highbury, I was surrounded by

Spurs fans at one game, managing to duck away before the fighting started. Trying to 'take' the home end was a matter of pride but ultimately pain. Any away intruders were massively outnumbered and relied on the police getting to them before the main body of home fans could.

The police didn't mess around. During fighting with West Ham fans, which took place in the panic caused by a smoke bomb going off, the police cleared the centre of the North Bank, banging their truncheons on the steel barriers, growling, 'Come on, you wankers.' Shoving a mass of fans backwards, one constable told a black fan to go 'back home'. The fan was incensed but other fans restrained his retaliation.

An Arsenal fan was stabbed to death after that West Ham game and at the next match a wreath was laid on the pitch. The appetite for fighting diminished.

Hundreds spilled on to the pitch that day, the absence of fencing allowing them to reach safety. Arsenal never erected fencing, forfeiting the opportunity to stage cup semi-finals. The FA's policy was soon to change in response to hooliganism when they decided to hold semi-finals exclusively at neutral grounds with full perimeter fencing. That decision contributed to the deaths of ninety-six Liverpool supporters at Hillsborough in 1989.

After one Spurs game police horses charged up St Thomas's Road near the ground, one of them barging me in the back. A skip full of rubble became a weapons store and a horse was hit by a brick. As they galloped on a lone constable was left surrounded. Fans encircled him as he kicked out. A brick hit him in the leg. In a rush there were police reinforcements. The lad in front of me and the one behind were targeted as they fled. The sound of a truncheon coming down on a skull was reminiscent of the popping made by kids at school pulling their fingers out of their mouths. Pop, pop, they were both whacked. I vaulted a fence and ran through some flats to the next street where there was no trouble at all, just people walking to Finsbury Park tube.

Nearly twenty years later, I hired a skip when I was having some work done on my house near Highbury and had to apply for a permit from Islington council. One of the conditions of skip hire is an undertaking to keep the skip covered when Arsenal are playing at home.

Arsenal and Juventus drew 1–1 at Highbury, leaving a daunting return leg to play in Turin. Listening to the scratchy commentary on Radio Two in the kitchen I could hardly make out what had happened at the end. Arsenal had scored? Rix crossed for Paul Vaessen to head in. Arsenal *had* scored! One nil! I was stunned and ecstatic, my dad and brother silent. This Arsenal thing was getting out of hand.

The club had reached two finals. I had enough programme vouchers for a ticket for the FA Cup Final v West Ham and queued round Highbury for two hours to get it.

Arriving at Wembley before they'd opened the ground, I bought a flag and joined the thousands waiting. Briefly, there was a panicked stampede as hundreds fled what they thought was fighting. My flag's wooden stick snapped in the crush. Not a good omen.

Trevor Brooking scored for West Ham early on. The goal was at our end but Wembley was so big that it was oddly silent momentarily before the roar from their end rushed in to us.

Arsenal couldn't respond and I had the dual displeasure of defeat and seeing Liam Brady trudging away. He'd agreed to join Juventus in the summer.

Sitting by myself at the tube station afterwards, a group of West Ham fans came and stood over me. A broken flag, a defeat, my last sight of Brady and now, probably, my head kicked in. Perfect. I looked up at them, my eyes shining.

''Ere,' one of them shouted down the platform, without any mockney affectation, 'this one's *crying!*' They laughed and left. An older Hammer came over. 'Don't worry, son,' he said, 'you'll win on Wednesday.'

Wednesday was the Cup Winners' Cup Final against Valencia. After two hours of goallessness came a penalty shoot-out, in which Brady missed and it fell to the likeable Rixy to save the day.

After the goalkeeper saved his kick, giving Valencia victory, Rixy broke down in tears. And so did I; back upstairs to that old pillow from 1978.

John McEnroe

Thirteen is a difficult bridging age, no longer a boy, not quite a man, often a prat.

Between boyhood and manhood, between instinctively liking things and thinking about what things to like, on the verge of a troubling hormonal nightmare for which boys are rarely prepared. They should be taken aside, aged eleven, for a quiet word:

'This won't make a lot of sense but in a year or two you will submerge and not listen to anybody for five years other than your peers, your pop stars and your penis. The dark tunnel you are about to enter will end and it need not be terribly difficult. Some people are on your side. You may not listen to good advice; indeed you may not receive good advice. You may listen to bad advice; certainly you will receive bad advice. You will be besotted with girls (or you will discover for certain that you are gay), you will want to paint your bedroom black and you will pretend not to like Abba, *Terry & June* and *Multi-Coloured Swap Shop* (you will be wrong about the first two but right about Noel Edmonds). You will be at odds with authority as you try to establish yourself. You will feel powerful and powerless simultaneously. You will behave like a fool and deny it, whilst suspecting you may have behaved like a fool. Older people will roll their eyes and try to ignore you, they may not offer you any encouragement, they may despair of you. This is normal. You are not a bad person because you are a teenager, in fact, you are about to discover the potential within you. Fly, spotty one, soar and be brilliant, follow your dreams, don't overdo the Oxy10, eat some fruit, please, be who you want to be. Look, there's Debbie Harry! What more do you want?'

For an idea of how strange it is to be a teenage boy, consider that, to a teenage boy, the behaviour of other teenage boys is in no way odd. They never wonder what on earth they are saying, or why they are doing what they are doing, or will they ever wake up, or will they ever go to bed, or will they ever eat anything, or will they ever stop eating one thing in particular? They don't notice teenagers' poor personal hygiene or, alternatively, their obsessive grooming. They understand a capacity to hang around bus shelters for fourteen hours and have no fear of a mosh pit. They never look at other teenage boys and wonder where the little lad who used to play in the sandpit has gone.

As a teenager watching John McEnroe playing tennis at Wimbledon I never found any of his behaviour questionable. His outbursts of rage and frustration, his duelling with authority and with his personal demons. All seemed perfectly understandable to me. He was behaving like a teenage boy. On a bad day.

McEnroe had made an immediate impact at Wimbledon when an actual teenager in 1977 by reaching the semi-finals as an eighteen-year-old newcomer. Bjorn Borg was the champion that year as he had been in 1976 and as he was to be in '78 and '79.

Who could stop Borg? The metronomic, ice-cool, un-expressive winning machine from Sweden. No one in sport has ever had greater control over his emotions than Borg. To me this made him soporifically dull. Someone had to beat him, please. Control over your emotions is the very thing an adolescent doesn't have. Show me a fourteen-year-old Borg fan and I'll show you a test case for a team of psychiatrists working round the clock.

Borg was admirable but he won Wimbledon five years in a row and that's a long period for a young fan to endure. Nothing seemed to happen in his matches. He just won and left.

McEnroe, on the other hand, brought an anxious, explosive petulance to the court that was sometimes less teenage and more pre-teen, or even pre-school. This sort of thing would, under no circumstances, be tolerated in the tennis clubs of Southern England. It's just not on. If you are upset, you jolly well don't show it and if there's been an injustice, shame on you for bringing it up. Just carry on and don't spoil everyone's day.

My dad had enrolled us all in Woodford Well tennis club and the etiquette of how to behave was as important as how to play. McEnroe drove my dad bonkers. So bonkers that no argument was brooked. He was a bad man, possibly evil. He should be THROWN OUT! The newspapers agreed, calling him 'superbrat'. McEnroe that is, not my dad.

The view of those fiercely opposed to on-court dissent and the tone of McEnroe's aggravating attitude was that the chaps in the umpire's and linesmen's chairs do a difficult job seriously, diligently and with absolute impartiality. Whether they are correct in their calls or not is, in many ways, irrelevant. They intend to make the right call and that's the point. No one could do it better than an honest Englishman volunteering from an English tennis club.

For people who are not English harbouring suspicions that the English believe themselves to be infallible, it's true, they do. For people who *are* English, who have nagging concerns that the rest of the world hate the English, for the self-regarding certainty of their infallibility, it's true, they do.

As the linesmen always intended to make the right call, so McEnroe always intended to make the right shot but the benefit of the doubt could hardly go with the player:

'The ball *was* out but it was *such* a good attempt, the crowd went "whoah" and I know you meant it to go in ... on reflection, the point's yours!'

McEnroe's arguments with officials accelerated the advent of neutral, professional umpires amid efforts to reduce mistakes, not least by changing the line judges every couple of hours. The argument was that mistakes were being made and if they cost matches then, as a professional, that affected your income and livelihood. It had validity in the late '70s when few players could afford a coach and prize money and sponsorship rewards were less than today.

It was as much the way McEnroe complained, as it was his audacity in complaining at all, that drew the most flak. I empathized though. He was rude and hostile and it was awkward for the umpire, who couldn't change a call because a player wanted him to, but when McEnroe began to receive catcalls and slow-handclaps, when those middle-class tennis club types yelled, 'Be *quiet*, McEnroe' or 'Disgraceful' or 'Get *on* with it', I rooted for him all the more. We played tennis as a family sometimes and my own on-court tantrums, whilst not inspired by McEnroe – they were all my own work – came from the same inability to manage frustration. My brother didn't speak to me, that was frustrating, my sister was the youngest and so was always right, that was frustrating, and my dad was irritated because I was spoiling the game, so when he came to serve to me, he would invariably hit the ball very hard so I couldn't hit it back before shouting, 'Oh come *on,* that was an easy one!' That was frustrating.

No surprise then, that when we watched those

Wimbledon arguments, I identified with McEnroe and my dad with the umpire.

When McEnroe beat Borg the following year, I watched the climax alone. As it became clear who was going to win, Dad stood up and left the room, followed, inevitably, by my brother, and dutifully by my sister. But he won, they couldn't stop him winning, and he was the most thrillingly gifted player to play on the centre court for years. When Federer played Nadal in 2008 it was the first time that the heights of the Borg v McEnroe finals in 1980 and '81 had been reached since.

I considered McEnroe to be like me. I saw bad behaviour and found solace in it, as I skulked around a school I wanted to burn down, on and off of buses I wrote on and in and out of shops I stole from.

The thieving was a thrill but also a way to impress at school. I'd go out nicking every week, usually staying on the bus down into Loughton after school and filling a bag (with a jumper in the bottom for silent depositing of the goods) with whatever I'd taken an order for. Initially, the theft was kleptomaniacal, taking things I didn't want or that had no monetary value and then hoarding them. Later though, when my peers found out how good I was at it (because I told them), it was entrepreneurial. O Level study cards were easy to steal and to sell. Bigger items were trickier but worth more. I grabbed a big book about the Lake District as a present for one posh boy's mum at Christmas.

Eventually I was caught, in a newsagent's, trying to get away with a magazine placed inside another, for a kid waiting outside. The game was up when the manager came to serve me. I should have left then but went through with it and then offered a 50p bribe once the second magazine had been revealed.

'Bribery as well,' he said. 'Perhaps I should tell the police.' I was revealed as a hopeless criminal, panicked and afraid after this pettiest of thefts. I waited in the manager's office for someone from the school to arrive. They wrote a letter that I had to give to my dad.

'What am I going to tell Uncle Pat?' said my dad. I liked Uncle Pat. One time Uncle Pat was cutting some cake and asked if anyone would like a finger – meaning a thin slice – the next thing was, he'd actually cut his finger. That was the funniest thing that had happened in my life since I was put in the bath by my mum, as a toddler, *with my socks on.*

'You don't have to tell Uncle Pat!' I said.

'Of course I do, *I have to tell everybody.*'

I'm sure they all found it a gripping anecdote. The key thing was that *everybody* should have a low opinion of me.

That was frustrating

I had to go back to the shop on a Saturday afternoon, missing a game at White Hart Lane that my dad had tickets for, in order to clear up their back yard. I quite enjoyed it, the first work I'd done in ages.

It turned out I wasn't like McEnroe at all. I was a petty thief and a liar with behavioural problems who was driving his family to distraction. McEnroe was a gifted athlete with a fierce will to, not so much win, as to avoid the crushing feeling of defeat.

His outbursts on the court were better controlled than I realized. He was remorseful and apologetic afterwards and never let loose in matches against Borg because he respected him too much. In fact, as McEnroe himself says in his auto-biography *Serious*, he had idolized Borg from his teens.

He idolized Borg!

That feels like a betrayal to me. A code violation for disappointing teenagers, Mr McEnroe.

1981

Chrissie Hynde

I was The Dead Beats' biggest fan. Never missed a gig. In fact I was almost part of the band. At one gig the bass drum kept edging forward during the set and I would be alerted by the drummer's facial tics and jerks of the head in my direction before heading onstage, in the roadie crouch, to push it into place. The roadie crouch came to me instinctively, uncoached. Something about being on someone else's stage, obscuring their audience's view, had me bending as if under fire.

It is so unnatural to walk with your hands nearer to the ground than your knees that, in itself, it is an argument against theories of evolution. There cannot have been a gradual transition for primates from four legs to two. It's so slow and ponderous to walk in a crouch, slower than both a four-legged and an upright two-legged animal. Why would there have been a phase where the primate began to move more slowly and vulnerably? That would threaten the survival of the species. Roadies, however, do it all the time.

An alternative argument in favour of evolutionary theory is that the roadies are an unusual sub-sect of the primates. Hunched over as they scuttle around the stage, closer to the apes' four-legged lifestyle (sometimes eating food that has dropped to the floor), but also able to stand on two legs, provided they are leaning on a bar.

Arriving at the venue first, humping and dumping several tonnes of equipment, waiting through the sound check and gig, before packing up again in the small hours. It is arduous work, with eighteen-hour days and little time to wash, shave, or take an interest in nutrition. It would come as no surprise to hear that roadies were offered artificial stimulants to help them through a tour, but with responsibilities to audiences, as well as their paymasters, they would never indulge in narcotic abuse and it would be wrong to suggest otherwise.

The Dead Beats gigged all around the Woodford area in the late '70s. It would not be entirely true to say I was their roadie. I was more their classmate. The road part of the 'loose drum gig' was actually the road on which the 20 or 20a bus travelled, which took me to school to see them play that night in the Great Hall. That may sound like an impressive venue but it was only where we normally had assemblies, prize-giving and the inter-house drama per-formances (which no one as cool as AL of AFC would be interested in, or indeed, considered for).

On guitar for The Dead Beats was Bev. Bev was a boy who took no pleasure in reminders that he had a girl's name. We sat next to each other in geography, which I was taking for A Level, with history and economics.

My dad persuaded me to take economics instead of English on the basis that it was 'much more interesting' than Chaucer and Milton, who were 'boring'. I was easily swayed as I had no intention of lifting a finger anyway.

There seemed no alternative to two more years at school, which had become more bearable now girls were admitted (co-ed began in the year below, the year I should have been in …). We also had a school skiing trip in my lower sixth year, during which some of the benefits of attending a Minor Public School finally became apparent. Sliding down an Austrian mountain, everyone tipsy on *Glühwein*, before spending the evening trying to get off with Julia Bradley, was one of the best weeks of my life. The laughter reached hysteria every day. I even found the confidence to conduct a survey of the entire group (best fall of the week, best zits etc), the results of which I delivered as part of a last-night party organized by the staff, who even performed sketches lampooning themselves. 'Al's Survey' went down well, and with hindsight, was a first taste of the joy of stand-up comedy.

Geography with Bev next to me was more fun than any other lesson. We had a nice beardy teacher called Mr O'Connor-Thompson who even let us hold a debate in one class. I forget the topic but Bev and I dominated proceedings on our team and this led to the first positive comments on a report card that I'd had in an eternity.

Bev also gave me access to a whole new peer group of punky gig-goers, including his older brother Nige, who had been among the gang protecting our classmate from the homophobic pursuit by my peers.

I was happy listening to The Dead Beats' version of 'All Day and All of the Night' by The Kinks but Nige and co. introduced me to venues in London I'd never previously heard of. We went to the Hope & Anchor to see The Little Roosters, to the Lyceum to see U2, the Rainbow to see The Stranglers and also a CND benefit with Gang of Four and Wasted Youth that featured a surprise appearance by The Jam. The Rainbow was a converted cinema in Finsbury Park that hasn't staged gigs for years but the Hope & Anchor in Islington still survives. The Lyceum was closed for a while before re-opening and immediately being hidden under a multi-layered Disney paint job in the guise of the musical *The Lion King*.

In December 1981 the chance came to see The Pretenders at the Lyceum. I had both their albums and Chrissie

Hynde's picture was on my wall. They were one of the best bands around and I knew all the songs.

Chrissie Hynde fronted the group and was hypnotically alluring with dark hair nearly over her eyes and tight-fitting leather trousers clinging to her slender legs. On some songs she'd sling a guitar over her shoulder, or she'd lean in to the microphone and huskily purr her way through the band's pre-indy post-punk repertoire. This included their number one, 'Brass in Pocket', which she sang so seductively it's possible that, as a minor, I shouldn't have been admitted to the venue.

The rest of the band consisted of three lads from Hereford who seemed happy to provide back-up, although the bassist, Pete Farndon, didn't mind attention. From the floor in front of the stage, the sight of the backlit Martin Chambers flaying his drum kit was spectacular. He appeared to have one drum that was full of liquid and when he hit that, as he bashed back and forth, an arc of spray would cascade up and in to the bright lights. It looked like milk but I doubt it was. Occasionally, he would allow a drumstick to fly out into the audience, which led to a surging mass of bodies trying to get a hand to it. I touched one as it flew by but couldn't catch it.

Throughout, James Honeyman-Scott dazzled with his expert guitar work. At least it looked expert to me but then I thought Bev was good in The Dead Beats.

Dead Beats gigs were a different affair, often dominated by Nige and his punk friends pogoing around a church venue like the Memorial Hall in South Woodford while spitting enthusiastically at my classmates on stage, much to Bev's amusement. Andy, the tall, well-spoken lead guitarist (for whose unwitting mother I had purloined a book about the Lake District), pulled out a handkerchief and wiped phlegm from his fingers as he tried to negotiate a song. Bev found this ridiculous and hilarious. I sympathized with Andy and realized that, for all the fun I had with Bev and Nige, I was never a punk. I failed to join in with a brawl at one gig when Nige, who had refused to be intimidated all night by the presence of the notorious NF-supporting 'Debden Skins', eventually went to war with about four of them. The Punks v Skins issue had passed me by. I was neither and didn't want to be.

Musically, by their standards, I was clueless. I was a big Stranglers fan by now and said that I thought people would jump on the bandwagon when they made it big, unaware that they'd had three top ten singles and five top ten albums by then already. 'They already are big, Al' said Bev, quietly.

I'd become an Adam and the Ants fan only after they'd changed line-ups, had commercial success, and Bev and his friends had dropped them. Bev scrawled 'Adam and the Ants are shit' on my rough book in geography, leaving me unsure what to do, since I'd bought their *Kings of the Wild Frontier* album and thought it was brilliant.

One night, a punk friend of theirs, who I'd been getting on well with, took umbrage at something I'd said and kicked me in the leg, as we walked past Snaresbrook Crown Court on the way to another gig. He didn't say which straw it was that had broken his camel's back. Months later, I chatted to Bev about it, and he agreed that it was a turning point. That, and the time I'd written a letter to a friend of theirs, Sam, who I'd gone out with for all of two weeks, expressing how upset I was and would she reconsider. Bev and his friends thought that I had only made things difficult for Sam, particularly as I'd written my plea on the wall of the subway between The Garage and The Shop, where half the school could see it.

Bev was unerringly honest. One night in May I went to the FA Cup Final replay between Tottenham and Manchester City dressed for a cold night, as was the norm for evening games, but it was a balmy evening that felt more like summer. Packed in amongst thousands of Spurs fans, I sweated profusely all night. There was a high moment, when Steve McKenzie scored with a stunning volley for City, but Ricky Villa set off on a weaving dribble directly towards us to clinch the Cup for Spurs. I travelled home in a pool of perspiration and chagrin. The next morning I was late for school and didn't wash. Arriving in geography I sat next to Bev and he instantly said: 'Phew, you pong, Al.'

Talking with Bev, about those days when I used to tag along with his punky brother and their chums, I said I just had the feeling all the time that no one really liked me.

'They didn't,' he said.

The Pretenders put on a great show that night and were wildly appreciated by the crowd. During the intro to one number the stage was flooded with dry ice. Clouds of it spilled out into the audience but it kept coming, filling the stage and enveloping Chrissie Hynde. She looked off to the wing and issued a volley of full-blooded American invective. In the shadows at the side it was possible to make out hurried movement as several *homo roadiens* scuttled to and fro in a panic, hunched over, trying to find the one pouring the dry ice pellets. The expanding cloud eventually stopped growing, The Pretenders emerged dramatically from the mist, calm was restored to the roadie community, and the gig carried on to even greater heights. Chrissie Hynde's flash of temper made her even more exciting, to an adolescent.

The house lights came on after the encore with the hot and happy crowd still banging their feet and yelling '*More!*'

before relenting to spill euphorically out into the night. My ears were ringing from the music.

It had been snowing and was icy underfoot. The tubes had stopped running out to Essex. I managed to catch a bus as far as Chingford Station which was about two and a half miles from home. I rang my dad and told him where I was, hoping he'd come and pick me up. He said: 'It's just a brisk jog from there.' Maybe I'd woken him and he'd forgotten that we had moved from Chingford to Loughton thirteen years before. Rangers Road, between the two, had no pavement, no streetlights and went straight through pitch black Epping Forest. Halfway home, tripping and slipping along an icy path that I couldn't see, a police car pulled up.

'Are you all all right?' said one of the policemen.

'Yeah,' I said.

I was fifteen, communicating with authority figures was a weakness. I should have said: 'Please help me. I can't see anything, I can't feel my toes. I've still got two miles to go. If I twist my ankle I could die of exposure. *Help me!*'

The other one said: 'Where are you going?'

'Home,' I said.

'OK,' he said and they drove off. Towards Loughton.

The following week I came out of a great U2 concert, at the Lyceum, into similar snow. This time the tube unexpectedly stopped at Leytonstone. There were going to be no more trains to Loughton that night. I went up to the street to wait for a 20a. An hour later I was still there. The buses had stopped running and no one had told anyone. Snow was falling heavily. I went into a phone box and smoked a cigarette for warmth. Six miles from home and frozen, I rang the police and told them I was stuck. They said I should walk a mile and a half down the hill to Redbridge roundabout where there was a minicab office. I had to sneak into my dad's room to find some cab fare without waking him up. He woke up and was livid. It was 2 a.m.

Despite the torturous journeys home, which I remember as well as the gigs, they were two nights that were rarely bettered in my teens.

A year later I went to see U2 again. This time they had flags flying and were singing passionately about Bloody Sunday. I bought the third album, *War*, but never liked it as much as the first two, *Boy* and *October*, so lost interest in them. They're still going I believe.

Ronald McDonald

On 28 March 1979 the nuclear reactor at Three Mile Island in Pennsylvania suffered a severe core meltdown, leading to an evacuation of pregnant women and pre-school children over a five-mile radius. Fortunately, radiation emissions from the plant were relatively low, but the accident had many consequences. Safety procedures, and core monitoring, were improved across all reactors in the USA, but public opinion turned against nuclear energy.

More than a decade previously, McDonald's Research and Development personnel began work on a product that could retain intense heat. This achievement in heat generation and its subsequent retention was unparalleled in scientific history, until the accident that led to half of the TMI-2 plant's core melting down.

The substance McDonald's had developed became the filling in what was marketed as a deep-fried 'Apple Pie'. Encased not in zirconium cladding, preferred by the nuclear industry at the time for the storing of nuclear fuel pellets, these pies were sheathed in simple heat-resistant card. The make-up of the pastry case, which completely enclosed the filling in much the same way as the containment walls at TMI-2 enclosed the melting core, remains secret. The pie's exterior, or room, temperature was cool to the touch giving an impression of edibility to the hungry McDonaldite. The moment the pastry exterior was pierced the molten fluid within rushed out, as if from a depressurized aircraft cabin, scalding and blistering tongue, gums, the roof of the mouth, anything in its path. The safest option, now widely accepted, is to break the pie and test the temperature with an extremity whilst at all times keeping the number of a good burns unit to hand.

The remarkable pastry, known to some as Pa-styrene or Polysty-stry, has unlimited potential for further development, as a lining for microwave ovens.

The first bite into a McDonald's hamburger I ever had came on a family holiday to America in the summer of 1981.

It was lush.

There was something in there I'd never come across before, a tangy flavour my taste buds had never previously had the pleasure of. I peeled back the bun to see what it was that could be giving this burger its unique specialness. There was the 'all-beef patty', there was the tomato sauce but there was something else in there, something green. A slice of vegetable. With flavour.

It was a gherkin.

I'd never had a gherkin before and considered this to be an ingredient included by a culinary superhero. Did Ronald himself come up with the gherkin?

It's possible that, at the time of the gherkin experience, I'd never before had anything pickled. Other than beetroot. There was always a jar of beetroot in the fridge. I'm never without it to this day.

My gran grew beetroot in her back garden. I watched her grabbing one out of the earth with her bare hands. She had dug for victory in the '40s. She made her own dumplings too and could bake for Blighty. All this was passed on to her daughters, my mum and aunt. Growing up in a haze of icing sugar and flour, I waited around the kitchen for the chance to lick the cake whisk and scrape out the mixing bowl, like a cat hanging around on the off chance a can of fish might be opened.

Our garden was replete with blackberries and apples. All through the autumn there was stewed blackberry and apple, blackberry and apple pie, apple pie, stewed apple, apple sauce. Not to mention the rhubarb (don't eat the leaves!), stewed or put into a crumble. If there were more blackberries (and the more we picked the more there seemed to be) there might be jam making. What a physical effort this was. To sit in the kitchen, just me and my mum (brother at school, sister yet to walk), and witness the straining and pushing, the heat and the steam of the jam making process was to sit at the heart of the family. Then all the little jam tarts went in the oven and there followed a great test of infant patience, once they were out, as they cooled down.

At the greengrocer's, an old holdall would be filled with muddy spuds, clouds of used farm earth dusting up the air at toddler level, before bags of carrots and sprouts were filled, and twirled at either end, while lifted in arc of performance-grocering.

Into the butcher to witness the strong-arm turn-handle mincing of something pink. No idea, until it was on the table in front of me, that it meant shepherd's pie for tea.

All the time we were out shopping, there was the chance that my mum's skirt would pull up alongside another skirt on Loughton High Road, and I'd have to wait for a bit until they'd finished whatever it was they did up there. If it went a little too long, this high-in-the-sky-above talk, then I'd be forced to tug at the skirt to hurry things along. Not that I had any pressing engagements, being four. Or three? I may have been five or even six. No more than that though, because at six she was gone, and all those steak and kidney pies and casseroles and the jam and those little tarts, they were gone too.

Since my mum went before we owned a freezer, and before Bejam appeared on Loughton High Road, it's hard to say whether she would have embraced the convenience of the frozen life or not. Would Mozart have used a synthesizer or Sophocles a laptop? As Patrick Moore would say: 'We just don't know.'

The answer is probably yes, though. The freezer and then the microwave changed everything and mums across England, raised in make-do-and-mend, Dig For Victory, wartime austerity, were bending with the times, though it must have felt wrong, wrong, wrong. Food in a box? In a sealed plastic bag? It certainly led to more peas on our plates with all that shelling a thing of the past. As an infant I had my mum's home-grown runner beans but after the freezer came along there were Bird's Eye peas a-go-go, not to mention fish fingers and the promised land of boil-in-the-bag fish, and casseroles.

Bejam was a room full of chest freezers. None of them had glass tops and they were not well labelled, but the regular customer with a keen memory could find processed meat, and more importantly Arctic Roll, without opening and closing endless lids. I did the searching for my dad. No more butcher, no more baker, never a candlestick maker, greengrocer not long for this world and no more chit-chat with busy skirts on the High Road. Bejam's for your frozen food and Sainsbury's for your spuds, baked beans, biscuits and Battenberg. Milk, eggs and bread delivered, all done.

Going by the names on the packets, the food sounded as though it would be the same. It just had 'frozen' in front of it. Frozen carrots. Same as carrots. Just frozen. If you boiled them, for a long time, they'd taste the same too. They'd both taste of nothing. And did we boil in England? Why certainly. All vegetables were boiled. Quite often the meat was boiled too. All the nutrients in England were boiled into pans of water and poured into England's drains. Peas were boiled in a pan, with a mountain of mini-bubbles rising out of it and, on top of them, a green spot, where the weaker peas who couldn't keep it together surfaced as pulp.

The boiling was a tradition and the frozen food manufacturers knew it. Cooking instructions: BOIL. At best: BOIL, then *simmer*.

The boiling away of flavour aided the transition, from a nation fed primarily on fresh produce to one fed primarily on frozen produce. Every vegetable, frozen or otherwise, carrot, bean, cabbage, spinach, broccoli, or cauliflower, tasted of nothing without gravy (all my meals for a large part of my childhood tasted only of gravy). So long as the same gravy was poured over the frozen food as was poured over the real food then the adjustment was small. The frozen food was close enough to the real thing that it made it worth cutting out the effort of preparing actual food. The art of eking out the remnants of a Sunday joint over a week slowly disappeared along with the joint itself. With sliced beef available in frozen tin foil cartons, the Sunday knife sharpening ritual, standing over the roast, became a thing of the past.

All this, like nylon sheets, was an *improvement*. Now we could have things easily that we hadn't had before and one of the things that we liked the most was a Bejam frozen beefburger. These were designed for the palate of children. Salty with no gristle and no fat on the edge. Easy to cut, easy to chew and equally good with ketchup or gravy. Any meal that could bring ketchup to the table was a good meal. Kids like ketchup. It's a sugar feast, working its neo-addictive magic on junior tastebuds over school-night teas all year round.

Ketchup, of course, was born in the USA. Cheap-as-chips fly-drive holidays had opened up the magnificence of the United States to lucky, well-off-enough package holiday makers like us. It was the last time we went on a trip as a family and it was the time that first-ever McDonald's burger was sampled.

Starting on the West Coast and travelling via Santa Monica, Disneyland, Universal Studios, San Francisco, Las Vegas, Yosemite, the Grand Canyon and then across to New York and Washington DC made for a hectic three weeks but it was the trip of a lifetime. There were certain things that had to be done. We flew in a light aircraft over the Canyon, we rode Space Mountain and saw Jaws leap out of the water at us. We went across the Golden Gate Bridge and sailed across to the island prison to see where Al Capone was held (and to buy a 'property of Alcatraz' T-shirt). We went up the Statue of Liberty, up the Empire State Building and up the now vanished World Trade Center and then we stood at Lincoln's giant feet and read the Gettysburg Address.

All the way across America we ate burger after burger after burger. Our palates had been transformed through the late '70s into processed-food processors. Familiar, now, with sausages every morning that had no skins, snatched from the freezer, sharply separated and grilled in non-splitting non-spitting sedate factory food fashion.

So we were ready for McDonald's. We wanted our food in a thick paper bag just as we secretly wanted our groceries in thick brown handle-free paper bags like they had on American TV shows of which we still could not get enough. In Santa Monica we bought a map showing where the stars lived. My dad chose Robert Wagner for Davies family surveillance. We pulled up a discreet distance from what was allegedly Bob's place and waited, eyes fixed on the front door. Minutes ticked by, then, success, a delivery arrived. Had it been a high-powered rifle, for taking pot-shots at stalking tourists, no court in California would have convicted Bob Wagner. The front door opened, my dad strained to see. The person who opened the door was not coming out.

'Is it him? Can you see?'

'No,' I said.

'Well *look*. Is it *him*?'

He was surprisingly agitated. My dad, not Robert Wagner. The door closed. We didn't see who'd opened it. We were truly wasting our lives, so we went for a McDonald's instead.

Lining up excitedly, we scanned the board for the options, seduced by the accents, the odd ordering of words in their sentences, the ubiquitous, 'Have a nice day!' My dad asked us what we wanted. He was in charge of ordering. I was fifteen. I *knew* I should be doing the ordering. I *knew* he'd be the slowest there that day. The slowest *ever*. This was someone who grew up in an age when the food cooked for a long time. When you could smell the stewing or roasting meat for an age, before you were dispatched to a sink to wash your hands so you were fit to eat it. There was a chance he'd take so long over it the staff would change shifts halfway through. I decided to help him. By *muttering things*.

The order did take a while:

'One hamburger please.'

'Fries with that?'

'I beg your pardon.'

113

'*Do you want fries?*'

'Fries with that?'

'Chips, yes, please.'

'Small, regular or large?'

'Medium, please.'

'*Regular.*'

'So that's one burger, one regular fries, anything else?'

'Yes, one quarter pounder with cheese, please.'

'*It's supposed to be fast food.*'

'Fries?'

'Yes, please, medium fries please.'

'*You don't have to say please every time.*'

'One Big Mac.'

That one was said with a hint of John Wayne in his voice.

'*Why are you doing the accent?*'

'And another hamburger, please, with fries.'

'Regular?'

'Yes, three Coca-Colas and one cup of tea, please.'

'It's McDonald's cola. Is that OK for you?'

'What? I don't know. Is it the same?'

'*Yes, yes.*'

'It's McDonald's cola, is that OK?'

'*Just say yes.*'

'Yes. And a tea, please.'

'Small, regular or large cola?'

Thanks in no part to my essential interventions, we eventually gathered up our food. It was unwrapped with an eagerness usually reserved for Christmas morning. It took less than a generation to wean a nation off real food and on to fake food and we were proudly in the vanguard!

Everything was processed and chemicalized so that the meat taste in our mouths was not the taste of meat. It was the taste of a laboratory. There was no discernible nutritional value that couldn't be replicated by eating the wrapping. As for the wrapping, we shovelled a mountain of plastic and paper in to their mammoth in-store repository. Happiness achieved, childlike palates sated, we could not wait for the next one.

That little bit of Gherkin In The Machine was the nicest thing there. The tastiest vegetable I'd eaten in my life. Unboiled, semi-raw and hiding in a food factory. It was like the little plant that *WALL-E* finds, the last green thing on Earth after it's been trashed. My gran may well have pulled it out, eaten it, and given the rest to her long-suffering cat.

Paul Weller

Vinyl Scrapyard was a second-hand record shop situated on the long downhill street that Walthamstow Market occupied and close enough to Walthamstow Central station that anyone arriving there from Loughton on the 20 bus to catch the tube to Arsenal could easily pop in for a snout round. I was usually after old Stranglers LPs

I had just bought their *TheMeninBlack* album. It was full of melodic keyboard arrangements with an oddly ethereal atmosphere intended to evoke alien life forms playing the piano and making up songs. Signing up for the Stranglers Appreciation Society, I began to receive their magazine, *Strangled*. Inside were equally ethereal articles about the mysterious Men in Black who control our planet, with their special knowledge of other worlds and other life forms.

Later the brilliant film-maker John Sayles, famous for gritty authentic tales of the American Dream gone sour, directed a comedy called *Brother from Another Planet* in which an alien, who happens to look like an Afro-American, ends up in Harlem and finds employment in a bar where he fixes fruit machines by closing his eyes and leaning on them. Eventually two Men in Black arrive to return him from whence he came. The Brother, by now, has discovered a world of illegal aliens in New York, not to mention some high-level drug trading and corruption. It's a good film but was principally of interest to me because of those pesky Men in Black the Stranglers had been on about. Subsequently, the movies *Men in Black* and *MIB 2* have shown a further comedic version of secret service types in black suits secretly protecting us all from the aliens amongst us. Then *The Matrix* trilogy drew heavily on the Men in Black idea, as multiple versions of Smith pursued Neo through a world that wasn't as it appeared to the populace.

The Stranglers were now my favourite band and, like Mulder in the *X Files*, I wanted to believe. However, having found some old LPs in Vinyl Scrapyard, I found that this Men in Black stuff was a recent interest. They had been at the forefront of punk rock and as such had been obliged to believe in nothing other than belligerent, rebellious posturing. Their old albums, like *No More Heroes* and *Black & White*, were potent, but they were old. It was while I was hunting for a copy of *The Raven* (with a hologrammed sleeve) that I came across an imported single by The Jam that I hadn't seen before. 'That's Entertainment' with a live version, from a gig in Germany, of 'Down in the Tube Station at Midnight' on the B side. I'd heard of this tube station song (it had been released as a single in 1978) but I'd never listened to it before. This imported version became the most played of all my records.

I couldn't stop listening to both songs. Turning it over to play the other side was frustratingly slow. I didn't want a break in the music. Headphones on, cigarette lit, sitting on the windowsill looking out over the Newbys' garden. I was transported. Hearing it now causes a rush of cold blood, a tingling of emotional memory. The songs came to mean so much that I can't listen to them any more without becoming teary-eyed. That's my youth, there, blazing, in spitting vocals and crashing guitar.

'That's Entertainment' had a poetically bleak view that chimed strongly with me. How had I missed The Jam? I hadn't bought their hit singles, 'Start', 'Eton Rifles' or

'Going Underground'. I didn't have enough money to buy many records and they were impossible to steal since only their sleeves were ever out on display.

Plus, I was loyal. Once I liked a band I stayed with them. The Police's most recent album, *Zenyattà Mondatta*, I'd bought on the day it was released, having gone all the way to Upton Park, where there was one of a selected group of shops offering a free poster with the record. That was devotion. The last single they'd released? 'De Doo Doo Doo De Da Da Da'. It just wasn't *saying* anything to me.

My favourite groups were playing songs I couldn't relate to. Singing along to U2's 'Gloria' or The Pretenders' 'Brass in Pocket', Blondie's 'The Tide is High' or The Stranglers' 'Just Like Nothing on Earth' felt meaningless. Even though I liked all those records, now I'd come across this apparent chronicler of my life called Paul Weller, they were rendered pointless. As for the Men in Black, what was that even about?

'Down in the Tube Station at Midnight' tells the story of a mugging by a gang of right-wing thugs, as told by the victim, a commuter on his way home to his wife. A few years previously a newspaper had run pictures of a mugging of a commuter on a station platform. When my dad came home from work he was surprised to be greeted by me with greater affection than normal. He asked me what was wrong and I said I'd been worried that he would be mugged on the way home. To me that mugging looked lethal in the papers and it triggered a huge amount of anxiety, obviously, in hindsight, related to losing my mum and the thought of losing the remaining parent. He assured me he wasn't going to be mugged, which seemed grotesquely naïve of him. Had he not seen the newspaper? The world was a *dangerous place*. I dried my eyes bravely.

I scoured Vinyl Scrapyard for Jam recordings. It turned out that 'Eton Rifles' was about a posh public school and the pupils' privileged, well-connected lives.

I went to a posh public school!

I wanted to burn it down!

I travelled on the tube!

I grafittied buses!

I was angry too!

I actually went to Mr Byrite to buy clothes because Weller had said they were all right and he didn't want his young fans wasting a lot of money on fancy clobber.

I even smoked Rothman's cigarettes (which were rank) because a packet was featured on the inner sleeve of the *All Mod Cons* LP.

Unfortunately, I wasn't working class. We didn't go on holiday to Selsey Bill or Bracklesham Bay like 'Saturday's Kids' but my dad did commute, even though his name wasn't double-barrelled like 'Smithers-Jones'. We were all certainly going through a 'Private Hell' even as we bickered our way around America on the holiday of a lifetime.

There was enough for me to relate to in every other verse of every song. By now I was having the *NME* delivered instead of *Record Mirror* and voted for Weller and co in their annual awards. They cleaned up. Every year. Best group, album, single, live act, everything, and Paul Weller was always 'Man of the Year'.

It didn't matter too much to me that they only released two singles in 1981, or that Weller wanted to break the cycle of album and tour every year, because I had a whole back catalogue to get through.

On top of all this, they supported CND too. Now a mass movement, the Campaign for Nuclear Disarmament was staging huge marches and demonstrations. The night before one such demo, there was a CND benefit at the Rainbow in Finsbury Park. I went with Nige and a punky-looking girl who I'd persuaded to go out with me (as usual for two weeks only).

On our way in the girl at the box office said:

'The Jam are here tonight.'

We took that with a pinch of salt but, halfway through the gig, The Jam were introduced. Everyone rushed down to the front, shocked and electrified.

They played three songs, including 'Going Underground', Weller's anthem of anti-nuclear protest. It's a good one to shout along to if you're a disaffected youth:

> *You talk and you talk until my head explodes*
> *I turned on the news and my body froze*
> *These braying sheep on my TV screen*
> *Make this boy SHOUT make this boy SCREAM*
> *I'M GOING UNDERGROUND!*

They'd turned up because they wanted to play for CND supporters, not just Jam fans. The next day they played on the back of a flatbed truck on the Embankment as thousands of CND protestors marched by on their way to a huge rally. A crowd of several hundred gathered just to watch The Jam, including scores of parka-clad Mod revivalists who had been inspired by the release of *Quadrophenia,* and who embraced the Two-Tone label's sound of ska-influenced groups like The Specials and The Beat.

Despite their impeccable taste in music, not all of these Mods were CND supporters. The Mods used RAF roundels and Union Flags to adorn their parkas. These suddenly seemed less decorative and more nationalistic when sported by an anti-CND mob.

Weller spoke to the crowd: 'Let's not forget what we're all here for . . .' he began, and continued to speak about the cause of ending an arms race that threatened world's end. At least I presume he did. I couldn't hear. The Mods jeered, drowning him out with: '*Mods, mods, mods, mods, mods!*'

The crowd behind the mods was larger and vociferously pro-CND but the dissenters were between the rest and Weller. He looked unhappy and, when they'd finished play-ing, disappeared from view. Rick Buckler, the drummer, came to the front and affably signed his name on a flyer I had, that read: 'Together we can Stop the Bomb'.

My memory tells me I saw The Jam play live on six occa-sions but it won't tell me where or when three of those gigs took place. I do remember the last one, at Wembley Arena, as part of The Jam's farewell tour. No sooner had I discovered them than Weller had decided to split them up. Jam fans were in mourning. He was adamant that this was it. No more.

Quite a crowd of kids from school wanted to go. We went up by tube. Outside the arena, one of our number bought six programmes for other friends from what turned out to be an unofficial opportunist. He then had to buy six more real programmes inside.

Big Country were the support act. Tough gig. The crowd didn't want to know and some cheered when they an-nounced it was their last number, chanting: 'Jam, Jam, Jam, Jam!'

After what seemed an age they appeared and the roar was deafening. As soon as Weller came up to the microphone and said: 'This one's called "Start"', there was bedlam.

> *It doesn't matter if we never meet again,*
> *What we have said will*
> *always remain*

Running from our seats, high up at the side, we couldn't find a way down to the floor where there was out-and-out mania. We had to stop at a barrier which, by the end of the night, we had pulled from its mountings.

knowing that someone in this world,
feels as desperate as me,
and what you give is what you get!

Everyone there knew every word to every song and sang all of them. It was raucous, emotional and unforgettable. They were absolutely the best live band, bar none, with a repertoire penned in a short few years by a young kid who was still only twenty-four when he broke them up. At Camden Market, a few weeks after the gig, I found a boot-leg, now long lost, of the very night I was there at Wembley Arena. I thought it would be the best way to preserve the feeling but I still remember it to this day. I have never felt anything like it since.

In 1983 Weller formed The Style Council and maintained his passionate support for many causes, including CND. I carried on buying their records and saw them in concert but they wore odd clothes that were not very Mr Byrite, and their pretentious sleeve notes took them away from me a little. There were already enough posers around, many vacuous bands I couldn't stand. For some reason, preening and posturing always seemed, to me, as low as a boy could go. Perhaps because I had no confidence in clothes and no money to buy any. Some of my friends, who'd been Mods one week, now announced themselves as New Romantics and raved about a Duran Duran gig.

I couldn't see the point, now I'd found a band who had a grasp and understanding of the reality of life for an audience they inspired, in listening to empty nonsense like Duran Duran. Classmates became fans of Haircut 100 and sang along to their 'Love Plus One' in the sixth-form common room.

'What does it even mean?' I said.

'Why does it have to *mean* anything?' said someone, scowling at me.

It just seemed so much better if it did. There were important issues in the world, causes to align with, but it seemed, if you didn't listen to Paul Weller or read the *NME* or go on a march, it was possible to miss them.

Violet Spalding

I had been a pathological joiner for years, following up membership of the Barry Sheene Appreciation Society, the Starsky & Hutch Fan Club and the Arsenal Supporters Club with a letter to U2's offices. I received an autographed promotional 'Post Card From The Edge' (and Bono Vox, and Larry Mullen, and the other one whose name I had to look up, Adam Clayton). The photo was from the *October* album cover with four scrawled signatures on it, in different-coloured inks. It went on my wall and the signatures faded but memories surface on the rare occasion I hear 'I Will Follow', 'Fire' or 'Gloria'.

U2's was the last fan club I wrote to. There were new organizations on the teenage *NME* reader's radar that placed issues above idols and passion above prettiness.

The most obvious organization to join was CND. It was clearly imperative that we should not have American missile bases on our island and that the independent nuclear deterrent was chronically expensive at a time of rising unemployment and social unrest. At least this was imperative to me, having read it in CND literature. It was hard to find such sentiments in any newspaper. All the papers I knew of, bar the *Daily Mirror*, were supporters of Margaret Thatcher and the Tories. None of them favoured unilateral disarmament and weren't likely to as it was never a policy that was going to shift any copies.

Despite the inspiring mass demonstrations, where crowds

of 250,000 people were estimated to have attended (by the organizers, 60,000 by the police), it was clear that CND's membership represented a tiny fraction of the population.

The significance of the split from the Labour Party of four senior former ministers to form the Social Democratic Party, or SDP, was lost on me but I picked up that Labour was in disarray and that arguments about unilateral nuclear disarmament were one cause of the rift.

Joining CND was a doorway to many other groups. Leaflets would arrive in the post with the assumption that, if you like this cause, then all these others will stir your interest too.

They did stir my interest, and my love of joining clubs. I began filling in forms and preparing stamped SAEs.

Public disturbances began to dominate the news, when the spotlight wasn't being either actively sought by the new SDP or directed brightly on to Lady Diana Spencer and her marriage to Prince Charles.

There were days of riots in Brixton and Toxteth which could be watched on television. Everyone became familiar with camera shots, taken from behind police lines, of people hurling bricks and petrol bombs at the constabulary, cowering in tunics, behind shields, while burning buildings collapsed and cars became flaming barricades.

The rioters were roundly condemned on all sides and the courage of the police commended. The causes of the riots were a mystery out in our part of suburbia, where the consensus was that hooligans were rioting and torching because they were bad people, while the police were valiantly containing and quelling the riot because they were good people.

There would never be a riot in our street. It was impossible to imagine one. Equally hard to imagine was the local force coming up our road using the 'SUS' stop and search powers they had been abusing in Brixton.

I knew about the SUS powers because I had joined the Anti-Nazi League. My membership card was on the wall next to my U2 postcard and just beneath my picture of Farrah Fawcett kneeling on a beach.

Though I was still reading *Shoot!* and *Roy of the Rovers* every week, I was less inclined to tear out pictures from them. I was developing a new personality and the bedroom wall was still the best place to post evidence of my attitudes and idolatry. At any rally there were satirical postcards to buy and flyers to read. These would find their way on to the wall as soon as I returned, particularly if they'd been signed by Rick Buckler from The Jam.

Soon included was Anti-Apartheid Movement material as I added membership of that organization to my list. *Anti-Apartheid News* joined the anti-fascist magazine *Searchlight* as required reading. I volunteered to help in the Anti-Apartheid Movement's offices and spent the day stuffing envelopes without really talking to anyone. It was a hive of activity with phones ringing, stuff on the walls, and people going in and out. They always needed volunteers to help and I wasn't the only one that day. No one asked questions or treated you with suspicion. They just found you a chair and asked you to fill envelopes with letters and leaflets. You could stay for as long or short a time as you wanted. It was up to you. It was voluntary. I stayed all day.

I don't know why I didn't go back. I was only fifteen and didn't understand much of the conversation around me. It was intimidating and serious, befitting the struggle to liberate millions of oppressed people, whose lives were blighted by the ruling elite's assertion that an acceptance of sub-human status was a wise alternative to resistance. Complaining about a teacher throwing a board rubber seemed less important. It was there I first heard the name Nelson Mandela.

The AAM was necessarily dealing with issues that were far from home. *Searchlight* chronicled brutality and terror happening only a few miles from the super-comfort of a detached house in the suburbs. The struggle against racism was immediately relevant. We were all racists and I knew from experience that it could take a while to even recognize it in yourself.

Two years after colluding in the baiting of the proprietor at The Paki Shop, I was a card-carrying anti-racist, opposing the National Front (whose insignia was graffitied all around Loughton) and the apartheid regime in South Africa.

These organizations were a gift to a teenager. Ready-made principles to adopt that were in direct opposition to the stifling, entrenched values at school and at home. Perfect. Unfortunately, the ANL and the AAM didn't have particularly good posters for my wall. There were some wonderful spoof movie posters from the anti-nuclear movement, including a memorable version of *Gone with the Wind* with Ronald Reagan and Margaret Thatcher as Clark Gable and Vivien Leigh. *Gone with the Wind* was my mum's favourite book. I knew this because her copy of it lay on her bedside table years after she'd gone. I've never read it and didn't really wonder what she would have thought of this poster, where the wind in question was a nuclear blast taking the world to kingdom come.

Another big seller was a print of an old B-movie poster with Reagan as an army officer in the thick of battle. This idea, of the American president characterized as regarding military conflict a little as he might regard a war movie, surfaced again over twenty years later when George W. Bush led America into the Iraq war with the apparent consideration of a B-movie film director shouting 'action'.

All of the organizations I joined had large and active memberships. They organized demonstrations, concerts and festivals attended by huge numbers, all staged with the compliance of the Labour-controlled Greater London Council under Ken Livingstone (who installed a scoreboard, on top of City Hall opposite the Houses of Parliament, displaying the unemployment rate accelerating upwards).

Other organizations had nothing like the resources, the volunteers, the metropolitan HQ or the funding to organize events, with their myriad costs. Other than the occasional publicity stunt, the only way these organizations could spread their message was to distribute eye-catching, affecting literature. There was nothing more diverting, among the stalls and leafleters at a big demo, than the words 'Chickens' Lib'.

The first time I saw it I thought it was a joke. 'Women's Lib' was an outmoded, populist term, long since replaced by the serious-sounding 'Feminism'. Perhaps someone had taken this old label and hijacked it for fun.

On the contrary, Chickens' Lib were real. Operating from a house in Skelmanthorpe, they distributed thousands of leaflets nationwide in a campaign against the battery farming of chickens. A thankless task in a nation of egg-beating carnivores who considered an animal well-done to be of greater interest than animal welfare

The squalor of the battery farms was unpublicized in the late '70s and early '80s other than by the founder of Chickens' Lib, Violet Spalding, who, with her daughter, Clare Druce, began a campaign that was to last for three decades.

The leaflets were simple. A black-and-white photograph

of a scrawny chicken, barely able to stand, with CHICKENS' LIB above it. Making space on my bedroom wall by removing people I'd grown apart from (Debbie Harry, Victoria Principal and Farah Fawcett survived the cull), I signalled my allegiance to this dishevelled bird and the millions like her, living in pain and desperation up and down the country.

More leaflets arrived and I went around Loughton putting them through doors. With the second batch came a larger poster of a size to replicate the floor area of a battery cage. The poster showed another desperately unhealthy bird and claimed that eight such birds would live their entire lives in a cage the size of the poster. Other cages would be on top and below, so the chickens would both defecate on other birds, and be defecated on themselves. All day, every day, for their entire lives. Like the turkeys kept packed into huge dark sheds in readiness for Christmas, the chickens would peck at one another, so would often have their beaks partially removed. That poster went on the wall too. This was the new me, the anti-battery farm, anti-nuclear, anti-Nazi, anti-apartheid anti-'me of two years previously'.

There were other animal groups who similarly progressed their cause through posters and literature. Animal Aid produced large black-and-white images taken secretly in a laboratory for animal experiments. Up on my wall they went: a cat with an electrode implanted in its head, a monkey being prepared for a heart transplant, rabbits enduring the Draize test, in which cosmetics are dripped in to their eyes to see if they go blind. Animals are killed after experiments so I knew that these awful images were precursors to death. I had a wall full of excruciating torture where I used to have 'Marco, Merrick, Terry Lee, Gary Tibbs and yours truly' from Adam and the Ants.

My dad wandered into my room one evening, as he was prone to do, at any time of day or night, to amuse himself. I wasn't allowed to have a lock on the door. He looked in horror at the ghoulish spectacle of tormented cats, dogs and other animals.

'What on earth are these?'

'Posters.'

'They're horrible. Where are all your footballers?'

'There're still footballers.'

'These aren't very nice for a bedroom wall, are they?'

I was monosyllabic until he left, probably thinking I'd turned at best peculiar, and at worst mad. I was *appalled* that he didn't understand or take any interest in my new passions.

My black-sheep status had long been assured. My bedroom was no sanctuary and just because I dreaded walking up the front steps every time I came home didn't mean I was able to make a plan to escape.

So there I was, fifteen and empathizing with animals in laboratories. I needed to get out more.

Chickens' Lib eventually became the Farm Animal Welfare Network, or FAWN. Animal Aid is still going strong. Both groups would be delighted to hear from anyone who has a spot that needs filling with a poster or two. Violet would be pleased, I'm sure.

1982

John Belushi

John Belushi was a product of the VCR age. Without the video cassette recorder there is no love for John in England. We would not have seen him. *Animal House* and *The Blues Brothers*, two of the finest comic films ever made, were seen, by me and my friends exclusively, repeatedly and somewhat surreptitiously, on tatty over-played VHS cassettes. We saw these films over and over again. My own tally was: *Animal House* eleven times; *The Blues Brothers* fifteen times.

Initially, *Animal House* was attractive to us teenagers because we'd heard tell of naked girls featuring, and there is a scene, shot through the dormitory window of a girls' fraternity house, that's devoted to just that intriguing subject.

Belushi's character, John 'Bluto' Blutarsky, is up a ladder watching a room full of nubile college students pillow fighting before bed. He gazes wide-eyed, agog, with his caveman simplicity caught in lady-headlights, as unattainable beauty frolics before him. Then the most attractive and senior girl, immaculate snob Mandy Pepperidge (played by Mary Louise Weller), exits to private quarters in the next room and Bluto, remaining at the top of the ladder, face set in determination, jumps inch by inch sideways to see her through the next window. As he settles in to his new position, he turns to the camera and raises a conspiratorial eyebrow of triumph. Half undressed, displaying much of her what Lloyd Cole and the Commotions would call 'Perfect Skin', Mandy enters a private reverie before the window, eyes half closed as if in a fantasy that many men would share as a dying wish. At this moment, Bluto's own half-closed eyes open wider, in the realization that something is wrong, as he tips slowly away from the window, falling backwards without ever changing his position, landing thirty feet below on his back still grasping the ladder on top of him. It's well-established by this point in the film that Bluto is impervious to pain, leaving the audience free to laugh as their own climax to a sequence of unparalleled sex-comedy. Bluto exists as a hedonista in a land of prim American college hypocrisy. Everyone else is obsessed by sex too, even the stuck-up ones, but he wears his primal urges on his sleeve.

Only after several viewings of *Animal House* did it dawn on me that it is Bluto's own unprecedented expansion, in the face of this beauty's unguarded flight of fancy, that forces his bulk away from the wall and outwards, past the vertical, into an irreversible concession to gravity.

Bluto, like Belushi's 'Joliet' Jake Elwood, in *The Blues Brothers*, also had an unerring, unconsidered reflex for the optimum anti-establishment stance in any situation. This made him a profoundly attractive character for adolescents. He is governed only by his instincts, which are for the breaking of Bad Law and the pursuit of pleasure: girls, drinking, music and the occasional high-speed pursuit. This is a fifteen-year-old boy's manifesto for a good life. It's a manifesto that manifestly cannot last, as all around adolescents, older young men can be seen, ditching said manifesto to take on responsibilities such as gainful employment. It's also a manifesto later returned to by some men, in what is commonly called the 'mid-life crisis'.

Speeding up the M11 in a friend's father's Ford Granada, I watched from the back seat as the driver, just seventeen years old, swigged from a bottle of booze before shouting, 'A hundred and twenty, boys!' as he looked down at the speedometer. We were happy to re-enact, in any approximate way, scenes from *Animal House*, in this case an epic 'road trip' in which a borrowed car is returned in ruins after a journey of alcohol-fuelled chaos. The Ford Granada in question fortunately came back down the M11 unscathed, with all its occupants.

Videos were usually watched, by now, in what had become the smoking room of our new house. We had moved next door into the Newbys' place. The reason for the move was the enlargement of our family as my dad had married the nice neighbour across the road from us. I now had a stepmother, whose choice to come and live with us seemed extraordinarily risky to me, but then my opinion was not sought as, of course, I was sixteen. My stepmother has since spent the best part of three decades striving to improve the lives of all concerned. A literally thankless task but one she approaches with great kindness and unflagging effort.

Also entering the fray was a new elder stepbrother, a keen smoker and VHS enthusiast, who offered advice and derision in equal measure as he watched me taking apart the Yamaha FS1M 50 cc motorbike handed down to me from my brother on my sixteenth birthday. Holed up in the garage, at the end of the drive that used to be part of my bicycle lap when I was imitating Barry Sheene, we would share cigarettes and Swarfega.

The little smoking room at the front of the house allowed access to the garage. It was as another viewing of *Animal House* neared its conclusion that it became apparent it would be a good idea to copy one of the film's highlights and stage a toga party in the garage, when dad and stepmum were away on holiday.

The garage was a source of huge anxiety to my dad. Full of car and motorcycle parts, unlimited dirty tea mugs, reeking of fags, oil, grease everywhere, it was a great place to hang out but not in any sense clean or tidy. In order to stage a toga party in there we were going to have to work to get it clean. By piling everything in to an Escort van on the driveway, we suddenly revealed the spacious tiled area that had once apparently served as Mr Newby's snooker room, above which he had built a large living room with a beautiful sprung dance floor (since carpeted after we turned up). The Newbys, they knew how to live.

To generate a party atmosphere we installed coloured light bulbs of low wattage. This was remarkably effective. Music came courtesy of a friend's portable record player. This piece of equipment, portable only in the sense that the rocks used at Stonehenge were portable when they came from Wales, played 12″ records in a vertical position. The size of a Mini Metro, the latest in cutting edge technology, it was to an mp3 player what Charles Babbage's Difference Engine was to, well, an mp3 player. But it worked and people always brought records to parties. All we had to hope was they could find the courage to leave their houses in bed sheets.

No one disappointed. Star of the toga line up was Danny, who arrived in a pink sheet with *Pontin's Holidays* embroidered on the side. Everyone had sheets on, about twenty of us in all. We did not have Otis Day and the Knights as they did in the film but we danced and we laughed and we managed to ignore the one-time NF supporter's astonishing body odour that was usually shielded by his New Romantic attire.

Around 11 p.m. my brother appeared, in striped pyjamas and a woollen dressing gown, like a 1920s housemaster coming to quieten an unruly dorm. He began telling people to go home. They did not. The next day he told our dad, phoning from Greece, that we'd had a party, perhaps in an attempt to spoil their holiday, having failed to spoil the toga fun. This could have caused a nuclear reaction but fortunately we now had a stepmum who presumably received news from *her* son that the garage had been cleaned, some friends had been over to listen to some records, and all the cats had been fed. The joy of two parents.

Animal House was a fount of inspiration for teenage misbehaviour. At school a Bluto-inspired food fight engulfed the dining hall. This was unimaginable rebellion in that place. It started when someone's jelly was put on their seat as they sat down and it finished with every surface covered in food scraps. A happy riot of chip-flinging and pie-dodging. Inevitably I was caught, with one or two others, while the majority made their escape. I was enjoying it too much and had long since stopped caring about the disciplinary regime, scoring an impressive fourteen detentions that term. The vile second master, Mr Millett, who, at five feet tall, suffered very obviously from Napoleon Syndrome had the capacity to terrify small boys but was laughable trying the same tactics in the face of adolescents taller than him. He would swish a cane in the face of small boys but not bigger ones, who may well have responded with the ubiquitous Essex challenge: 'Come on then.'

A long afternoon of dining hall cleaning could not eclipse the joy of the food fight though I felt a familiar pang of unfairness when my school report stated that I had taken part in the fight but *not* the clean-up. Outrageous! Cleaning that hall was the only work I'd done all term and now I was being denied credit for it. Injustice!

John Belushi and Dan Aykroyd's creation on *Saturday*

Night Live of the Blues Brothers led to a film that transcended cult status to become a classic musical comedy. Belushi's performance in *Animal House* and their ratings-pulling turns on *SNL* gave them a popularity that enabled them to attract an extraordinary array of musical stars, such as Aretha Franklin, James Brown, Ray Charles, Chaka Khan and Cab Calloway, not to mention Steve Cropper and Donald Dunn from Booker T and the MGs.

At house parties I would always carry a cassette of the soundtrack album and, with friends, try to re-enact dance routines from the movie. We'd quote lines and sing along to their version of 'Rawhide'. We never adopted the Men-in-Black-style suits they favoured – it would have felt like school uniform – but I did have a T-shirt that read:

> *It's a hundred and six miles to Chicago, we've got a full tank of gas, half a pack of cigarettes, it's dark and we're wearing sunglasses. Hit it.*

Dan Aykroyd now talks about the Men in Black as possibly real, having seen one, the day his television show about UFOs was cancelled. What John Belushi would make of that is impossible to say: he died from a massive drug overdose on 5 March 1982.

Six months after I saw them play live, and soon after Belushi had gone, James Honeyman-Smith of The Pretenders died from a heart problem brought on by excessive cocaine abuse. Ten months after that a second Pretender, Pete Farndon, was also dead from a drug overdose.

All these deaths made little impact. I knew nothing about drugs. No one I knew even smoked joints at that time. We just went to the Reindeer on a Friday night, drank beer, smoked fags and played records on the jukebox. There was no such thing as ecstasy and no one talked about drugs.

Some time later, after we'd all left school, one of the kids who we'd been skiing with died from a drug overdose. I don't know what drugs he took but I was told it was suicide. He was liked, prone to risk-taking, but funny. His parents were wealthy and they had a big place out in Essex. We would go over there sometimes and swim in their pool. I don't know what happened but all of us who knew him were shocked and ignorant of the danger he'd been in.

John Belushi died in a Los Angeles hotel room while his wife and his best friend, Aykroyd, were desperately trying to contact him from New York, and another man, hired to help protect him, was travelling to save him. That they were unable to reach him in time remains a terrible tragedy.

He was the ultimate hedonist in *Animal House* leading to a generation of imitators but, thankfully, teenagers playing at hedonism is only play. However wild we thought we were at the time, we knew nothing.

Kenny Roberts

Riding a 50 cc motorcycle gave me freedom. At sixteen I had my Yamaha FS1M. It was not the FS1E, or fizzy, but everyone called it a fizzy anyway. Fizzm didn't seem to work.

The bike had been run in by my brother, who was now crawling around Loughton in a Ford Escort. With L plates and a provisional licence, at a restricted top speed of 30 mph, you were free to go. After brief instruction from my dad on how to operate the clutch I was loose.

It was an immense and undimmable thrill, being a buzzing danger to myself and others. With my customarily chronic dress sense I paired the navy blue paintwork of the bike with a bright red open-face crash helmet. My dad purchased an unbelievably uncool waxed Belstaff jacket, not the *über*-cool distressed-leather versions favoured latterly by Hollywood stars, but a waxy, multi-pocketed affair, such as may have been worn by a special constable on a wet night in 1958.

Clothing had always been a problem. As kids, our casual wear came from Shattins on Debden Broadway. Shat tins. Shat in. Shat. If they'd called it Shit-Shat it would at least have had a ring to it. T-shirts in Shattins must have cost minus four pence, since they appeared to shrink on the way home, never mind in the first wash.

Fortunately, I was never embarrassed by having cheap and tasteless clothes at primary school since, although the school did not have a uniform when I went, my dad thought it should, and dressed me and my brother in grey shirts, black trousers and black school shoes. The only kids in uniform at the school. Put that together with short back and sides haircuts and we looked like extras from *Lord of the Flies*. Still, it was preferable to the misshapen catastrophes from Shattins we wore at weekends, which carried enough static electricity to power your bike, if you could only harness the current.

Waxy jacket and open-face helmet in place, I would career out on to Loughton High Road and venture forth to the Reindeer on a Friday night. There I met a couple of lads who rode Honda XL250s. They were seventeen and had passed their tests. Another kid had a Yamaha DT125 and took me on the back of it for an exhilarating ride through Epping Forest.

High Beach, up in the forest, has long been a meeting place for bikers and I'd heard tell of gangs. One night, as I was sitting on my fizzy chatting to my mate Ji (pronounced to rhyme with eye and short for Jeremy), two big bikers throbbed up alongside and asked where Queen's Road was. I said I'd show them and buzzed off, they cruised alongside me, it was only two minutes away. When we got there (Ji had run up on foot) they said we could come into the house they were visiting. The living room was entirely empty except for a crowd of leather and denim enthusiasts and a huge keg of beer. The furniture was in the garden. We were in the middle of what appeared to be a Hell's Angel party. Several people had jackets with 'Sidewinder' stitched on to them so I presume it was their do. Everybody was very civil but we struggled to keep them interested in our conversation so we were basically ignored until we left.

When hacking along Epping Forest's bridle paths after dark, the way ahead would be a sea of reflective rabbits' eyes which became bouncing furry bodies as you approached. Riding in there in daylight was risky and on one occasion I was spotted by a forest ranger who pursued me through Buckhurst Hill, Woodford and down to Chingford Plain. I was reckless but nimble. He had power but not the abandon of the teen, who is happy to leave forty feet of rubber alongside a line of cars as he locks up his rear brake before swinging right into traffic and away down Ranger's Road past Butler's Retreat. I lost him and went home with adrenaline pumping. Ten minutes later he rang at the door, having tracked me down via my pesky number plate. He never even managed to speak to me. My stepmum stone-walled him on my behalf. I saw him walk back to his bike and leave. I was so grateful for her protection I went and thanked her immediately. She told me that he'd said I had been riding 'like an idiot'. Doesn't he mean 'brilliantly'? I thought. Just because he couldn't keep up. And me on a fifty.

Except I wasn't on a fifty now. My fizzy had a big bore kit on it which meant a larger piston and increased engine capacity. *60 cc of mayhem!*

This piece of kit had been purchased from a lad in Buckhurst Hill who had a garage full of bike bits. I went out to a parts shop on Eastern Avenue that sold me a larger rear sprocket and over to Walthamstow for a bigger piston and piston rings. I had to make that journey twice as, after I'd fitted the new big piston, I kick-started the engine without putting the cylinder head back on. The piston shot up and out of the engine before crashing into it on the down stroke and breaking. I was below competent as a mechanic but I really wanted more speed. The big bore kit took top end up to a mind-blowing 42 mph.

The engine did run a little hot and I would have to make sure I didn't touch my jeans against it as there was a clear fire risk. If I went through a puddle a cloud of steam would billlow around me as the water hit the engine. Eventually, blasting down the hill into Loughton after another flat-out, full-throttle-the-whole-way journey back from Epping, I heard a 'ping' and the engine lost power. When I took the cylinder head off in the garage, there was a hole the size of a halfpenny in the top of the piston. Tiny shards of piston were everywhere down inside the cylinder. The whole engine would need to be cleaned out. As only a moron would, I took a wet cloth to the inside of the cylinder and tried to wipe away pieces of metal.

It was going to be too big a job for me. I'd have to take the whole crank case apart. I was too lazy to try, so took the coward's way out and told my dad the bike had 'broken down'. When it came back from Woodford Motorcycles fully operational at a cost of £200 (it cost £400 new) the mechanic there told my dad that the engine had completely rusted up. I feigned ignorance and felt the shame of my idleness and my ham-fisted introduction of water to the machinery.

Meanwhile, down at the Reindeer, a plan was afoot to ride up to the British Motorcycle Grand Prix at Silverstone.

Four of us went on three bikes with me on the back of an XL250. The numbness in my behind was absolute by the time we reached the circuit. My buttocks could have been gnawed off by badgers and I'd have felt nothing. We put the bikes into three sides of a square and hung a fly sheet over them to sleep under. Approximately two million inches of rain fell on Northamptonshire that night. No one could sleep so people amused themselves by sliding prodigious distances through the mud on their bellies. Water raced down the sides of the lanes knee deep. The flysheet reduced the rain to a fine mist which we slept in.

The next day was Sunday, 1 August, and one rider turned up with a new bike carrying the brand new Y plate. How he managed to pick up a new bike on a Sunday made for a fascinating discussion.

We looked for a spot near Stowe or Club corner and dried out in the sun, waiting for the main event, the 500 cc race. Everyone wanted to see Barry Sheene race against Kenny Roberts, the legendary American rider who had taken Sheene's World Championship title in 1978 and won it again in '79 and '80. Sheene was adored by all the British fans but secretly we all felt Roberts, with his remarkably smooth, almost cruising, knee-down riding style, may have been the better rider. They were friends and rivals. Sheene had memorably flicked the Vs at Roberts while passing him in the British Grand Prix three years previously, though Roberts came back to win.

Unfortunately for us, but more for him, Sheene couldn't race. He'd collided with a fallen bike at 175 mph in practice and the bones in his legs had been smashed to pieces. X-rays after surgery appeared to show a Meccano set holding him together.

We could hear the bikes on the other side of the track but the tannoy was hard to understand. There was a roar of engines as they set off. There would be a minute or so before they arrived. In the distance, as the first bikes appeared, we could see a tall column of smoke rising up. The bikes roared past us, the engines screaming as the riders changed down through the gears for the corner and then up again to blast away. There was no Kenny Roberts. The riders came round again on the second lap but there was still no Roberts. Perhaps he was the cause of that column of smoke? No one knew if he was injured or not. No one knew if he was dead or not. Barry Sheene was already lying in a hospital bed. A few weeks earlier, many riders had boycotted the French Grand Prix because the track was unsafe. The race was loud and exciting but I didn't hear who'd won over the tannoy (it was Franco Uncini, who would take the title that year).

Later we heard that Roberts was injured but alive. He raced brilliantly again the next season, winning six races but losing the title to 'Fast' Freddie Spencer (always my favourite nickname that).

Riding home, we lost our way and ended up being buffeted by winds on a newly opened section of the M25 which was being built a few miles away from Loughton. One of my stepbrother's friends, a nineteen-year-old lad called Adrian, who had lodged with my stepmum and stepbrother over the road from us until our families merged, lived in a caravan out near the construction site. One morning he was found dead next to his bike up there. He'd been riding on the construction site without a helmet, possibly chasing a thief away from the caravan site. Security patrols, which should have been hourly, did not find him and may have saved him had they done so. But they didn't and he died.

By this time I was attending Loughton College and I went in that morning dressed all in black with the intention of heading up to Parndon Wood Crematorium and Cemetery for the funeral.

In the end I didn't go. I couldn't face it and didn't want to turn up on a bike and upset anyone. He had been estranged from his parents but my stepmum went to see them and persuaded them to attend. There was a huge turnout. My memory of Adrian is of the two of us, sitting on our bikes outside the Chariot chip shop in Loughton, with me laughing and laughing while he picked the corner of his bag of chips away to let the pint of vinegar he liked to add drain out. He was always smiling and it was unbearably sad when he went.

I'd come to know Parndon Wood. Another friend and fellow fizzy rider lived near to it. Everyone called him Ernie because of a past resemblance to the *Sesame Street* character. We used to ride around together, often to see the pretty girls, both called Anna, we liked to chat to down at the stables in Buckhurst Hill.

Ernie sold me a Beeline race exhaust which made my bike satisfyingly loud. People could hear you coming from miles around. When leaving the Gardeners Arms in Loughton, having given 'backies' up and down York Hill to ra-ra-skirted fourteen-year-old beauties from school like Natalie Clarke, I would rev my noisy exhaust and ride away with a cigarette dangling from my lip. Fifty yards down the road, it would be necessary to stop and rub hot fag ash from my eye.

Ernie too had a noisy pipe on his bike. He pulled up outside my house one day and my dad appeared:

'That's far too noisy,' he said.

'No it isn't,' said Ernie.

'Yes it is,' said dad

'No it isn't,' said Ernie.

I knew Ernie could go on like this because when he'd sold me the exhaust he'd asked for £10 and I'd said:

'Nine.'

He then said:

'Eleven.'

I said:

'Nine.'

He said:

'Twelve.'

I said:

'You can't say that.'

He said:

'Yes I can.'

I gave him ten.

'Far, far too noisy,' said my dad, going indoors as if to end the argument.

'No it isn't,' said Ernie, grinning at me.

Ernie asked me where my real mum was and I told him she had died of leukaemia. He asked me where she was buried and I said I thought she was in Harlow. I hadn't attended the funeral. It was coming up to the tenth anniversary of her death. Ernie said there was a cemetery at the end of his road in Harlow and did I want to go up and look for her? I said I did so we went.

Parndon Wood has a modern crematorium with fields full of headstones sloping away from it. All around the back of the building is the wood itself.

We went down and began to look along all the graves, looking for my mum's. There were dozens of headstones, row after row. We split up to look but there was no sign of her anywhere. We walked up the slope to see if there was anybody around to ask. There didn't appear to be a funeral going on that day. Eventually a middle-aged man with a concerned expression came out to see what we wanted. I said I was looking for my mum's grave. He said that, as it was a Sunday, there was no one about and everything was locked up. There was a moment's silence. Then he asked me if I knew the date she had died.

'August 22nd 1972,' I said.

He opened up an odd little room that stood alone and housed the Book of Remembrance. I thumbed through it and came to 22 August. There was my mum's name. It was a relief to know she was there. Assuming she'd been cremated, we were directed into the wood where an area had been divided into months of the year. We scoured August for a little plaque where an urn might be buried, or for a small flower holder, as some had names and dates on. There was still no sign of her. Nor was her name engraved on any of the commemorative benches. I wondered if her ashes had been scattered. After a while, we thanked the man who had shown us the Book of Remembrance, took our bikes and rode away as quietly as our exhaust pipes would allow.

Michael Foot

The heaviest thing in the cold store at Doug Smith's green-grocer's on Loughton High Road was a green net sack of eight white cabbages. Great heavy solid football-size things they were, much more difficult to carry than sacks of spuds because one or two could slip within the netting, shifting a good part of the weight suddenly, causing you to stagger as you emerged into the shop itself. Serial killers must have similar problems when disposing of bin liners full of heads in Epping Forest.

After my first week working for Doug, I received my first ever pay packet, £55. Unprecedented wealth! I went straight to the little clothes shop at the bottom of Church Hill to buy two shirts that didn't suit me in any way.

Doug was my stepmum's best friend's husband. I'd been told that I would be allowed to leave school early only if had a job to go to. The greengrocer's was it.

I preferred it to school: using the big old scales, twirling paper bags, doing arithmetic, saying, 'Can I help you?' to old ladies wth tartan shopping trolleys and a keen eye for an apricot.

On a Tuesday for some reason, no one came in and it was boring, but never as boring as school.

A regular customer was Len Murray's wife. Len Murray was General Secretary of the TUC from 1973 to 1984. There were so many labour disputes during that time, particularly with the Winter of Discontent, that Mr Murray was often on the news and, along with Terry Venables, he was Loughton's best-known resident (such people were not called celebrities then). Later in life Mr Murray became Baron Murray of Epping Forest.

Since I'd joined a new group calling itself Epping Forest Young Socialists, I could have passed a message to Len: 'You're not the only lefty in Loughton.' He might have liked that, but I don't remember him ever coming in the shop. Mrs Murray was in charge of veg while the Gen Sec was going toe to toe with Thatcher and the Tories.

In the sixth-form common room I had been a CND-supporting 'Commie' to some. Though actually, we spent all our time playing four-card brag, and I'd decided against communism. As a pathological hoarder, with no capacity to tolerate loss, no matter how insignificant, the concept of 'all property is theft' was anathema to me. My intolerance of loss also meant I took no pleasure in gambling. Even when I won I couldn't enjoy it since people almost never paid up and that felt like a loss.

I decided to be a Socialist since this was a movement that accommodated my three principal concerns:

1 A passionate anti-public school stance with
  pyromaniac tendencies towards said schools.
2 Going to see The Jam at CND benefits.
3 Being Leader of the Opposition to my dad.

The first meeting of the Epping Forest Young Socialists was mentioned in the local newspaper, the *Gazette*. I showed it to my dad:

'That's where I went on Tuesday night,' I challenged.

He sighed wearily and went to watch telly. I stuck the clipping to my wall.

When I decided to leave school I called round at the

Gazette's offices in Loughton to offer my services. Bafflingly, they declined.

I was adamant that I was going to leave school though, despite this knockback. A couple of my best friends were leaving and it was proving a waste of my time and my dad's money.

Economics was suffocatingly tedious. It was taught in a Liverpudlian monotone, tinged with menace, by Mr Pearson, who wore brown and cream two-tone shoes, with a pale-blue three-piece suit, topped off with a thick blond moustache and permed hair, grown longish to distract from his bald patch. He droned at us, suppressing his murderous rage, and we took notes. He usually looked out of the window rather than at his pitiful pupils. The good thing about him was that he didn't give a toss if you bunked off. It was your loss as far as he was concerned. He also liked *Hill Street Blues*, which he said was the only decent American TV show and the best thing on television. It was, I agreed, though my dad and brother hated it. I had perked up but he didn't elaborate. Despite liking him after that, I still bunked off.

I did have a last hurrah as a public schoolboy in the shape of a geography field trip to the Isle of Arran. Twenty of us slept in a dormitory shared with six lads from a school in Keswick. One night me and one of the Keswick boys snuck in to the nearby girls' dorm. I was keen to fumble around in the dark with a particular girl from a Bradford school with peroxide blonde hair and a mini-skirt. Once we were inside their pitch-black dorm, the door opened and one of their teachers appeared.

'Ooh, Sir,' squealed the Bradford lasses, 'we're not decent! Don't put t'light on! We're in t'nude! You'll see us! Have you come in to see us in us knickers, Sir?'

Me and the lad from Cumbria stood unspied in the dark.

Hanging around with the Bradford girls was fun but it did mean missing a night in the pub. Our dorm was in the roof and, on their return, one of our drunken class leant out of the skylight to be sick. We held his ankles until one of our teachers came in when we instantly let go leaving him inches from tipping out. We distracted the teacher by swaying from side to side, as he was clearly the worse for wear himself, and we wanted him to think the room was moving.

Later that week that same kid, while sleepwalking, climbed into the bed of a boy who was covered in such coarse body hair we called him Trog. When Trog awoke he found the school's biggest poser and wannabe ladies' man in his bed.

I hadn't laughed so much in a week since the previous year's ski trip. Whenever we were let off our usually tight leash there was chaotic and gleeful misbehaviour. It had always been the same on school trips. Within the school the regime was petty-minded, patronizing and sadistic if you didn't toe the line. Given the slightest slack few of us had a sense of social responsibility or self-restraint. We'd been treated the same way since we were eleven and our emotional development had stopped then. Institutionalized people struggle to function in the outside world and under no circumstances should they be in charge of anything until they can do so. Like camps holding prisoners of war in Iraq for example.

There was a feeling of a split in Britain and posh schools like mine were on the wrong side of the line for me. Margaret Thatcher was the most unpopular prime minister since polls began, but everyone I knew, rather than being enraged by Thatcher, instead regarded Michael Foot's leadership of the Labour Party as a joke.

The previous year, Michael Foot had worn what was regarded as an inappropriate coat to a Remembrance Day service at the Cenotaph. It was universally described as a donkey jacket (it wasn't). The queen mother famously complimented him on his choice, as it was cold, but the Tory press savaged him as scruffy and disrespectful to those who had made the ultimate sacrifice.

During the war, Foot had trained as an assassin, as part of a group, known as 'scallywags', who were prepared to risk their lives to kill English collaborators in the event of a successful Nazi invasion.

Remembrance Sunday came only a couple of weeks after I'd stood amongst a quarter of a million people in Hyde Park to hear Michael Foot, a founder member of CND, speak passionately and eloquently on the subject of unilateral nuclear disarmament to cheering and applause. He seemed genuinely moved by the sheer numbers and I found his inherent grandfatherly decency endearing and worthy of respect. He was erudite, considered and inspiring but he faced a bullying barrage from the press.

With a desperately unpopular prime minister, and a hugely popular peace movement, it seemed, to my naïve eyes, that Labour could win a general election. Michael Foot would become prime minister and Britain would lead the world in efforts to eradicate both nuclear weapons and poverty.

Unfortunately, such a scenario was unthinkable to the press, whose influence was enormous. Furthermore, the SDP breakaway gathered strength and terminally split the potential Labour vote. On top of that, Argentina invaded the Falklands and England (described as Britain by Mrs Thatcher) went into a patriotic fervour as a task force was dispatched, placing thousands of forces personnel at risk of death in the South Atlantic.

I found a postcard at one demo that contrasted the front page of the *Morning Star* and the front page of the *Daily Mail,* the day after HMS *Antelope*'s magazines had exploded, due to an Argentinian bomb landing on board, during the Falklands War. Both publications carried the same picture which showed the ship illuminated by a vast spray of flame and sparks.

The headline in the *Morning Star* read:

SENSELESS SACRIFICE

The *Daily Mail* read:

ANTELOPE DIES IN A BLAZE OF GLORY

Now the Tories were making a comeback. A victorious war led to some (Tories) comparing Thatcher to Winston Churchill. Foot was portrayed as a disorientated, unpatriotic pensioner, unfit to hold office. His sympathies lay with the victims of the Tories' policies, in particular the hundreds of thousands who had lost their jobs as an economic recession culled the workforce.

Foot's treatment by the press seemed heinously unjust and even anti-democratic. A principled, intellectual orator, author and political philosopher, with decades of knowledge and wisdom to draw on, was trampled underfoot, having already suffered the self-interested betrayal of the defecting Labour members who went on to waste their political careers in the SDP.

The following year there was no chance for Labour. Thatcher was re-elected by a landslide. Michael Foot resigned to be replaced by a younger man, fellow unilateralist Neil Kinnock, who had given many rousing speeches that Foot doubtless approved of.

Elected unnoticed to Parliament for the first time in 1983

were Tony Blair and Gordon Brown, beginning their fourteen years in opposition. Like the rest of the Labour party, they turned their backs on the 1983 manifesto, which had included plans to nationalize the banks, lest the forces of unrestrained capitalism were allowed to follow an inevitable path to excessive greed and profit, thereby putting the entire world economy at risk. It's conceivable that more people have re-read that manifesto since than read it at the time.

The Tories, for their part, distracted the country from troubles at home by invoking Britain's military history, with political broadcasts showing Spitfires taking off in the Battle of Britain, as if the Falklands conflict was connected somehow to the defeat of Nazism.

Back home, I suffered the fate of millions during Mrs Thatcher's first term in office. I was laid off. After two weeks at the greengrocer's, Doug took me to one side and said that his son Russell was coming back from his holiday, to take his job back. I hadn't known that was the arrangement. Though I didn't see myself in a greengrocer's in the long term, it seemed early in my working life to be tossed on to the scrapheap. Now what would become of me? Cast out with nothing but two terrible shirts to show for it.

My dad told me there was a college in Loughton that offered a media studies course and perhaps I'd be more interested in that. My stepmum may have put him on to it as my stepbrother was attending the college, studying to be a mechanic. I had an interview and was admitted.

Immediately my life was turned upside down. My new classmates (bar one non-committal church-going one with thick glasses) *hated* Thatcher. Many of them loved dear old Michael Foot and admired his brave oratory in the face of vicious press attacks. Now we had two years of communications studies A Level to discuss the mass media and its portrayal of the left and the unions. We were to be thoroughly absorbed by a compelling Marxist reading of press and television influence, on both politics and the public.

On top of this we could make TV programmes in their little studio and take O Levels in film studies and drama. I took only two A Levels as I was unmotivated after school. Communications was one and I could choose between sociology and theatre studies for the other. I went to see the sociology teacher, a serious man called Dave, with a beard and an earring. The drama teacher, who was called Piers and had silver-painted boots with rainbow laces, said: 'Try it for a week and if you don't like it you can change.' We spent a week playing juvenile but effective get-to-know-you theatre games like 'stick in the mud'. I loved it and stayed on in his class. Within a few weeks I'd decided I wanted to be an actor. Or a Labour MP. But probably an actor.

Piers and Dave, it turned out, had formed a comedy double act and were trying out on the London comedy circuit.

Rik Mayall

Those shopping centre dispersal devices that emit an intolerable mosquito-like tone only young people can hear, thereby driving anti-social teenage urchins out, while tormenting babies and toddlers, have their polar opposite. It's a pile of VHS cassettes with episode after episode of *The Young Ones* on them. Between 1982 and 1984 there was no more effective teenage boy magnet.

Hopeful youths would trek up the hill to our house for a *Young Ones* double bill. My dad memorably went out on to the front drive to shout 'clear off' at a group of five friends who were mooching towards him, slowly and discontentedly, as if weighed down by acne and the continuous exhausting production of reproductive seed.

It was perhaps because me and my peers were slouching and sauntering our way into our late teens that a programme about four students living in a mouldy old house, constantly bickering and insulting each other, was appealing. At least they had their own place! They could do what they wanted! What set them apart from their directionless teenage audience was the spring-tight energy of Adrian Edmondson and Rik Mayall as Vyv and Rik.

Rik Mayall was known to us as Kevin Turvey, the Solihull-based 'investigator' whose monologues were the weekly highlight of BBC2's *A Kick Up the Eighties*. In that show, though, he was seated, and meandered edgily through surreal tales. Now he was near-manic. A couple of years later I saw him on stage at the Dominion Theatre in a double bill with

Ben Elton (with whom Rik and Lise Mayer had written *The Young Ones*). At the climax of the show his underwear exploded, while he was still wearing it. It looked painful but people laughed, as they had throughout his entire Tigger-style performance. He turned the tables and chastized us for laughing at someone blowing up.

With Nigel Planer as hippy Neil, the ultimate victim of bullying, and Christopher Ryan's Mike, the business-minded mature student, the quartet was uniquely memorable.

Despite its teenage following the popularity of the show was achieved without sexual content. Unlike *Animal House*, with which *The Young Ones* had to compete for space in the VCR's busy timetable, there was no nudity in *The Young Ones*.

That's not to say the youth of Loughton were unmotivated by carnality. In fact, the most requested videotape I had was one I'd found in the gutter outside a house in Stratford, after me and my friends had been thrown out of a party being held by some people we'd met on holiday in Majorca that summer.

Three of us had shared one room in a cheap Palma Nova hotel, which was also home for two weeks to a group of nine predatory Geordie women in their early twenties. We had very little money, so we worked out which bars and discos (they weren't called clubs in 1982 – clubbing hadn't been invented yet) had free admission between certain times.

Armed with packets of condoms and convinced that sex was inevitable, we joined in the booze'n'snog culture that was being exported from the UK to all of Spain's costas.

One of the Geordie girls decided I would do and we headed back to my shared room. At twenty-one, five years my senior, she would, I hoped, offer expertise and guidance, but in those days the nervous, incompetent boy still had to take the initiative in all aspects of the mating ritual (asking for a dance, buying drinks, asking for a date, asking for her hand in marriage, asking for forgiveness, asking for access to the children – actually much of that still applies in the twenty-first century). The role of the semi-inebriated girl was to offer neither resistance nor assistance in the removal of her underwear. If you couldn't unclasp her bra while she was lying on your arm, causing numbness and the onset of pins and needles, then you weren't to be trusted in other departments. A boy knew this was the first challenge of the game and success here was mandatory for progression to other levels. Eventually, both my room-mates returned to lie on their beds, either side of me and my Geordie *amour*. Unable to suppress their giggling, and refusing to sod off for a bit and leave us to it, they succeeded in spoiling the mood sufficiently for her to bolt back to her mates upstairs. That, it turned out, was to be my opportunity. Those condoms never did see the light of day.

Sitting down opposite some Mancunian girls in a burger bar one evening, me and a lad from Enfield we'd befriended began trying to chat them up. He was nineteen to my sixteen so he did all the talking but they were soon goading him about his diminutive stature and showing general disdain. They behaved as if we'd sat down at their table uninvited and butted in to their conversation without considering whether we were welcome. Which we had. One of the girls then squirted ketchup at us.

We were now engaged in a squeezy bottle battle with mustard and ketchup spraying everywhere. The girls ran off but the lad from Enfield was set upon by four Spanish burger chefs wielding the iron bars that they used to pull the shutters down at the end of the night. They were beating him on the back as he cowered beneath their blows. I tried to grab him so we could run and one of the Spaniards turned to me and raised his iron bar high in the air. I put my hands up to protect my head just in time as he brought the bar hard down across my fingers. That was enough of a diversion to break up the attack and we escaped, but there was no sign of my mate who had been at the counter ordering burgers.

We went back and snuck in to the gardens of a hotel opposite, to see if we could see our innocent accomplice. I was bleeding and the knuckle of the middle finger on my left hand had moved oddly out of place. The boy from Enfield had red welts all over his back. He was appalled that my mate had only spectated rather than helped, and had little sympathy when we saw him handcuffed and being loaded into a police car.

They returned him to our hotel later with instructions to pay a 'fine' for 'damages' to furniture. It was our last day and none of us had any money. I knew my mate's dad had given him a £50 'emergency fund' which would more than cover the fine. He said that this would not constitute an emergency in his father's eyes. Wrongful arrest and a dodgy fine, dished out by a copper who issued dire warnings over non-payment, seemed an emergency to me. I suggested he tell his dad that I'd been arrested and that he'd used the money to help me. We made up any number of stories he could use but he was so scared of his father we ended up having to give him our few remaining pesetas and then go begging around the pool for more.

I was surprised how spineless and fearful he was. He was a big lad who played rugby and was forever posing by the pool, flexing his muscles and pouring oil on himself. He'd been especially scornful when I borrowed a big Geordie girl's one-piece swimsuit and come down to the pool in it for a laugh.

We managed to raise the money, for which he didn't thank us. Those girls with their ketchup had caused no end of trouble. My finger still has a scar, if you look closely, in a certain light.

We were chucked out of that party in Stratford because I'd taken a girl into the parents' bedroom and pulled a plant in front of the door to stop anyone interrupting us. A minute later the door opened and the plant went over, spilling earth all over the carpet. Standing outside on the street I noticed, in the gutter, a VHS cassette with *Mother's Wish XXX* on the label.

The plot of *Mother's Wish* concerned the visit of a randy aunt who arrived to stay with a family and immediately coaxed them into incestuous acts played out to an un-listenable '70s soundtrack. XXX was an understatement.

Once I'd shown this film to friends, the requests for another look were unending. No one else had any porn. Inconceivable as that must seem in the twenty-first century. It was necessary to turn to the underwear section of the Freeman's catalogue to see any scantily clad models. Mys-teriously, pages from soft porn titles would sometimes appear in hedgerows around Essex, a phenomenon every bit as interesting as crop circles and with little or no plausible explanation.

I tired of *Mother's Wish* after repeated screenings but those who hadn't seen it had real urgency in their requests to view. A college lecturer said he'd like to look at it for research. He handed it back with a remark about the soundtrack or camerawork but I suspect he may have just been watching it in his leisure time.

Despite the popularity of *Mother's Wish*, it was never

watched as much as those *Young Ones* episodes. Adrian Edmondson's first entry as Vyvyan had him crashing through a wall, which was hilariously surprising and set the tone for the series.

Cartoon violence, infantile teasing and bullying between characters, talking inanimate objects, live appearances by bands like Madness and Motorhead, all seemed designed to appeal to us boys.

The continual references to the political climate of the time, including the peace movement, the police as the government's private army, jokes on racial issues, and constant references to Thatcher and the 'fascists' gave the show a contemporary edge and made it incomprehensible to suburban parents or indeed almost anyone over thirty. In the same way as the shopping centre buzz can only be picked up by teens so could Rik and Vyvyan's banter only be enjoyed by the young.

At parties, when we weren't dancing to *The Blues Brothers* soundtrack we were doing impressions of Rik and Vyvyan and quoting lines from the show.

On 2 November 1982, those of us on the modern communications (with special emphasis on television) course at Loughton College of Futher Education sat in the small TV studio at the college (in between the vast cameras that had once been bolted on to Citroën estate cars and driven around race tracks alongside galloping horses) and waited for the historic opening of a new TV channel.

Channel 4 started with no fanfare or big budget event that presaged the huge impact the channel would have, particularly with regard to comedy, in the next few years. The animated logo and sting that were to become so familiar appeared and they opened with *Countdown*. That night they ran a spoof of the *Famous Five* novels I'd loved as a child,

Five Go Mad in Dorset. Dawn French and Jennifer Saunders appeared with Adrian Edmondson.

It's likely that without Channel 4's imminent emergence the BBC would never have commissioned *The Young Ones.*

This new comedy was astute, vibrant and confident. It was an alternative to the offerings on the established channels, a wilfully politically correct strain that, with juvenile irreverence, mocked the race and gender stereotyping of the dominant comedy programming of the day. All other shows were ripe for attack and many were lampooned on *The Young Ones.* Also ridiculed, in Rik Mayall's hilarious performance, was the posturing intolerance of 'right-on' types epitomized by his self-styled People's Poet.

Not much was aimed at teenagers back then, since we had little or no disposable income. Even if we'd had the money to spend on magazines it's doubtful that anything like *Nuts* or *Zoo* would have emerged. The campaign to ban the Page 3 girl in the *Sun* was in full swing and it was to be well over a decade before *Loaded* magazine rebranded the objectification of women and the PC storm of the '80s died down. In 1982, though, it was just beginning. Political correctness invited you to approach women as if they were thinking creatures with a sense of humour. There was no fake tan, no fake breasts and everyone had full pubic hair.

1983

Antonin Artaud

There are only two sound effects, or SFX as we learnt to call them, in Harold Pinter's *The Dumb Waiter*, in which two hitmen await instructions for their next job. The first is of a toilet chain and flush, heard offstage left. The second is of a dumb waiter coming down.

In our O Level drama production of *The Dumb Waiter*, we had no set, just a curtain behind. There was a gap in the curtain through which me and the other actor, Guy, would reach into an imaginary dumb waiter to retrieve notes vital to the plot.

Unfortunately, our fellow drama student, Dean, who was operating the reel-to-reel tape machine that would play the two SFX, became confused and mixed them up.

The dumb waiter crashing down, with another message for the two hapless and baffled characters, is a charged dramatic moment in Pinter's tense little tale. This tension can be undermined when the actors are anxiously drawn to the sound, not of a dumb waiter, but of a Victorian high-tank toilet cascading its two gallons upstage, before apparently issuing a memo.

Again and again poor Dean played the wrong sound. When one of us went into the wing (just to the side of the badminton court in the college main hall) ostensibly to use the lavatory, the sound of a dumb waiter would be heard, as if our personal waste was being delivered for service to a sewer bistro.

The audience found all this amusingly tolerable, Dean

was mortified, but he had superb flammable 80s highlights in his hair, so was impossible to dislike. Me and Guy found it challenging to concentrate. Harold Pinter ... wasn't invited, which was a shame, he might have enjoyed it. He would surely have approved of my Methuen copy of his play, as the 'o' in Harold had been made into a CND symbol with a Biro. Piers the drama teacher was encouraging and asked us to write up notes on the assignment in which our group had split up, with one group putting on Pinter's *The Room,* and ours *The Dumb Waiter.*

I concluded my notes enthusiastically in my new role as a motivated student:

> Over all successful – working steadily vastly more self confident – enjoying it immensely – Drama has opened up a whole new part of my life – fun

I'd only read two plays before. *Macbeth*, the night before my English literature O Level, when much that Mr Giles had been talking about for two years fell into place. What a story! I managed a C. For the same O Level I'd also read Marlowe's *Dr Faustus*, which was compelling, particularly if you:

a) Believed in the Devil
b) Had sold your soul to him and could therefore relate to the protagonist.

As it was, Faustus' dilemma is a no-brainer for an adolescent. Twenty-four years of unparalleled pleasure in exchange for ... it doesn't matter what the exchange is, where do I sign?

Now Piers had introduced us to this Pinter play in which people spoke uncannily like people in actual life. Raised as I was on a culture-free diet of American cop shows, westerns and the parallel universe of the English sitcom, the notion of theatre like this was alien to me. Pinter immediately became My Favourite Playwright, which put him in front of Shakespeare and Marlowe in a list of three.

Meanwhile, in film studies O Level classes, we were watching Hitchcock films: *The Birds*, *Marnie*, *Psycho*, *Spellbound* and, my favourite, *Strangers on a Train*. These were our actual lessons, illuminated by our lecturer, Allan Rowe, who would twist and squirm on his chair, so unable was he to contain his fascination with his subject. When we watched Channel 4 start up, I thought Allan might faint with excitement as he peered at the screen waiting for action, leaning forwards, daring his chair to tip him out. At the end of the year, he threw a party for everyone at his house in Clapton, where he made lush Indian food and I had my first poppadum.

I was enjoying everything. In communications, we studied inter-personal communication with our psychologist teacher Andy (even his kids were to call him Andy – prescribed gender roles were a no-no), who had us unnervingly observing body language wherever we went, which probably gave other students the creeps.

For a general studies mock O Level we were asked to correctly lay out a letter. I wrote to my MP. My teacher's comments follow:

Sir John Biggs-Davison MP
1 Whitehall Place
London
SW1

12th May 1983

Dear Sir,

Recently, I am sure you will have become aware of the controversy surrounding the construction of the latest nuclear power station. For the following reasons, I, as one of your constituents, urge you to support the proposed ban on such power stations in this country.

Firstly, nuclear power stations are potentially very dangerous. The near meltdown at Three Mile Island in America endangered thousands of people. Such a catastrophe in such a densely populated country as ours could kill millions of people.

Secondly, the C.E.G.B. has admitted that, for the amount of money involved, the current nuclear power stations are producing very poor returns in terms of energy.

Thirdly, the new Pressurized Water Reactors which your party are intending to build are even more dangerous than their predecessors. Some workers may be exposed to up to five times the radiation levels previously encountered in other nuclear power stations.

Fourthly, investing in nuclear power inevitably leads to the development of nuclear arms, the biggest threat to civilisation as we know it of all time. Never before have we been on the verge of total destruction as we are today. "We are living on borrowed time" to quote Paul Weller, an idol of thousands of young people. The banning of nuclear power would be an excellent start in the struggle for nuclear disarmament.

Fifthly, the money spent on a PWR station could be used

to insulate hundreds of thousands of lofts, or to research in to wind, solar, and wave power.

It is for these reasons I implore you to grant your support for this campaign to ban nuclear power.

Yours faithfully,

Alan Davies.

An excellent well-organized letter that I happen to agree with! Even if I did not, the letter would be impressive for the clear way in which you have presented your arguments in a logical sequence. You also urge your MP to act on your behalf. 20/25

Sixthly, life at college was suiting me; you could cite Paul Weller in your mock O Levels!

I was becoming highly suggestible and eager to please and it was this as much as anything that caused me to embrace Antonin Artaud.

Piers loved Artaud, a French theatre practitioner who, in 1938, had published *The Theatre and Its Double* in which his stated theatrical aim was to stage the innermost desires and fears of humankind: the lust, the crime, the dreams and the fantasies experienced or perpetrated by humans. The audience's attention was to be inevitable and the performance to run through them like their own blood. He called for a Theatre of Cruelty, in twin manifestos, and exhorted others to follow his desire to create a new language of sound and expression to fuel it. He believed that the multi-layered conventions of human behaviour concealed and controlled true impulses and desires, which emerged in dreams or terrible acts and that such impulses needed to be expressed, with the theatre the only place to display them. The human race could be purged of cruelty only in a

Theatre of Cruelty. A functioning crucible for the cleansing of all humanity.

This was going to be a tall order for our drama group, particularly if Dean was going to be on sound.

Willingly I tried to follow the teachings of a maniacal dead Frenchman passed on by a nice man from Derbyshire in pinstripe dungarees.

Artaud's anger was bottomless. Theatre's true potential was being mocked by a devotion to revered masterpieces and bourgeois social conventions. I could imagine him throwing up all day after an evening at the theatre.

'No more masterpieces,' he declaimed, and it was a compelling mantra to follow. If we don't understand the so-called classics, if they are elitist or elusive, then we can express those ideas in our own way for our own times. This was excellent news as I didn't really understand any great masterpieces and could now legitimately stop trying to, having read only three plays.

Before we did anything Artaudian though, we first had to stage a panto. Though I had no aptitude for being a dame, I was the most shameless performer in first-year theatre studies, so I donned a purple frock (with some football socks beneath, to be hilariously revealed) and screeched my way through a show we concocted.

I have no memory of any compliments afterwards, which does not mean I have forgotten them. Piers was pleased though, perhaps because all the cast had turned up for once.

The college hall was the site of all our attempts at theatre. Continually pushed to create our own shows, our best was a short play about the abdication of Edward VIII, in which I played the self-interested king (piece of cake) and a teenage girl called Kathryn was a remarkably able Stanley Baldwin.

Every effort to produce something Artaudian was

defeated by a collective failure to really understand what he was on about. Still, it was beneficial trying to be creative, even if there was more often failure than not. Artaud had influenced theatrical greats like Jean Genet and Peter Brook. His work hadn't been wasted on them even if it was wasted on us.

We were encouraged to go to the theatre and taken on regular trips to the homely and unpretentious Stratford Theatre Royal in East London as well as the Barbican to see Judi Dench and Zoë Wanamaker in *Mother Courage*.

In college, SNAP Theatre would visit and stage daytime adaptations of books on the English syllabus like *To Sir with Love* and *Cider With Rosie*. With the audience on all four sides of a rectangle, no lighting or set and only a few props, they made a big impression on me with their innovative staging. I still remember two actors combining to make the shape of a sash window and then a third lifting an arm to 'open' the window and shout down into the imaginary street below. The pleasure was as much in how they told the story as in the story itself.

The next event in the college hall that I was involved in, though, was to be the hustings for the student union elections.

We politicized media studies types decided to field candidates and make a TV programme about it. I put myself forward to be president. When Andy, the psychologist, found out, he said: 'Another promising student wasted.'

He needn't have worried. Far from being the opportunity to synthesize my twin ambitions to be an actor and an MP, the hustings, where candidates were to make a short speech and take questions, were an excruciating embarrassment.

Months before, during a three-day blockade of the college refectory over inadequate common room facilities (we had our picture in the local paper, which made up for not changing anything), we had decided that the principal of the college was 'really bad'. I had extrapolated from there and, though I knew nothing about him, was adamant he spent all his time playing golf and drinking scotch.

Come the hustings at lunchtime, I took to the stage and began to rant, about the effing principal and his effing golf and his effing scotch and the effing previous president of the effing students' union who was effing useless, and on and effing on.

I don't know what I was thinking. I stood on the North Bank at Arsenal every week and adopted the tone of those terraces whilst trying to emulate the impassioned speeches I'd heard at rallies in front of tens of thousands, but this was in the college hall, at lunchtime, in front of maybe eighty students. I would have to go next door to the refectory in a minute and sit amongst them, seriously diminished.

I had no policies, no ideas, no humour and could not stop swearing. Exiting the stage to near silence with my media colleagues still filming I passed a lecturer, who I'd seen at Greenham Common at Easter.

'Do you think I laid it on a bit thick?' I said.

'Just a bit,' she said, looking worried.

The outgoing president, Winston, leapt up to the stage to defend himself. He pointed out that I was only seventeen so wasn't eligible to stand anyway (a point he'd previously been prepared to overlook since there were no other candidates). Winston was black; so were many of his friends who came in to college each day from Leyton and areas less suburban than Loughton itself.

From my extensive understanding of political campaigning I quickly surmised that all the black kids were going to vote for Winston, who announced his intention to stand again. I was now unpopular with them for putting Winston down. I don't even know why I did it; he was absurdly apolitical for a union leader and had no agenda, other than he liked to be called the president, but he was quite a nice bloke. He'd play the piano at lunchtime occasionally and people would sing songs. He wasn't angry enough for me, I suppose, but then no one was.

An all-black union committee was elected, since the majority white vote were the abstaining working-class Thatcherites who believed unions to be evil. I had hoped to have the support of Gary Cranston, a charismatic Jamaican who was a good speaker and had become a friend and confidant. He was no longer a student, though, and he couldn't be there that day.

Gary had started PROCS, the Progressive Cultural Society, to encourage black and white students to mix. I attended the PROCS meetings and was the only white person there.

Confident in my status as a card-carrying anti-racist, I endeared myself to them immediately with questions about Caribbean names, asking if, as I believed, so many black people were called Winston because their parents named them after Winston Churchill in an effort to ingratiate them selves on arriving in Britain. There was a moment's silence before I was calmly disabused of that notion. The looks I received during that silence stayed with me for a while. Since then I've had less trouble noticing when someone thinks I'm a fool.

Watching the footage of my speech back in the TV studio, there was an uncomfortable silence, followed by an awkward chat. Gill Bucknall, the 23-year-old mature student in our group who undertook a great deal of teen counselling at different times, came up to me and grinned:

'Don't worry about it, mate, I thought you were brilliant!'

A few months later, during a shambolic union general meeting, I proposed a vote of no-confidence in the committee, which was passed. To my irritation, a Tory-supporting lecturer muttered, 'About time,' as I proposed the vote and the black kids were kicked off the committee. Soon afterwards, there was a college investigation into the union funds. The new committee had embezzled £200, which caused a bit of a stink and led to proper elections being organized the following year.

I should have listened to Andy, the psychologist. I was no politician, and not being involved had left me free to pass my A Levels, and meant the avoidance of further humiliation at union meetings with the effing principal.

Tony Benn

In December 1982, 30,000 women travelled to Greenham Common in Berkshire where a US military base was to become home to cruise nuclear missiles. Their intention was to encircle its nine-mile perimeter in a demonstration called 'Embrace the Base'. The right-wing press, led by the *Daily Mail* and *Daily Express*, made mention, in large print on their front pages, of the presence of a Russian TV crew filming the demonstration. The implication was that the state-run Soviet news agencies would only broadcast, to the abject Russian populace, propaganda that intimated Western resolve was weakening in the Cold War and that the women at Greenham were therefore unpatriotic, putting the interests of the Soviets ahead of those of their own people. Media slurs on the women of the Greenham Peace Camp were sustained throughout their long and arduous stay outside that airbase.

At the time, CND reported a survey showing that 60 per cent of Britons did not want cruise missiles based in the UK. These missiles could strike directly into the Soviet Union and while the US government, with the British characteristically following, stated that the threat of Soviet SS20 missiles needed to be matched with missiles of a similar range, the reality was that SS20s, based behind the Iron Curtain, could not reach the USA.

Plans appeared to be afoot for a limited nuclear war, should it come to that, within the confines of Europe, leaving America unscathed. Britain, or Airstrip One, as

CND members referred to it, was now a target like never before and CND's membership grew exponentially as the British people, at least those not in thrall to their daily papers, woke up to the danger they were being asked to face.

Margaret Thatcher cited the special relationship between Britain and America and could barely conceal how thrilled she was whenever she was seen with Ronald Reagan. Thatcher, from a generation of Britons in awe of American silver screen stars, seemed hypnotized by the down-home charm of Reagan, while he was in awe of her bossy energy and her tack-sharp brain, not a requirement for the presidency of the United States.

Newspaper attacks on the left were a feature of the 1980s. The only way to guarantee a fair hearing for left-wing politicians, who were opposed to arms proliferation and the spending of billions on weapons while unemployment was rising and North Sea oil revenues were sustaining social security, was to hear them speak in public. Which they did frequently. The most impressive speaker at all the rallies I went to at that time was Tony Benn.

I'd heard of Benn before. My history teacher, the one with a penchant for picking out the Jews and Catholics in his classroom, never tired of telling us that Anthony Wedgwood Benn, once a Viscount, came from 'one of the richest families in Britain' and made much of his privileged background.

Benn had rejected his peerage when he inherited it in 1960. He had been an MP for ten years by then but could no longer sit in the Commons as a peer. A bye-election was held in 1961 to replace Benn, after his succession, but he stood as an independent and won. The seat was awarded to the Conservative runner-up but two years later legislation was passed allowing hereditary peers to renounce their titles.

Benn renounced his twenty minutes after the law was passed.

As a speaker at CND rallies in the early '80s, Tony Benn often shared the stage with Joan Ruddock, chair of CND and Monsignor Bruce Kent, the general secretary.

Ruddock always seemed taller than Kent. It may have been her heels. She was dark-haired and articulate with a metropolitan air and a resemblance to Joan Bakewell. The acceptable face of the peace movement to the media, with her matching boots and handbag, she was made-up, groomed, and in full grasp of the arguments. No paper could drag her into attempts to dismiss the women's peace movement as a bunch of hairy-legged lesbians with no make-up and no dignity, wallowing in mud, smoking roll-ups and making soup. She was a Labour MP within a few years and later became Tony Blair's Minister for Women, which seemed, to many, to be the job she'd been doing throughout the '80s, if only in a shadow capacity.

By contrast, Kent, with his weary smile and dog collar, offered an avuncular, morally resolute demeanour with, appropriately, dogged determination. His conventional kindly pastor looks again gave the lie to media portrayals of CND as fools led by extremist fools.

Ruddock and Kent commanded wide respect inside the peace movement and beyond, but both had to live with constant MI5 and Home Office surveillance, as the attempts to prove that CND had appointed figureheads to disguise a Soviet insurgency in dungarees continued.

Tony Benn delivered, in his speeches, historical context, a rational understanding of the dangers faced, and the motives of those in power, while addressing the moral issue of such frightening destructive powers being wielded by governments over their people. He spoke not in anger, but with a smile. Afterwards, you were left feeling the collective was strong, that you were not only standing on the shoulders of those who had gone before you, but that to offer your shoulders to the next generation was a noble calling.

No arms race had ever ended without war and history told Benn and the leaders of the peace movement to maintain a struggle. Many people at the big rallies, and CND supporters came from all walks of life, were there following their instincts and to have their own half-formed ideas crystallized, and eloquently expressed, was rewarding for a crowd who craved someone to speak for them.

Sometimes I'd find myself arguing with people who regarded the prospect of unilateral disarmament as tantamount to an open invitation to Russia to invade unopposed. Each time, to have had Tony Benn at my side would have made things so much easier.

Being at Loughton College meant I'd heard, at last, of the *Guardian* newspaper and its alternative view of the Conservative government, unemployment and the arms race. The *Guardian* reported the peace camp at Greenham as if it were a protest by principled women taking a stand. Elsewhere they were ridiculed for spelling Wimmin without using 'men' (thereby disassociating themselves from men as the creators and users of all weapons of war), while they were mocked for their songs and for their hippy naïvety. If they were straight, it was emphasized how dirty they were, if they were lesbians, that was further evidence of mental instability.

The favourite targets, it seemed, were women who had 'abandoned' their husbands and families, to be part of the camp. If they said their families supported them, they were assumed to be lying.

The women at Greenham, who camped outside all year

round, who faced changes in local law to enforce their eviction, and who faced constant harassment, took solace in one another and strength from worldwide messages of support. They had no interest in conventional views of the 'fairer sex'. In this fight they were seen by many as the saner sex, with an anarchic, spirited defiance that came to symbolize the efforts of ordinary people standing up to a government acting at the behest of a foreign power against the will of the majority.

In Easter 1983 the 'Wimmin' at Greenham co-operated with CND, who organized a mass demonstration that was to be open to all.

The plan was to link Greenham, by a human chain, via the research facility at Aldermaston, with the nuclear weapons factory at Burghfield. It was a fourteen-mile route through the so-called 'nuclear valley' that was going to need tens of thousands of protestors to cover.

Piers, my drama teacher at college, had a friend, Martin, who lectured in the physics department and who was keen to go down to Greenham for the demo. They asked if any of us wanted to go. In the end nine people climbed into Martin's old VW camper van and headed down towards Newbury.

Arriving the night before, we had to make sleeping arrangements. I was on the front seat of the VW, which was not long enough and left me unstraightenable in the morning. That was far from the short straw though, as people squeezed into contorted positions. We must have had tents as well, I suppose, but I can't think how we managed, what we ate, or what facilities there were.

The atmosphere was convivial though. It was exciting to be there, to be participating. No one really knew what was happening most of the time. We found a stretch of road with pine trees on either side and sat on a roadside bank awaiting further instructions. Everybody had to spread out to make the chain reach as far as possible, though there was confusion as to whether we were going around the base or not.

Enthusiastic runners charged up and down the line to keep us up to date. In some places, the crowd was too great and people were two or three deep. In others there were not enough. Passing us continually were streams of like-minded revellers, there to protest together. It was an uplifting gathering.

At one point a Loughton CND banner came past. We'd never heard of Loughton CND! There were so many banners from so many parts of the country that it was unlikely, and for some reason highly exciting, to see one from our own town. We ran over and took photographs of them and they of us.

Meanwhile two hundred of the 'wimmin', dressed as teddy bears, were at the main gate trying to gain entrance with a picnic. This was tricky one for the people on the gate since excessive force in the face of an army of teddy bears would be a publicity disaster.

We did not see any Russians, TV crews or otherwise.

As we waited for the signal to hold hands and complete the chain of protest I became increasingly smitten with Martin's sixteen-year-old daughter, Becky. Tall and slim, beneath the baggy old coat and leg warmers uniform that we all favoured, she was quiet, but not unreceptive to my constant attention. Would it be wrong to try and get off with someone at the radical feminist peace camp? What would the 'wimmin' think?

They'd never know, being on the other side of the base singing, 'If you go down to the woods today you're sure of a big surprise.' I'll give you a big surprise, I'm going to get off with someone at Greenham, surely a coup. I can't help myself, this is what happens if you let blokes in, that was your first mistake.

Should I not have been concentrating on the peril the world faced with thousands of nuclear warheads poised for launch? Probably. But Becky and I had matching CND badges. I intended to snog her as the day reached its climax. It had felt like an all-day party so snogging a girl at the end was not entirely inappropriate. In the end I settled for asking for her phone number.

Piling into the VW camper after the euphoria of the final hand-holding moment, we headed down a country lane past scores of coaches that had come from all over the country. In front of us an old red Citroën 2CV, with its vinyl top pulled back and happy protestors hanging out, ambled along, inviting attention from the stream of people hunting their coaches. A little gap allowed the car behind to speed in front of us and the 2CV. It then stopped and three or four angry-looking men emerged. They began ranting at the driver of the 2CV, apparently for being too slow.

Suddenly, the men lifted the side of the little car, whose occupants had now shrunk back inside and tried to tip it in to a ditch. People came and remonstrated, shouting things like: 'We're supposed to be here for peace, man!'

They dropped the car back on to its four wheels, went back to their own vehicle, and drove away. It had been a harsh back-in-the-real-world moment for us lefty college types about to re-establish contact with the unlike-minded.

Back at college we found out we'd been on TV.

'We saw you on the news, tramping through the mud!' they said.

It was very exciting to be on actual telly and not just the

odd little programmes we made in the TV studio at college. We were national news, openly defying Thatcher and the state. MI5 were very likely poring over that footage and bugging my dad's phone even as we regaled our fans in the refectory.

Me and Becky went out a few times and listened to The Doors while drinking Special Brew in her bedroom but, without the fervour of the demo to fan it, our flame burned less brightly.

Then, one night, outside the Horse and Well in Woodford (where I had once produced a photocopy of my brother's birth certificate in order to be served underage), an old schoolmate asked her:

'Do you spit or swallow?'

She didn't complain, or even grimace, but we were a long way from Greenham.

We went our separate ways and, tactfully, I then went out with one of her mates. That was short-lived too. Staying over at her house one night, we were awakened by her ex-boyfriend breaking in to see if she was with anyone. For a moment I thought he might attack me but he began crying hysterically instead. Her parents ushered me into the spare room, where I came across several novels by Tom Sharpe.

I read most of *Wilt* that night and still regard Tom Sharpe as the funniest comic novelist of the '80s. Every cloud and all that.

Woody Allen

Thaxted, in Essex, has a fourteenth-century church, thatched roofs and Morris dancers. It may have brothels and crack houses too but I refuse to accept that. It is pretty and idyllic. Or at least it was in 1983 when the nine students on the Loughton College media studies course visited for a residential study week.

As second years, we could be entrusted with a philosophical retreat. The theme for the week was 'Culture'. What is it? How do we define it? Is it a good thing? These questions were intentionally open-ended to generate discussion between fag breaks.

We discussed the world we actually lived in, leaving me in danger of becoming over-stimulated. We talked about, read about, and wrote about 'Culture' all week, with enthusiastic teachers who enjoyed the discussions, appeared to be interested in what we said, used our first names and spoke to us without being demeaning, patronizing or threatening. Sometimes the teachers laughed *at the same time* as the students, unheard of at the Minor Public School, which seemed a long way away.

The unexpected bonus I found in Thaxted was a little shop with a rack of books on display including a copy of *Side Effects* by Woody Allen. I'd enjoyed one or two of Allen's films, like *Take the Money and Run,* but this book made me laugh out loud even more than Spike Milligan's *War Memoirs* had done, which was saying something. Particularly hilarious were Allen's tales of Sandor Needleman, who fell out of a box into the stalls at the opera and went back every night for a month to repeat the action, so people thought it was deliberate. There was page after page of expertly wrought comic prose, which inspired me to try and write my own, though I never showed any of it to anyone.

Inside the front cover of books I would obsessively record my name, and the place and date of purchase.

Within *Side Effects* it reads:

> October 1983
> From a small
> shop in Thaxted.
> Thank you, small
> shop owner;
> unwittingly you
> have brought so
> much joy into
> my life. Ha Ha,
> Hee Hee, ouch.
> It hurts to
> laugh anymore.
> Alan Davies

Twelve months later I was a student at the University of Kent at Canterbury and found Woody Allen's first book of prose, *Getting Even,* in the campus bookshop. I wrote another bizarre 'note to self' inside:

> 9/10/84 Dillons UKC
> Alan Davies.
> I treated myself
> + now my sides
> are hurting.

Six months after that I found *Without Feathers*, which I enjoyed as much, though you wouldn't know from the sober inscription:

Alan Davies.
Albion Bookshop,
Canterbury.
Monday 25th March 1985

The jacket of *Without Feathers* carries a quote announcing Allen as a genius in the tradition of Groucho Marx and James Thurber. So I read Groucho's *Memoirs of a Mangy Lover* and Thurber's *The Middle-Aged Man on the Flying Trapeze*. Both were enjoyable but, for me, neither compared to Woody.

I then discovered that he had recorded a stand-up LP. The internet makes life unimaginably different now compared to the 1980s. Without leaving the house it takes minutes to find out what an artist has produced and then to download it, or arrange to have it delivered. While you wait for the download, or for the package, you can scour websites where the character of your new interest may be eulogized:

'I love him, he's brilliant, he looks like my dog'

or assassinated:

'He was in our hotel on holiday. After dinner he just went to his room. Miserable sod.'

Back then, trawling through book and record shops could result in unexpected finds and Allen's double LP of stand-up, recorded in the '60s, was one such gold nugget, discovered after lengthy sifting.

His crafted, hilarious monologues were surely scripted by a wordsmith, rather than having evolved through a natural talent to riff like Richard Pryor's, or to playfully create a unique comic atmosphere like Steve Martin. That would be my ideal comedy club line-up. Allen, Martin and Pryor hosted by Morecambe and Wise with John Hegley and The Popticians to close.

I watched all the Woody Allen movies I could find on video: *Annie Hall, Manhattan, Sleeper, Bananas, Love & Death.* Through the '80s there was a new gem every year. *Zelig, Broadway Danny Rose, Purple Rose of Cairo, Hannah and Her Sisters, Radio Days.*

On the opening night of *Hannah and Her Sisters* in London when Max von Sydow's character says: 'If Jesus came back and saw what was being done in his name, he'd never stop throwing up!' there was spontaneous applause in the packed cinema. Allen offered wit, satire, hypochondria and gags by the pound. He's unsurpassed in the creation and execution of comic dialogue.

The trip to Thaxted wasn't the first time I'd spent time away from home that year. I went out one night to a friend's eighteenth at the Traveller's Friend in Epping Green, where they had a regular singing duo on Mondays. They would always end with 'Hey Jude' and the whole pub sang 'la-la la-lah!' throughout drinking-up time. There were no classes in college until two the next day so I didn't go home until the la's had finished.

At home, my dad confronted me because I was 'half-cut', we argued and he said he'd wake me up at seven o'clock the next morning as it was a 'work day'.

Before seven, I was on my way to Gill Bucknall's house in Waltham Abbey. She'd become like an older sibling to me at college and I couldn't think of anywhere else to go. She answered the door and listened with concern to my woes before going upstairs to talk to her then boyfriend.

When she came down she said she was sorry, that if it was up to her I could stay as long as I liked, but that he wouldn't have it. I rode my bike down to college and fretted in the refectory until another classmate, Jamie, said he knew of a 'safe squat' I could use. I went with him that evening.

The squat was in a dilapidated Victorian mansion in Buckhurst Hill. It was derelict but one room was occupied by a large skinhead called Mark and a lad with a mohican known as Strawb. Not much explanation was needed for them to accept me. Jamie stayed as well. We had to be careful going up to their room, as there was a hole through the stairwell from top to bottom, where a safe had been pushed off the top landing when the house was being cleared.

Out on the roof we looked over grand gardens that were wild and overgrown. Some large greenhouses tempted us and we hurled roof tiles at them. The distance was considerable but the tiles spun and cut through the air in great arcs down into the undergrowth. Eventually Jamie hit the target and we listened to the eerie sound of distant breaking glass.

Mark and Strawb had sleeping bags. Strawb went to start a fire in the big old fireplace. As the flames grew, a huge shadow of him, with his mohican spike hanging out over his forehead, was cast up on the wall. We lay down four abreast and slept.

Around three in the morning, there was much banging and crashing in the house and I became increasingly fearful in the darkness, as the noise came nearer. The door opened and a man entered, holding a hatchet. He stared at the four of us. Thankfully, Mark the Skinhead stirred and spoke to him. He was stealing the Victorian fireplaces. Mark asked if he'd mind leaving ours and he decided that he would.

At seven the door opened again and a man in a suit with

a clipboard came in and asked for our names. Mark broke the silence:

'Mark,' he said.

We all gave our names to the bailiff who had come to evict squatters.

Walking down the Epping New Road, Jamie was apologetic that the accommodation he'd laid on had turned into such a temporary solution. I was grateful for what he'd done though, it was just bad luck. Walking past a boarded-up house, Mark and Strawb spotted a way in. We said goodbye and watched as they clambered through a window with their bin-liner each of belongings. I never met them again.

At college, Steve Caley, my tutor, sympathetically lent me a fiver and offered to speak to my dad. Piers said that he was going home to Matlock for a week and, with remarkable generosity, offered me the use of his flat in Forest Gate. I had £5, my motor bike, keys to a flat and a tin of Big Soup. Things were looking up.

I went to Newham Council to speak to a housing officer who asked me:

'Would your father take you back in?'

To which I had to answer: 'Probably.'

No flat for me.

Steve asked me if it was OK for my dad to ring me at Piers' place. He sounded quite worried when he rang and said how much my sister was missing me, which was surprising. He then asked what I wanted for my seventeenth birthday, which I'd spent at Piers's flat.

When my £5 ran out, and Piers returned, I went home. There was a new stereo in my bedroom. I sat in my room and played records. If I'd had that Woody Allen LP then, it may have been just the tonic. Though, for cheering-up purposes, it's hard to top the scene in *Broadway Danny Rose* where Allen, as Danny the talent agent, is showing off an act to a promoter. She plays music on wine glasses filled with water, while Danny stands behind her saying:

'Never took a lesson. Self-taught.'

Twenty-five years later I went to visit Gill in hospital. Her cancer meant she only had a few days to live:

'Forty-nine, Al, I'm not even fifty, it's not enough.'

We laughed about the time I'd arrived at her house one February morning, with a bag of clothes and a tin of Big Soup bungee-strapped to my fizzy, saying that I'd run away from home. I'd dug out some pictures of us all at Thaxted and we reminisced happily about that week. For both of us, Loughton College was a saviour. I'd only just dropped out of school but Gill had been through various jobs and was twenty-three when she returned to college. She was as good-natured and helpful as anyone I ever knew.

Gill went on to university but promptly dropped out of her sociology degree, when she was told the Marxist angle she'd found so compelling at Loughton was not in vogue in her new environment: 'Basically, Al, they're telling me that everything I've learnt in the last two years at Loughton is wrong.'

So she left and had a productive three years at Middlesex Poly before devoting over twenty years to charity work and fundraising. After her death, UK Fundraising announced that their Fundraiser of the Year award was to be re-named the Gill Astarita Award in her honour. I was grateful to her husband, Mark Astarita, for contacting me and giving me the chance to say goodbye.

Jimmy Cliff

The *New Musical Express* (every Thursday, 40p) created compilation cassettes which you could send off for. In 1983 they produced NME 010, *Smile Jamaica*, 'a musical celebration of 21 years of Jamaican independence'. There were two other tapes produced at the same time, both excellent, one of blues and soul, the other of new contemporary artists like Lloyd Cole and the Commotions, The Smiths, Billy Bragg and The Art of Noise.

Smile Jamaica featured a song from every year since Jamaican independence, beginning in 1962 and going all the way to a Black Uhuru track for 1983.

Soon after my seventeenth birthday I began to have driving lessons and soon after that my dad bought me a second-hand Mini. He wanted me to have a Ford Escort like my brother but I was adamant about wanting a Mini 1275GT. This was the clubman version of the Mini Cooper, the British-designed and British-built classic, tuned by John Cooper and utterly dominant in the Monte Carlo rally in the mid-'60s. My dad and his driving partner entered, and finished, the 1964 Monte Carlo rally, in a Mini Cooper.

In the garage at home, my stepbrother was putting a roll cage into an old Mini Cooper, with a view to entering it in rallies himself. I took photos and completed a project on Mini rallying for my general studies O Level. The entire text was plagiarized, but the rallying books I had found in the local library were so obscure, I imagined I was undetected. The reality was a blind eye turned by my tutor. I'd been gratefully copying for all of my last year at the Minor Public School (usually from affable Marc Freeman) and hadn't yet shaken the habit.

With *Smile Jamaica* in the cassette player, I drove around suburbia singing, 'Do you remember the days of slavery?' along with 'Burning Spear'. I didn't of course. Nor had there been 'police and thieves in the streets' round our way in living memory but then I didn't imagine Junior Murvin's Jamaica resembled Essex too much.

Until I passed my driving test I had to have a passenger with a full licence next to me in the Mini to offer guidance. This was daft given the excitable teenagers who were available to volunteer. Pulling away from the zebra crossing on Loughton High Road one afternoon, the front-wheel-drive Mini squealed its tyres on the black and white strip. 'Wheelspin!' shouted my seventeen-year-old passenger. It was the day before my test and I was being supervised by a kid whose nickname, Wally, was appropriately granted.

Wally spotted friends of ours in a Triumph Herald. Kneeling on his seat, facing out of the back window, he tried to organize a liaison with them. He yelled:

'They're behind us, turn in to the car park! They're following, go, go, go!'

I spun the wheel and accelerated, still in first gear, in to the car park behind the shops on the High Road.

'They're turning in!' shouted Wally, as the Mini, with its lively 1275 cc engine revving freely, jerked and then bolted forward under my untrained right foot. I went for the brake pedal, hit the accelerator instead, and drove into the back of the Co-op.

Once the pride of Loughton, the Co-op had opened its doors as one of Britain's largest supermarkets in the 1960s. It was an immovable object.

Minis are hopeless in a frontal impact. The radiator is immediately in peril and the engine is inches behind it. The front wheel arches are inevitably near the impact and are likely to bend in to the tyres.

Our friends pulled up in the Herald, with barely concealed glee all over their faces. You could hardly blame them. I had driven into the back of a shop and they'd seen the whole thing.

Only ten feet away were the main rear doors for the Co-op. Had we crashed through those, we might have enjoyed some *Italian Job*-style Mini driving down the aisles, with some *Blues Brothers*-style dialogue about the product lines on offer. But we hadn't. This was real life and now I had to get the Mini home to show my dad. I climbed into my friend's car while the others tied it to the Mini with a tow-rope. Wally sat in the Mini's driving seat. He tried to bump-start the broken car while being towed, which led to some slackening and tightening of the tow-rope that nearly detached the rear of the Herald.

My dad lost his no-claims bonus as I was on his insurance.

'I suppose you were doing a "racing turn", were you?'

He was cross, so as per our established routine, I lied, making him crosser:

'No I wasn't. I got my foot caught under the brake pedal.'

'But people have been driving these cars for over *twenty years!* I've never heard of anything like that!'

'It got stuck between the pedals, they're really close together.'

I was convincing myself now. It was no use for my dad. I would not admit responsibility. I'd never experienced any reward for confessing to errors, the ensuing rage didn't diminish, so I had long since developed a personality defect, in that I had no capacity for acknowledging when I was in the wrong. At best, diffidence, at worst, hostility, would come before any contrition. In fact, death before contrition!

Once I'd asked if I could have Shredded Wheat instead of my normal cereal because they were giving away some collectable item. I'd never eaten it before and quickly established that, though it is marketed as such, it is not food. I climbed over the fence into next door's sideway and hid the box in the back of their shed. Some time later my dad said Mr Mendoza from next door had been round with a box of Shredded Wheat, missing one piece. Backed into a corner with no other culprit possible, but safe in the knowledge that there were no witnesses, I denied all knowledge. Brazen.

The Mini went off to be repaired and I had to rebook my test, which I then failed anyway. After reversing round a corner, I went to pull away and carried on backwards. I hadn't changed gear. If you're going to fail, fail big. Always ready with an excuse, I blamed the presence of lots of school children, causing me to wait for ages. I didn't make the connection that therefore, in my world, children crossing the road was a legitimate excuse for me to drive away in the wrong direction and that, despite this flaw, I believed I was not unfit for a licence.

I passed second time and prepared tapes for the car. By now I had *The Harder They Come* soundtrack, which featured Desmond Dekker, Toots and the Maytals and Jimmy Cliff's 'Many Rivers to Cross'. His was the most amazing voice in all of reggae. I was accumulating second-hand albums from a little shop inside Wanstead tube station, where I found LPs by Culture, who, alongside Gregory Isaacs, were my favourites now.

I had piles of Motown and still listened to The Style Council (whose *Long Hot Summer* kept me and three mates happy for all of our five-day summer trip to Devon) but the only other band I really liked was The Fun Boy Three, who I'd seen at the Hammersmith Palais in February when their second album, *Waiting*, was out and they were in the charts with 'Tunnel of Love'.

It wasn't a great year for music, other than New Order's 'Blue Monday' and Heaven 17's 'Temptation' and despite *The Tube* showing plenty of live acts (including Madonna singing 'Holiday'). *The Tube* was very popular. Jools Holland was amusing, Paula Yates was highly fanciable and they had Mark Miwurdz on every week who, as Mark Hurst, became one of the best comedians in the country. Everyone left the pub early the night Michael Jackson's 'Thriller' video was on television but somehow, inexplicably, I loved reggae, and this without an accompanying interest in marijuana.

One night ten of us were going to a party in Toot Hill, which is some way from Loughton along pitch black lanes. We had two cars but I was reluctant to take more than four in my Mini, having just passed my test. Wally was driving his dad's small Fiat saloon. He drove at breakneck speed everywhere with all the calmness of someone fleeing a fire. One time several of us were standing outside the Chariot chip shop on the High Road when Wally's Fiat swung in to the slip road in front of the shops. He'd seen a liaison opportunity and hurtled towards us before slamming into reverse and thrusting back into a parking space. Leaping out, he strode towards us. I was all for not letting on but someone kinder than me told him:

'You've left the handbrake off.'

'What?' he said, before turning to see his dad's car rolling towards its neighbour. Trying to stop it with his hands he screamed:

'It's not funny! Help me!'

'You can manage,' said someone else.

Wally offered to take six to Toot Hill in his dad's car. He was a bit miffed. I should have taken five but the Mini was tiny. We set off with me leading as my passengers knew the way. Wally drove inches from my rear bumper. Eventually, lost, we pulled over. Wally walked down to us and spoke to my passenger.

'I could have taken him on every corner,' he muttered.

He offered to lead as one of his passengers knew the way from there and sped off. The Mini 1275GT was a better cornering car than the Fiat, but we were skidding to keep up. Memories of friends of mine, who'd recently rolled a Triumph Herald, rendering one of them impotent, having broken his pelvis, were fresh in my mind.

I followed Wally's rear lights. It was becoming difficult to keep up. Screeching round a left-hand bend, I saw the brake lights of the Fiat moving up and down. I realized they had left the road and that I probably shouldn't follow. The Fiat jumped up in the air, with its six occupants, including three fifteen-year-old girls, bouncing around inside. It came to rest on top of a hedge with all four wheels spinning in the air. The passengers were unharmed and climbed down tentatively. They had ploughed through a front garden and narrowly missed a house, the owners of which came out to see what had happened. The huge tree in their garden had lost some of its bark, stripped off by the Fiat. Wally remained in the driver's seat, furiously revving the engine with the rear wheels spinning in mid-air.

Not all the teenagers I knew drove fast. I did though, as I became more confident and as a consequence was regularly breathalysed by keen policemen, who were eager to use their new equipment to catch offenders under the recently enhanced drink–drive laws. I wasn't going fast because I'd been drinking. I just liked it. The melodious, ever-present reggae didn't slow me.

A friend of mine suggested swapping the Mini's front tyres over to even up wear. He knew nothing about cars but had a confident manner so we swapped them. Driving along the next day, my girlfriend, Justine, said she could hear a banging. I listened and began to speculate authoritatively, for her benefit, on what it might be, although I had no idea. I didn't consider pulling over and having a look. Justine mentioned it was getting louder. I dropped her off at her house in Chingford and headed back to Loughton. Pulling out on to Ranger's Road the nearside front wheel came off and bounced away in the darkness on to Chingford Plain, leaving the Mini sliding on its axle.

I had no spare wheel as the 1275GT had special Denovo tyres that ran flat when punctured. Recovering the wheel, I found the holes for the wheel nuts had ripped open. I found a telephone box and rang the AA.

Two hours later, a vehicle normally dispatched to tow home articulated lorries arrived. It had more flashing disco lights than *Top of the Pops*. Spinning lights, pulsating lights, blazing white spotlights at the front that illuminated the forest.

Those lights made a mockery of my dad's lined curtains as we pulled up outside the house. He stared down from his bedroom window in disbelief.

On this occasion I confessed the truth because I could hear my stepmum sticking up for me:

'It's just bad luck, it could happen to anyone.'

No, it could only happen to an idiot who needlessly changes his wheels and doesn't tighten the nuts up enough.

That day was a missed opportunity to introduce my dad to the music of Jimmy Cliff, particularly his famous track, 'Better Days are Coming'.

1984

James Dean

I was introduced to James Dean by Louise Burgess. Louise told me that Dean was:

'The best-looking man there has ever been.'

'Really?' I said.

'Oah . . .' she gasped.

She clearly meant it. I'd never heard of this guy. The most beautiful man in the world? Ever? How had I missed this?

Dean, it turned out, had died in a car accident in 1955 and had only made three films, *East of Eden*, *Rebel Without a Cause* and *Giant*. I'd never seen any of these, though I'd vaguely heard of that *Rebel* one, or maybe it was just the phrase I'd heard before, which surely wasn't coined for the movie.

If I could have metamorphosed into a Dean look-a-like at that moment I would have done so, because I fancied Louise something rotten. I had completely queered the pitch with her though, by spending much of 1983 in the throes of a crush on her younger sister Melanie. It was calling round after Mel that allowed me to meet Lou in the first place. One summer afternoon this older girl appeared and began dancing to whichever song was playing at that moment. 'Come on!' she said, as the teenage boys sitting round gazed at her skin-tight white shorts and bare legs. Who was this? As if Mel and her friends weren't enough, now there was a new, virtually adult, vision of female excellence.

Mel was a year younger than me, and Lou a year older. It seemed impossible to have a girlfriend who was older than you. To ask an older girl out was to risk humiliating, mocking rejection. So when I did chat to Lou, I'd be trying to persuade her to persuade Mel to give me a go.

I'd known Mel for years as we went to the same primary school. The Burgess household, at times, resembled a drop-in centre for teenagers. Mel and Lou had an older sister who offered haircuts to their friends and a nice line in droll remarks, their mum appeared to enjoy the noise of a busy house, and Mr Burgess sat wearily in the front room while the noise of three competing stereos and four competing conversations rang cacophonously around him day and night.

Many Sunday nights were spent with Mel listening to Tommy Boyd's phone-ins on LBC. In common with most households then, there was one TV, in the front room. Out the back at the Burgesses' there was a room, with a hatch through to the kitchen, where you could listen to the quirky ranters who would phone LBC, which had some very good presenters at the time. Brian Hayes was on in the morning and he, rather than encourage dimwitted, ill-mannered bigotry, would give it very short shrift. They weren't grateful to you just for calling, they wanted intelligent conversation. Tommy Boyd, who was on late in the evening, had a lighter show which was often hilarious. Mel found almost every caller funny and kept a stream of her own chat going to me and to Tommy on the radio.

At the end of the show though, I'd have to go home, unrequited.

Sitting alone with Lou in the small hours one night, again talking about Mel, she turned to me and said, somewhat exasperatedly:

'What about me, Alan? Don't you fancy me?'

I looked at her in shock: 'Of course I fancy you, Lou, *everyone* fancies you.'

'Oh right, of course,' she scoffed. 'You're just saying that now.'

'I'm not!'

'It's too late.'

'No,' I spluttered. I really did splutter ('To utter incoherently with spitting sounds' – *Collins Gem*) which I had previously thought only happened to characters in *Cheeky* comic.

'I *do* fancy you.'

'You *can't* fancy us both.'

'I fancy you *more*.'

This was true, Lou was the most attractive girl I'd ever spoken to. Of course, I'd seen the Barnett sisters from Woodford County High and tried hard to spy on them sunbathing in their back garden. I'd watched Jane Smart, the most beautiful girl in the sixth form, from the top of the bus every day as she drifted away to her home, but these were distant untouchables. Lou actually talked to me, and laughed with me, and had apparently had enough of her 21-year-old boyfriend with the Golf GTI who seemed impossible to compete with, what with his being twenty-one and having a Golf GTI.

I implored her to forget all that I'd said about Mel, who was patently never going to want me, had a crush on my best mate, and only came with me to Arsenal sometimes because she quite fancied Charlie Nicholas. Had I even thought it possible that Lou would consent to even five seconds of closer proximity, I'd have been overjoyed. She wasn't having it.

So they were like sisters to me, the Burgess sisters, and I remained one of their many surrogate brothers, and Mel laughed at Tommy Boyd and Lou told me about James Dean.

James Dean became My Favourite Icon and the first one I'd adopted from another era. Dead over a decade before I was born, his life and times were so remote from '80s Essex as to be recognizable only by virtue of both periods being populated by humans.

There was something about Dean though, that instantly chimed with me at seventeen. His three films were run on television at this time and I videotaped all of them. Watching him was easy, he compelled you to look at him even though he often seemed to do little or nothing; everyone else almost shrank in his presence, so much did he dominate the screen. Even when he stood or sat still, the sense of the churning within him was palpable.

Dean's torment, expressed vividly in those three characters he played on film, was real. He had lost his mother to breast cancer when she was twenty-nine and he was eight. His father, who had sold his car to pay for his wife's last operation, couldn't cope with his job and caring for James, so he sent him to live with his sister and her husband.

The loss of his mother was a mortal blow. She had nurtured him unconventionally, giving him the middle name Byron, apparently after the poet, and taking him to singing and dancing lessons, which set him apart from other boys. He was different, raised to be artistic and told he was special, perhaps better than his peers. Then she went away. He was left by her and left different.

His father sent him away and gradually his sadness, grief and despair hardened into an anger, an 'I'll show you' rage that pushed through him, surfacing from within like emotional floodwater whenever he was required to portray emotion for the camera.

A child's emotional development can be hindered, or

even halted, by significant trauma, such as bereavement. In the improvised opening scene of *Rebel Without a Cause*, James Dean appears to draw on child-like feelings as he portrays a young man drunk in a gutter. Dennis Hopper, who was in the cast, is quoted in David Dalton's biography of Dean (which I read in 1984):

'I have a script in my hand that says this guy's in the gutter, drunk, and he gets taken to the police station and is angry about it. Well, first of all, the guy is in the street playing with a toy monkey? And doing baby things – trying to curl up, to keep warm … Then he's searched, and this angry drunk guy is suddenly ticklish? Where did that come from? It came from genius.'

It reads like a description of the arrest of a lost eight-year-old boy. Dean would exhibit the vulnerability of the bereaved child in all his roles.

Cal Trask's desperation to please his father in *East of Eden* is as heart-rending to watch as is his lonely, sad search for his mother. John Steinbeck's compelling novel is too huge to be committed to film in two hours so a piece of the book was chosen that encapsulated the trauma of a family with no love at its heart and rage there instead. James Dean's performance, or rather his controlled exposure of the edges of his real pain, made him a movie star overnight.

He made two more films and then crashed his lightweight super-fast silver Porsche into a station wagon that did not see him coming as it turned left across the highway in front of him.

Four days after he died, *Rebel Without a Cause* was released, providing confirmation of the young talent that had been destroyed at twenty-four. At the heart of it all was James Dean's anguished man-child with his lament to helpless parents:

'You're tearing me apart!'

Even in *Giant*, his last film, in which he shared top billing with Rock Hudson and Elizabeth Taylor, his boyish surliness is to the fore. He plays a ranch hand who refuses to sell a small piece of land he has been left, by the ranchowner's sister, and then strikes oil there. In confrontation with Hudson and Taylor's characters, there remains the upset vengeance towards parent figures, as he smears an oil-stained palm on their white mansion.

When I first saw Dean's photo I understood immediately what Louise was talking about. To resemble Dean would be perfect (the perils of being beautiful are lost on, or disbelieved by, those who aren't).

The search for a red jacket similar to that worn by Dean as Jim Stark in *Rebel Without a Cause* was a long one. Despite the rails of '50s Americana on sale at Camden market, the loose-fitting slightly pegged jeans and plaid shirts, and the flying jackets at appropriately sky-high prices, there were no red bomber jackets. I had the soundtrack to *American Graffiti*, which made for an authentic '50s atmosphere in my Mini but I had no aspiration to replicate the '50s. I just wanted to look like James Dean. To turn my own churning into an irresistible broodiness rather than a resistible moodiness.

It wasn't feasible to wear a ten-gallon hat in Loughton under any circumstances so the silent pose, favoured by Dean on location on *Giant*, with the tipped Stetson over the eyes, was out. I didn't wear glasses so the 'actorly bespectacled artist in a polo-necked jumper' look was out too. How was I to look like Dean?

I had youth, which was a start, I had no discernible muscle definition which was a similarity. The sight of James Dean shirtless in *Rebel Without a Cause* would, were it fifty years later, have led to calls to his agent from personal trainers angling to give him the gym body of the age. He was pale, hunched over and sorry-looking as befitted the scene.

I grew my hair a little like Dean and I tried to wear jeans like him and, fortunately, checked shirts, which were so readily and cheaply available in Camden, were fashionable, so I could pretend I was James Dean whilst not standing out too much.

At my eighteenth birthday party at Epping Forest Country Club, the assembled throng of teenage boys in plaid looked like off-duty lumberjacks, the uncalloused hands of suburbia poking pinkly from sleeves being the principal giveaway.

Also pink that night were my cheeks after my college mate Jamie invited me to try some blue pills he had in an envelope. I had five. '*Five!*' said my older, wiser friend Gill when I told her. I didn't fall asleep until six in the morning. I had never heard of amphetamines and assumed I was just too drunk. I'd been swigging from a half-bottle of vodka all night, which I'd received as a birthday present and proudly shown to my stepmum. 'Oh dear,' she'd understated. Four coffees and four pints of water later I was still wide awake. Justine, my girlfriend of five months by then, was sound asleep as I lay twitching in the dark. I had enjoyed myself, with everyone I wanted there; Mel and Lou, mates from school and college plus Justine and her friends. It's one of those nights from the '80s I remember well, mainly because I was up all night reliving it.

The urge to look like James Dean reached its nadir when

I spent my time trying to smoke cigarettes like him. He was often photographed with a cigarette shoved into the corner of his mouth while keeping it pointing straight forward. It's not possible to overstate how absurd I looked standing around house parties in Essex with a fag poking out of my mouth in this odd way. Then I came across a red jacket at last but that didn't help as it was a slightly effeminate blouson affair with a wide plastic belt, incorporated in to the waistband with a series of loops. This was not the garment of a rebel, with cause or otherwise. Wearing it on campus in my first year at university, one of my friends shouted, 'Belt!' from some distance away. I went with empty hanging loops after that. Eventually, I forgot I wanted to look like James Dean and, having experienced performing in a few plays, also dropped my hopeless aspiration to act like him.

Charlie Nicholas

The new darling of Glasgow Celtic, scorer of fifty-two goals the previous season, including a stunning hit against Old Firm enemy Rangers after a mesmerizing stop–start dribble, wanted a transfer.

For some reason, possibly the loss of playmaker Liam Brady, to expand his bank balance and his horizons, with Juventus of Turin, and the further loss of striker Frank Stapleton, to expand his bank balance, and train in the rain each week, at Manchester United, Arsenal had decided they wanted Charlie.

This was out of character for the club, who were not usually in the market for skilful mavericks, partly because they'd been let down by the small impact made by another Scot, Peter 'the new George Best' Marinello, in the early '70s. They had signed teen goal machine Clive Allen from QPR in 1980 but promptly swapped him with Crystal Palace, for left back Kenny Sansom, in a deal that smacked of a set-up, since Allen never played for Arsenal. Then in 1982 they signed England's Tony Woodcock to play up front.

With Graham Rix in the side there was potential, and Charlie was to be the creative spark that would hopefully fire the team to great things, even though he was only twenty-one.

The 1982–83 season had been a disappointment as Arsenal had lost to Manchester United in the League Cup semi-final (with Stapleton scoring in the face of torrents of abuse from his former congregation). The two clubs were drawn to play again, in the FA Cup semi-final at Villa Park.

Aston Villa's ground can be seen from the M6 principally because of its vast Holte End terracing, which was divided down the middle for semi-finals with rival fans on either side. I travelled to Villa Park on my own and walked up the huge terrace to the back. It was uncomfortable, with fans drunk and drinking. No matter, Arsenal went 1–0 up and we sang of going to Wem-ber-ley. During half-time the ground beneath my feet was wet and I looked round to identify the source. All along the top of the Holte End, men were lined shoulder to shoulder, facing the corrugated iron, relieving themselves of imperial gallons of urine, which cascaded down the terrace, possibly all the way to the pitch.

The game restarted and some tough tackling saw Arsenal's best defender off injured when United equalized. The momentum was with them now and they won 2–1. Feelings of bitterness and injustice were conjured up by the chemicals in my brain, carving out a synapse of their own, which was to be well used over the next three decades and counting.

Manchester United also wanted Charlie and so, more to the point, did Liverpool. To a football fan, this was a no-brainer. Liverpool had won the league six times in eight years. They were three times winners of the European Cup in that time, and three times winners of the League Cup too. Kenny Dalglish, the finest player in Britain, now Brady had gone to Italy, and like Charlie a former Celtic hero, was in his playing autumn. Over the next couple of years Liverpool would be looking to groom a successor. Charlie had to go to Liverpool if he had any sense.

Manchester United, who had the FA Cup and the cash to pay big wages, would be most people's second choice. If Charlie had any sense.

To the disbelief of the club's fans, the best young player in Britain decided to sign for Arsenal. Various reasons were suggested. That he thought there would be less pressure at Highbury was one, which didn't augur well, and the idea that he fancied London's 'bright lights' was another. This is a strange concept to Londoners, implying the rest of the country lives in near darkness with excitement consequently hard to come by.

Whatever the reason, a big crowd expectantly attended his debut against Luton. I even took a camera and stood down the front of the North Bank to try and snap our new hero. He looked a bit short and dumpy, but he had good close control, and a mullet.

The next game was at Wolves and, when Arsenal scored, a goalflash, Wolves 0 Arsenal 1, appeared on BBC1's *Grandstand*, which was normal, but it included the scorer's name: Nicholas, which wasn't. His first goal was of national interest. It was followed by a second in the same game. Now he'd started, would he stop?

Yes, he would. For three months.

Arsenal lost their next three games, including home defeats against Liverpool and Manchester United. Charlie was not living up to the hype by November when Arsenal went to Spurs for a League Cup tie. He scored though, and Arsenal won.

Then he went into hibernation again (though he was technically on the field for every game bar the last one that season) until Boxing Day when Arsenal returned to Spurs, whose fans were eager to delight in Charlie's tribulations. He scored twice as Arsenal won 4–2.

Later in the season, he dribbled through the Spurs defence at Highbury to score his fourth goal in three games against them, as Arsenal won 3–2. This three wins out of three record against Spurs, together with his rejection of the northern giants, made Charlie the archetypal 'darling of the North Bank'. He was cocky, flash, and underachieving, but adored.

Sometimes, for a skilful sportsman like Charlie, everything comes easily. Like a kid at school, placed one set below his ability, who doesn't have to work too hard. Arsenal were a level below the top sides, which meant he could be a hero. Not that Liverpool and Manchester United were going to come back for him now. He lacked speed. Had he been as fast as Woodcock he could have been one of the best in Europe. For Arsenal fans, now unused to challenging for the title, what mattered was to beat Spurs and try to reach a cup final.

Charlie had a little bit of Jimmy White, the snooker player, in him. Nearly the same age, they shared a slight physical resemblance: both were dark-haired, with a half-smile a permanent feature, and neither was averse to browsing in a jeweller's shop. Both were entertainers. Whether they liked it or not, even on a bad day, there was more interest in them than their immediate opponent or, for Charlie, than in his team-mates.

The unpredictability of their play in itself defines the appeal of spectator sport. It may be that winning is the sole motivation for those less gifted (certainly those that become the, often sociopathic, obsessives known as football managers). Certainly it is the less gifted players for whom a desire to win probably took them closer to the top than their talent would merit, but it is the players who offer the element of surprise who bring in the crowds.

Every unique populist needs his nemesis though. It's that contrast in styles that completes sport's appeal.

It's rare, but memorable, that two thrilling entertainers meet head to head, as Nadal and Federer did at Wimbledon in 2008. More often the maverick repeatedly encounters the same automaton. If he's unlucky, he'll meet two. As McEnroe met Borg and then Ivan Lendl so White met Steve Davis and then Stephen Hendry, in a career that would see him reach the World Championship Final six times and contrive to lose every time.

1984 was White's first final. He had to play Davis, the champion and regarded as one of the best of all time. Davis was from Essex and, in normal circumstances, I would have supported him, but I couldn't, as he was the most infuriatingly perfect bore in sport. He never missed, he never betrayed emotion, he never gave the opponent a point if he could help it, and he never let things go a little loose when he was clearing up the balls with the frame already won, suddenly firing a dramatic swerving shot off three or four cushions to break the tension, as a little bonus for the paying customers, who had respectfully watched him crush another man's spirit.

Not for Jimmy the moody patrolling of the table with an eternity between each shot. He was rapid, he was the 'Whirlwind'.

Me and my sister bonded over disliking Davis and wanting White to win. Previously untapped reservoirs of rage were revealed in her as she glared at the screen while Davis lined up another pot:

'Miss, miss, *miss* . . . *oh*.'

'One,' said the referee as the white ball rolled in behind the black.

'Miss, miss, miss, miss, *misssss*.' It was an incantation now. I was impressed. Maybe there was hope for this family yet.

We stayed the course as Jimmy fell just short and everyone agreed that he was so young his time would surely come.

Later that summer the Olympics were held in Los Angeles. Here was an event without underachievers. To qualify you had to be in the top two or three at your event in your country, and even then, Olympic qualifying standards may exclude you. No sitting happily in a lower set there. You were at the top, or absent.

Four years previously in Moscow, Steve Ovett had shown you could be a bit flash and still be the best in the world when he beat Sebastian Coe to win gold in the 800 metres.

Like Borg v McEnroe and Davis v White, Coe v Ovett was a national litmus test.

On holiday one year, I stood with my dad on a cliff top as we looked at waves crashing against rocks.

'Would you rather be the sea or the rocks?' I asked.

He breathed out, frowning: 'The rocks,' he said.

'I'd rather be the sea.' He didn't respond.

'It wears the rocks down in the end,' I added in an 'I win' voice.

I was spiteful, but the appeal of the restless water, over the unchanging rock, was genuine.

Predictably, given the way the family went three to one in the Borg v McEnroe stakes, a split emerged over Steve Ovett.

My dad was enraged by him.

If he was winning on the home straight, Ovett would celebrate by waving to the crowd. Some saw this to be adding insult to his rivals' injury, gloating, and – this is the cardinal sin – unsporting. Of course, the more he was disliked in our house the more I warmed to him; he was an oddball with natural talent and none of the advantages of

Coe, with his freakishly perfect motion and his well-spoken 'take me home to meet your mum' manner.

Ovett looked like he was running away from a shop after nicking something (I may have been projecting that on to him).

Coe had been expected to win the 800 metres, but prevented Ovett from taking a double by winning gold in the 1500 metres instead, which was Ovett's speciality. They left with a gold each and another medal each, which neither seemed interested in, for coming in behind the winner.

Along with Allan Wells in the 100 metres and Daley Thompson in the decathlon, they were the British heroes of the Moscow games, which had been spoiled by the USA team pulling out over Russia's fruitless attempts to control their uncooperative neighbour, Afghanistan, by military force.

The Russians, along with some of their allies, refused to participate in the Los Angeles '84 games in retaliation, clearing the way for an impressive US medal haul, with their drug-addled Eastern European rivals at home.

Coe won the 1500 metres brilliantly again in 1984 but this time my dad turned on him for his behaviour in victory, when he pointed furiously at doubters in the press box. To win without displaying emotion is the ultimate achievement to some English people. Or to feel none at all. No wonder Britain maintains Olympic standards in heart disease.

We were encouraged to feel that the Americans had boycotted out of principle and the Russians out of spite; that the American gymnasts who therefore cleaned up in '84 were wholesome cheerleader types, who were not chained to the asymmetric bars during infancy on an intravenous growth hormone drip; that Carl Lewis, the four-time gold medallist, was the epitome of human perfection and that such a specimen could only flourish in the all-American dreamworld of the US Olympic team.

Lewis was later disgraced, having failed three drugs tests at the US Olympic trials in 1988. He went unpunished and escaped a ban, along with over a hundred other American athletes. The sheen of American glory was dramatically muddied.

That was all to come though. In August 1984 when Lewis turned up at a packed Crystal Palace to race in a special 300 metre event he was the most famous high achiever in sport. The man at the top of the top set.

I went to that meeting with Justine and my sister. Lewis didn't win but we saw him and that was exciting enough.

For some reason, Arsenal players were there giving out the medals, to boos from the South London crowd. We squeezed through to try and collect autographs. On the way we had a photo taken with the enormously popular boxer Frank Bruno, who was the most solid individual I've ever brushed up against, a wall of muscle. Then Justine saw Charlie Nicholas.

She edged along the row and appeared in front of him, a tanned and pretty seventeen-year-old with curly hair and a beaming smile. Charlie signed her programme and asked her if she'd like him to write her phone number on it. She was a bit confused and flushing slightly but told him her number. He wrote it down and then tore it off the back of her programme with a cheeky grin. Justine moved away and the burly bloke next to Charlie indicated me and said: 'Look out, it's the boyfriend.' Charlie's smirk was supplanted by a more Glaswegian expression. There was a moment of tension as we made eye contact but I kept going right towards him. I expected his minder to stand up and intervene but I was by now staring at Nicholas, inches from his face in the scrum of the crowd. He met my gaze and then I spoke:

'Can I have your autograph please, Charlie?'

We were slightly disappointed that he never called.

Billy Bragg

The *NME*'s special compilation cassettes came up trumps for me by including a Billy Bragg track on NME011, *Department of Enjoyment*.

'Fear is a Man's Best Friend' didn't appear on Billy's short album, *Life's a Riot with Spy vs Spy*; nor did it turn up on *Brewing Up with Billy Bragg*, his first full LP and my most played record of 1984.

It was typical of Billy Bragg that, should he be asked to provide a track for a compilation cassette, he would give them something unreleased and then consider it gone. To release it again and put a price on it wouldn't sit right with him. It would be exploiting young fans without much cash.

Life's a Riot came with the instruction:

PAY NO MORE THAN £2.99 FOR
THIS 7 TRACK ALBUM

Brewing Up carried the tag:

£3.99 OR LESS

Each song was crafted and witty and many were clippings from the plants nurtured in Billy's growbag of heart-rending emotional truth. If he didn't want a dry eye in the house then he could have it that way. Usually he'd make you laugh just when you were having a wobble over songs like 'St Swithin's Day' or 'The Man in the Iron Mask'.

He was a one-man band and, with his guitar in hand and an amp and speakers on his back, he had busked all over the place, bawling out his own songs in an entirely untrained, unaffected and personal way about subjects dear to his heart: love, betrayal and trade unionism.

I thought of him as heroically honest, warm and funny. In a Radio One live concert which I, and probably several thousand others, recorded and played back hundreds of times, he told a story about how he and his ever-present mate Wiggy were playing Subbuteo:

'Wiggy's Mum moved something from behind the sideboard and a dartboard rolled out, went once round the pitch, and then went *foom!* [much laughter from the live crowd]. It was worse than the Munich air disaster, except it was Everton or someone ... [then you can hear a voice offstage] oh, Crystal Palace, Wiggy says it was Crystal Palace.'

The reference to Munich may seem in poor taste on the page but it wasn't, being thrown away, a bit off the mic like a good stand-up comic, which he was in many ways. It was just another example of the ordinariness and the unpretentious style of Billy Bragg that belied the powerful impact he made when bursting forth in full committed performance.

His music came along at a time when The Jam had split up and Paul Weller had disappeared into a gentlemen's boutique while 'The Cappuccino Kid' wrote the amusingly upbeat sleeve notes for The Style Council's poppy releases. The edginess of The Jam was gone and while I bought everything that Weller released for years it was Bragg who now sounded like the young Weller of *All Mod Cons* and *Setting Sons*.

There were some bands, like The Redskins, with a political agenda, but there was as much infighting amongst left-wing musicians as there was amongst left-wing politicians. As usual, most pop music avoided anything approaching thought, never mind expression. All bland and all vain, it was all unpalatable.

Then Frankie Goes to Hollywood jumped up and injected the charts with some adult content with 'Relax', their pounding sex anthem. They followed that with 'Two Tribes', and its extraordinary video, featuring two actors in masks portraying the US and Russian presidents, Reagan and Chernenko, ripping into each other in a ring, while a baying mob of world leaders urge them to fight to the death, before descending into violence themselves while Reagan and Chernenko watch, wondering what they've started. Frankie Goes to Hollywood provided thrilling music with something approaching actual content.

'Relax' was number one for five weeks at the start of the year and re-entered the charts in the summer while 'Two Tribes' was at number one for nine weeks. For a period in July '84 the two tracks were at numbers one and two.

Me and Justine spent two weeks travelling through France in my Mini that summer, with 'Relax' blaring out across the manicured gardens of various exquisite *châteaux* in the Loire valley. We drove first down to Paris, becoming hopelessly lost on *le périphérique* before seeking help at a service station. I showed the man behind the counter my map of Paris which he threw away from us to the other side of the room. He pulled out a map that showed the outskirts of Paris and jabbed his finger at it. My map was for inner Paris, the old city. I was clueless.

With a new map we found our way into the chaos of the city itself. My main thought was to avoid the Arc de Triomphe as I'd been told that no insurance company paid out for accidents on the notorious roundabout surrounding it. As we hesitantly navigated towards our hotel, which

Justine had booked over the phone using her best O Level French, we heard someone shouting at us.

'Paris?' he called, pronouncing it Paree. He was hanging out of the driver's window of a white Renault van.

'Paree?!' he called again.

'Yes!' I shouted. '*Oui!*'

He gestured for us to follow him and we dutifully did, eventually turning on to the Champs-Elysées.

'Paree!' he yelled happily, before veering off into another lane, never to be seen again. We were soon swerving our way around the Arc with cars zooming in all directions.

Eventually we parked underground beneath Notre-Dame and checked in to our hotel, thrilled and happy.

After one night in Paris we travelled down, staying in campsites, until we arrived at a caravan we'd hired for the week in Argelès-sur-Mer. We'd found that in the small ads. It belonged to a barrister's clerk who worked in a chambers in London. I went to see him. He was a bit of a wideboy.

'I know what you're going down there for! Two eighteen-year-olds, going away on their own! First time away together is it?'

I didn't say that Just was only seventeen. Not that it mattered. After much disagreeable 'nudge nudge wink wink' he gave me the keys and the directions. It was a happy fortnight. We arrived home after 2,000 miles in total and I took Just back to her house. Her mum was furious. We hadn't called home once; it hadn't occurred to me to do so. Also, we hadn't used up our duty-free quota. No cheap fags! I sloped off home to get out of the firing line.

Soon afterwards me and Justine were back in the Mini heading for the University of Kent at Canterbury. It was my first choice on my UCCA form and I'd been offered a place for two Bs in my A Levels. I'd managed an A and a C.

Theatre studies had gone a bit wrong. Thirty-five per cent of the mark was to come from a devised show and we had concocted a stage version of *The Sweeney* so bad it beggared belief. Our mockney accents alone ought to have had us down for a fail.

Two of us managed Cs, the rest D, E or nothing. Piers, the drama teacher, despaired. We could have dusted down the old *Edward and Mrs Simpson* show we'd done the year before. Would wandering around a badminton court in Essex, with a pompous look on my face, pretending to be Edward VIII have pushed me up to a B? Perhaps not, now I think about it.

Steve, my tutor, said I had eight points with five for an A in communications and three for theatre studies, the equivalent of two Bs. I was safe.

I wasn't convinced and so headed down the A2 to try and convince someone in admissions to admit me.

We arrived, found the Registry and were immediately told there was no one there to help. Looking out from the campus over Canterbury with its beautiful cathedral I hoped I would be allowed to come.

Not that settling on Kent had been easy. With only two A levels I wasn't able to apply for any of the more famous and over-subscribed drama departments at places like Manchester, Bristol and Hull. I went for Kent, East Anglia, Loughborough, Warwick and a teacher training course at a college in Cambridge.

At interview the teaching college gave me a polite brush-off as theirs was the only such course on my form; Loughborough couldn't have gone well as there was no offer from there; but the other three all offered a place for two Bs, largely on the strength, I suspected, of Steve Caley's helpful reference.

UEA had a nice campus and, as it was in Norwich, they had a first division football team to go and watch. Warwick too had Coventry City only up the road, also in Division One, with the other Midlands clubs nearby. I'd be able to see Arsenal at plenty of away games.

I was surprised to receive an offer from Warwick as I'd gone into my shell a bit during an afternoon of drama exercises with other hopefuls.

We were invited to find some space in their large drama studio and then told that we were to act as if making our way through a blizzard. I started to squint as if snow was blowing in to my face and put my hands out in front of me to shield me a bit from the weather. Moving forward I took small steps as the wind was blowing in to me and the ice was slippery underfoot. Now I was making gradual progress around the room, hoping they'd call a halt to this quickly. Should I be raising the stakes? Perhaps a bear could leap out at me from behind a tree? How would they know it was a bear though? Or that there was a tree. Were they mentally filling in the scenery as they watched? I'd have to mime being afraid of a bear in a blizzard very well. I might just look as if snow made me scream. Would they admit a chionophobic to a prestigious institution like this? Too risky. Perhaps I could become increasingly stuck in a snow-drift and, being unable to continue, gradually weaken through exposure, eventually succumbing to frostbite. In that scenario I may become delirious and begin talking to myself, even having two-sided conversations, that would allow me to show off my flair for making amusing remarks during improvisations, though it would be foolish to risk irony. Hallucinations were plausible for a dying man in an arctic tundra. Hallucinating what though? That only pre-sented the same problems as the bear plan. Becoming trapped and deteriorating was feasible but now the timescale of the exercise was against me. To fully portray decline, illness and death (unless I had a St Bernard rescue me) could take hours when I was looking at sixty seconds tops. Just then my train of thought was broken as a supple interviewee, legs spread wide apart, bent double, and walking backwards around the room, nearly collided with me. She was having trouble seeing where she was going as she tried to look between her legs. Who walks backwards in a blizzard? Had I misheard? Had they said: 'Walk as if in a hail of gunfire?' Then, to my relief, they stopped it.

We also had to do audition pieces chosen from their list. I did Lady Macbeth which drew an appreciative remark. Or was it an ironic smirk? I probably thought it would show me as enterprising and fearless. They probably thought that they should have taped it for a good laugh later. See the eighteen-year-old boy – who smokes fags like James Dean with a stroke – give his Lady Macbeth sleepwalking in Essex routine.

Kent had a couple of things going for it, including a special fourth year with the option of specializing in directing or theatre in education but a more pressing concern was that the university I went to should have a karate society as I had decided I was going to take that up. Kent had 'tae kwon do soc', which was the clincher.

I settled on Kent. They accepted my results. I started in October.

I packed up the Mini and set off for four years away. I had a long goodbye with Justine. Several people had told me that relationships rarely survived one half heading to university. With no phone it would be difficult.

Justine followed me in her old Ford Escort (top speed 35 mph) for a few miles before turning off. As I watched her go in my mirror I began to cry. Any separation was hard for me, bringing to the surface all the sadness over my mum, but I loved Just, we'd been together for a year and, although I wanted to leave home, I was scared of going away. I cried most of the way there and then queued up at the college payphones for ages to speak to her later. This was going to be hard.

Two weeks into my first term I saw a poster for a concert in the college dining hall. I bought a ticket and went along. There were hundreds there. A couple of support acts played and then the main act came on. The singer walked to the microphone and introduced the first song by saying:

'For the first time ever in a dining hall in Kent.'

Everyone laughed, but then he was known for his sense of humour, that Billy Bragg.

I never did any tae kwon do.

Arthur Scargill

The miners' strike began in March 1984. By the time it was over, almost a year to the day later, it had exposed and entrenched rifts in British society to an extent unseen since the depression of the 1930s.

During the course of the strike, Billy Bragg revived and adapted a song called 'Which Side are You On?' written by Florence Reece (a coalminer's daughter and a coalminer's wife), in Tennessee during a miners' strike in 1931. This moving song tells a tale of hardship in the teeth of a dispute. It's a rousing cry for unity, a plea for strength in numbers. Travelling up and down the country playing at countless fundraising gigs for the miners, he sang the song over and over again. For many people, the question remained relevant for years, only with a small change, becoming: 'Which side were you on?'

If you did not back the miners and their families in their struggle you probably lived in the south. Or Nottinghamshire, where the miners were resistant to the leadership of the National Union of Mineworkers' president, Arthur Scargill.

Scargill was an abrasive Yorkshireman and a prominent figure, not just as the leader of the NUM, but as part of the far left wing of the Labour Party. With his frizzy red hair and dogmatic, aggressive manner he became a hero to those he led and a hate figure for those trying to break the strike.

A series of anti-union measures had been implemented by the Conservatives under Margaret Thatcher, in an effort to control the power the unions had to orchestrate mass walk-outs, with voting at huge meetings where dissenters were in plain sight and potentially open to intimidation. Secret ballots were to be held in order to stage strikes in the first place. On top of that, it was made illegal to join picket lines in sympathy with members from other unions. A limit was placed on the number of pickets allowed by law.

All of these measures were intended to make it impossible for the NUM to run a strike as they had done in the past, when they had caused terminal damage to a Conservative government with strikes first in 1972 and then 1974, during which Prime Minister Ted Heath called a general election on the issue, only to lose to Labour. Prior to those strikes the miners hadn't been out since the General Strike of 1926.

The NUM's success of 1974 was assisted by cooperation from other unions, notably the dockers, who refused to unload imported coal, and to organized secondary picketing. The movement of coal into power stations was stopped and soon all power stations were targeted, as well as other heavy coal users.

A new pay deal was won and the three-day weeks, called because of the energy crisis created by the strike, were over.

In 1974, similar tactics yielded a similar result, and a catastrophic defeat for the Conservatives, who spent much of their subsequent time in opposition plotting the legislation and the tactics to win a similar battle the next time it occurred.

Pit closures were announced in 1984 that were to cost 20,000 jobs. They were announced in the spring, when demand for coal was about to drop off, and after coal had been stockpiled.

The NUM refused to comply with what they considered to be anti-union legislation in calling their strike and opted for mass and secondary picketing once again.

These mass pickets were now illegal, allowing the police to be used to uphold the law. Local men stood toe-to-toe. Men from the same towns and villages, some with miners' helmets, some with policemen's helmets. As the picketing grew, however, policemen from across England were sent to take on the miners.

The picketing became riotous in particularly brutal encounters at the Orgreave coking plant near Sheffield. Five thousand miners were confronted by police in riot gear from ten counties. There were many injured on both sides. The miners, now cast as lawbreaking thugs, were vilified in the right-wing newspapers, but the sight on television of police horses charging, and the striking men being struck with batons, made it clear to many that the Tory government had created an environment where they could use the police as a force against the people.

The NUM suffered from further new legislation that allowed the courts to sequester funds from unions that participated in illegal strike action.

There was real poverty in the mining communities while the police were earning large sums in overtime, a fact that some were not slow to mention as they taunted the miners in increasingly unpleasant battles.

There was never a full strike as East Midlands branches of the NUM refused to join in, believing it to be folly to break the new laws. Scargill was convinced there was no way to win without adopting the successful tactics of 1974.

The miners' wives, struggling to feed their families, carried placards that read:

THATCHER PAYS POLICE TO
STARVE KIDS

As the summer wore on it became clear just how much coal had been stockpiled and how successfully the Tories had plotted their new legislation. The miners were resilient and their communities received support from all over the country. This strike was different from those in the '70s that had been about securing good pay for the miners. It was about the closure of pits and the permanent decimation of the industry in favour of cheaper imported coal. Arthur Scargill's assertion that these closures of the so-called 'uneconomic' pits would only be the beginning was repeated throughout the bitterest and most divisive labour dispute in post-war British history.

Down south, in suburban areas like Loughton, the notion of uneconomic pits, i.e. those pits where it is unprofitable to continue to mine, was an open-and-shut case. Rarely mentioned was the social cost of closing down communities, with the resultant economic cost of providing social security and housing benefits to the thousands thrown on to the dole, never mind the other businesses that would now go under because of their reliance on the wages of miners.

The extent of support for the miners in middle-class areas was slim to none. In our house it was me. By now I was a card-carrying member of the Labour Party, with Clause 4, printed as it was on the back of that membership card, learnt off by heart:

to secure for the workers by hand or by brain the full fruits of their industry and the most equitable distribution thereof that may be possible upon the basis of the common ownership of the means of production, distribution and exchange, and the best obtainable system of popular administration and control of each industry or service.

Well, I knew the first line anyway.

I knew my dad thought the injuries to the police were disgraceful, and that he was scornful of Scargill, who was so strident and uncompromising that he was a hard man to like, even if you considered the defence of the miners' communities important. I had no money to help the miners, so I just watched the strike on TV while wearing badges saying 'Coal not Dole'.

Sitting in my Mini one evening, talking to my stepmum about my dad and our differences, she drew a distinction between the two of us by saying that he was a more establishment figure than me. This pleased me. I warmed to this theme and said that maybe when I was having disagreements with him I was:

'. . . taking a subconscious swing at the establishment'.

Out of the corner of my eye I could see her stifling a laugh. We'd spent a good half an hour on the subconscious with our psychologist in communications studies by then, so I was an expert of course.

I was determined to establish clear ideological water between myself and the rest of my family. It dismayed me that my stepmum sympathized with McGregor of the coal board (who, to my mind, was evil) because of the difficult decisions he had to make, with millions of pounds at stake.

It seemed an accident with money was always the big fear in the south, since there was no industry left to speak of, so the notion of a decimated community had no relevance.

The Sloane Rangers' Handbook came out at the time and I bought it for my dad's birthday since it was about posh people and he spoke in a posh voice. The book made fun of 'Sloanes', the posh Fulham and Kensington girls epitomized by the new Princess of Wales. My dad was no more a Sloane than he was a member of Chernenko's politburo. He looked at it bemusedly and I failed again to point up our differences.

If anything, I was closer to the Sloanes than he was, being a regular at workshops run at the Royal Court Theatre in Sloane Square by their Young People's Theatre Scheme. It was a long way from Loughton on the tube but it seemed worth it to be involved at such a famous theatre.

The Royal Court had been at the forefront of new writing in the British theatre since the '50s. It prided itself on discovering and nurturing new writers and on fostering the expression of challenging ideas on its famous stage. Upstairs at the Royal Court was a smaller theatre, called Upstairs at the Royal Court. I went along hoping to one day be cast in a play, but my eagerness to please and garner attention led to my spoiling one workshop, when I asked if the game we were about to play was going to be 'the one where . . .' and gave away the ending.

'Yes,' said the man running the workshop, 'and now you've ruined it.'

I felt small and embarrassed. Still, I kept attending. I liked the politics there too. There was no shortage of sympathizers with the miners. Perhaps coincidentally, it was Stephen Daldry, artistic director at the Royal Court in the '90s, who directed *Billy Elliot,* a film set against the backdrop of the miners' strike.

I stopped going to those workshops when I went to university in Kent but I was never as enthused about the theatre there as I had been at the Royal Court, where there were many talented kids and good new plays.

What there was at university, though, was support for the miners. There were three pits in Kent and bucket collections daily on campus. If there were demos to attend there were always coaches organized. I was a bit disappointed in my fellow freshers, many of whom had just left school and seemed a bit over-excited at being in the bar legitimately. My time at Loughton had been a big leap from school and more of an undergraduate life in some respects. There always seemed to be someone vomiting in a stairwell during that first few weeks on campus.

The miners' strike bedded in for the winter and became attritional. The Labour Party leadership and some at the TUC wanted Scargill to hold the ballot he was required to by law.

Only the Nottinghamshire miners were not on strike, and they had the option to go to court to ensure they had the right to a ballot of their own, should the result of a national ballot be to strike (Tony Benn points out in his *Diaries 1980–1990* that they had previously done just that over an incentive scheme they wanted to adopt that the NUM had rejected under a Labour government). This made a ballot pointless in the NUM's eyes.

The Yorkshire miners picketed Nottinghamshire heavily and a divide opened there between miners from the two areas.

Ultimately Nottinghamshire established their own Democratic Union of Mineworkers, with Conservative government encouragement, ironically.

Divisions widened for the duration of the strike: between miners in different areas, between miners and police in the same areas, between unions, between factions of the Labour Party, between family members inside and outside the dispute, and between the North and the South of England (with the exception of those pit areas in Kent). Margaret Thatcher had come to power promising harmony where there had been discord and had delivered the opposite. A more divisive leader it is hard to conceive of.

Scargill, too, polarized opinion, but what can never be

doubted was his commitment to the members of his union, tens of thousands of whom lost their jobs.

It was my nineteenth birthday the day the strike ended. That they all went back to work brought no relief, only sadness. So much lasting damage had been done. The NUM's struggle continued, as pits were closed year in year out, and every effort was made to bankrupt it. Scargill remained its leader for another fifteen years.

1985

Anton Chekhov

*'It is with perplexity that I look upon religious people
among the intelligentsia'**

That quote from Anton Chekhov was on the front of my A4 pad at Loughton College. What is it with teenagers and slogans? I owned any amount of badges, posters and T-shirts that had phrases printed on them. They had to be funny or political – they were the general criteria – preferably both. If they couldn't do both then I'd double up: 'Together We Can Stop The Bomb' on my back and *The Blues Brothers* on my front. I was a part-time activist and comedy VHS collector. Karl Marx beard with Groucho Marx moustache and eyebrows.

I found that Chekhov quote myself, though, and displayed it for all the world (or all *my* world) to see. I was warmly satisfied when Allan Rowe, our film studies lecturer, leant over to inspect it and offered a wry grin. Look out world, I have views! Here is a thing I believe. Religious people are flawed intellectually.

I could not consider myself part of the intelligentsia, at a further education college in Essex, but wielding that quotation around the place betrayed a desire to be part of something resembling a clever club. It was a 'think better of me' plea, betraying self-doubt that people could think well of me, that I might be bright or humorous.

*From *The Theatre of Revolt*, by Robert Brustein

It was, at least, a great leap forward from scribbling *Al of AFC* on the buses but perhaps only in the sense that I was no longer writing on buses.

I now revered people who said things that I agreed with. I wanted to follow them, read more of what they'd said and pursue other ideas that I might find agreeable, but why that particular statement of Chekhov's appealed I'm unsure.

Chekhov's tormented childhood, in mid-nineteenth-century Russia, with a father who regularly beat him, upset him throughout his life until tuberculosis killed him at forty-four. His father, a grocer and local church choirmaster in the port of Taganrog, six hundred miles south of Moscow, coerced Anton and his brothers into long hours of rehearsals for the choir. Those who admired their singing were unaware of the gruelling regime they undertook. As an adult he said that whenever he passed a church it brought back the memories of an unhappy childhood. His low opinion of religious people has a clear origin.

His father enrolled them in a Greek Orthodox school even though they didn't speak any Greek. They didn't learn any either and moved to a Russian school after half a year at their mother's insistence, though there was often one or more of the six Chekhov children at home, due to unpaid school fees.

The imposition of this enforced singing practice with siblings by a devout and bullying father, rather than leading to a Russian precursor of the Jackson Five or an earlier von Trapp family, resulted only in resentment. Eventually his father was declared bankrupt and fled to Moscow, leaving him behind. Anton thrived in his new freedom despite the financial hardship and trained as a doctor, whilst all the time maintaining literary aspirations.

Chekhov's despising of the devout is understandable, but

religion played almost no part in my life, other than my dad's insistence on watching *Songs Of Praise* on a Sunday evening, in the hope they'd sing 'Onward Christian Soldiers'.

There was Sunday school in the '70s, which I'd enjoyed. The Bible stories were entertaining, especially the Good Samaritan and the one about not building your house on sand. To illustrate this, our Sunday school teacher had two doll's houses, one resting on a firm surface and the other on a pile of sand. She then showed us the effects of pouring the contents of a watering can over the respective houses. A watering can indoors! I liked that for a start. The house built on sand tilted over slowly and rested at a sick angle, listing. It looked disturbingly wrong, while our teacher looked relieved and pleased. This had given us much to think about, but what?

None of it left any flicker of belief in me. Those who expressed faith left me baffled by the time I was a teenager, and contemptuous enough to highlight my views on the front of my A4 pad. My only belief was that you had to be a fool to believe in something that is a man-made construct. This was conventional wisdom readily adopted. Church was boring, the Adam and Eve tale nonsensical, and the desperate attempts of the modern clergy to attract young people laughable. Any good works done by the Church were unconsidered. It was an easy victory over the establishment for a rebellious adolescent. There's no such thing as God, you fools, and you believe in it and still expect me to listen to another word you say with anything other than a dismissive smirk. Take this short shrift!

It wasn't his views on religion that first attracted me to Chekhov, but his plays.

We'd been introduced to Chekhov by Piers the drama teacher as we had to study *The Seagull* for A Level.

Fortunately, there was an excellent production of the play running at the Greenwich Theatre during May 1984, starring Maria Aitken as Arkadina, which I went to see three times for revision. I've always loved the play's opening, where Medvedenko, the smitten but hapless schoolteacher asks the world-weary but young and attractive Masha why she always wears black.

'I'm in mourning for my life,' she replies.

That tickled me the first time I read it and seems as good a test for an appreciation of Chekhov as any. If you don't find that funny, this stuff may not be for you and you need to raise your game. In 'mustn't grumble' Britain where many people, in fact, grumble all the time, that poetic complaint from a woman tired of much else besides batting away the affection of someone who doesn't appeal, while at the same time failing to shift through her own gears to improve her lot, ought to resonate with every narky, wound-up, passive-aggressive resident of the British Isles. I've liked every production of *The Seagull* I've seen, if only for hearing that opening line. When I was a teenager I decided that if I ever ran a pub I'd name it the Seagull, which is of interest now only because it betrayed the onset of a lifelong devotion to public houses.

Our other A Level 'text', as we learnt to call them, was *Comedians*, Trevor Griffiths's 1975 play about a stand-up comedy workshop preparing would-be comedians to perform in a showcase for a talent scout. The character Gethin Price, who wants to try an experimental act in the search for 'truth', rather than follow the derivative style the others on the course favour, was an appealing anarchic figure. He was the rebel in the play so I tried to empathize with him. It was a struggle: his views were close to incoherent to me, and the comedians he idolized were from a bygone age. He hated

Max Bygraves though, which was of interest as my dad adored Bygraves. That was a point of contact for me and Gethin at least.

The play offered a foretaste of some of the arguments shaping over the so-called alternative comedy scene that was emerging in London.

The Tower Theatre in Islington was running an amateur production of *Comedians* which I also went to see three times (parking in Canonbury each time, I decided I'd like to live in the area and thirteen years later I moved into a house round the corner from the theatre).

I learnt a speech from the play, that Price gives as his stand-up act towards the end, for my A Level exam, without ever really understanding it. I tried to make it funny but it isn't that funny, it's more angry. I hadn't cottoned on yet that anger is the source of much humour.

The first year at university we were given a choice of two plays to perform scenes from for our exam at the culmination of our performance course, Chekhov's *Uncle Vanya* and *Comedians* by Trevor Griffiths.

Our group consisted of twelve women and four men, two of whom were already going out with each other. *Comedians* was an odd choice with its cast of eleven, mainly Mancunian, blokes. We discussed how to split the group, with each half tackling a section of one of the plays. Shamelessly, I announced I was more interested in which part I would play, either Price in *Comedians* or Astrov in *Vanya*. There was a silence as the collective ground its teeth. No one else had made any requests about casting. It was decided there would be a female version of *Comedians,* leaving the boys to take part in *Uncle Vanya*. No one else wanted to be Astrov.

I enjoyed the subtle nuances and naturalistic style of

Chekhov's comedy but had no self-awareness of my inability to portray them. As with many would-be actors, I was convinced that a prominent role would be the best one for me, and in this case Astrov was funny too, and I thought I was funny.

At the UKC (University of Kent at Canterbury) Dramatics Society meeting in my first term, new members ticked boxes on a form to alert the society to their talents: acting, costume, set design, knowing all the lyrics from *The Rocky Horror Show* etc. I wrote down one side of my form that I was interested in writing and performing comedy as well as acting in plays.

The BBC had a series on at the time called *Comic Roots* in which famous comedians traced their personal development as performers back to where it all began. For many, their roots were at university, in all-night undergraduate mirth, leading to sketches, revues, and Edinburgh Festival shows. Michael Palin said his room-mate, who wasn't part of *Monty Python*, was the funniest man he knew at university.

As Rik Mayall had met Adrian Edmondson at Manchester University, so I fantasized about meeting a collaborator, but no reply was ever forthcoming from UKC Dramatics, so I wasn't involved in any drama in my first term. I did some writing, in secret.

Occasionally, I would ask the pair of earnest teachers of our performance course whether they wanted a particular exercise or improvisation to be funny, irritating them, as they struggled to immerse us in the ideas of the great Russian actors' guru, Stanislavsky, and his quest for truth.

I had already 'done' Stanislavsky for A Level, and, bringing my natural diffidence to bear, decided that these two could teach me nothing. Then they had me take part in an exercise where three of us had to run into the room, one at a time, desperately try the two other exit doors, only to find them locked, before running out the way they came in, panicking. I was third in and the rest of the group were in stitches as I wrestled with the two doors, eyes wide in terror, before fleeing. No one had laughed at the first two.

The group had been told that the first person was fleeing a fire, the second a murderer, and that I, in third, desperately needed the toilet. Our teacher apologized for setting us up but his point was made. Comedy wasn't about playing for laughs which I would certainly have done if I'd been told to run around as if needing the lavatory.

Chekhov wrote, in one of his scores of fascinating letters:

Let the things that happen on the stage be as complex and yet just as simple as they are in life. For instance, people are having a meal at the table, just having a meal, but at the same time their happiness is being created, or their lives are being smashed up.*

That's a fair description of teatime at home in the '70s but more importantly the key to making the plays work. His intention was to show the very people he was portraying, the Russian middle classes, how dreary their lives were, in the hope that they might change, before the world changed them. That they might recognize their foibles and listless-ness and, while finding them exquisitely and humorously observed, be inclined to work hard and pull away from such decaying wastefulness. Chekhov died thirteen years before the Bolshevik Revolution did change the lives of all Russians. In Chekhov's *The Cherry Orchard* a sound, like a breaking string, is heard in the distance and different char-acters speculate on its cause according to their own view

*From the Introduction to *Chekhov Plays*, by Elisaveta Fen

of the world. Could it have been machinery? The onset of industrialization, foreshadowing the future, is mooted but ignored.

We rehearsed and learned our lines for our performance. There was to be an external examiner who would sit with our teachers to pass judgement.

Stanislavsky wrote:

The theatre has invented a whole assortment of signs, expressions of human passions, theatrical poses, voice inflections, cadences, flourishes, stage tricks, and methods of acting which become mechanical and unconscious, and are always at the service of the actor when he feels himself utterly helpless on the stage.*

Unfortunately, out of my depth, and self-consciously awkward, I offered the full range of Stanislavsky's dreaded 'signs', adding one of my own by blushing furiously, my face burning as I struggled without a clue. Acting Chekhov well is as difficult as acting can be. I was afraid of the external examiner's inevitable damning judgement. In a lull in the scene (I considered any moment in the drama when someone else was speaking to be a lull), I steeled myself to look across and witness the examiner's disappointment.

He was sound asleep.

*From *The Theory of the Modern Stage*, edited by Eric Bentley

Bertolt Brecht

Conversations with a Golliwog, by Alexander Guyan, was staged by UKC Dramatics in early 1985, directed by a vaguely intimidating young Scottish woman with short red hair, prominent cheekbones, and what looked to be a very attractive figure, concealed beneath the statutory baggy old trousers and jumper to discourage objectification. To me she was the Most Beautiful Girl on Campus.

Three of the cast were second-year girls, one of whom was an effortless boy-entrancer with long spiky blonde tresses and exhibitionist tendencies. Her surname was Fox, and, as her first initial was A, she appeared on college notices as A. Fox. There were three boys: one a refugee from a P.G. Wodehouse story, another a serious-minded Boer (is there any other kind?) and me.

This was my first play at university. It was a sad tale of a teenage girl, suffering from mental illness, who confides in her golliwog, which then talks to her. The Boer, the white Boer, played the golliwog.

There were no black people in the drama department, which alleviated some tricky casting choices. Is it worse to ask a white man to play a golliwog, and have to apply full make-up, or is it worse to ask a black man to play a golliwog?

In a period of intense political correctness, during which we were all being asked to reconstruct ourselves, it was a considered choice not to replace the golliwog with another soft toy that could come to life, though that could have resulted in a serious play about mental health resembling an amateur production of *Rainbow,* with Bungle in a counselling role.

The women in the cast were pathological smilers, and highly exotic to a lonely boy living in a college room, with a car park (as opposed to cathedral) view and a much-missed girlfriend miles away at Loughton College.

The director and the actresses were rapidly becoming radicalized by the Women in Theatre course that ran during the second year of the drama degree. The course had a successful history of both politicizing previously indifferent students and creating trial-period lesbians from the ranks of its more advanced devotees. These subsequently enraged undergraduates, together with the spread of Radical Feminism generally, made it tricky to be an unevolved straight boy. Compliments to women would back-fire; in fact any comment could easily be misconstrued by newcomers to the battlefield of sexual politics.

I had chosen to live in Keynes College in my first year because it had a reputation for being left-wing. It wasn't, and it also had no fellow drama students in it, which made settling in difficult. On one occasion a woman was chain-smoking in the Keynes dining hall, making eating unpleasant. There were a few no smoking signs about. I said 'excuse me' a couple of times, as she was sitting right behind me. I really should have left it, I didn't mind that much, maybe she was having a bad day, but everyone knew you couldn't smoke in there and she was ignoring me. I reached out and tapped her on the back of the shoulder.

'*DON'T TOUCH ME!*' she yelled, recoiling violently to re-establish her personal space, her voice echoing around the rafters of the high-ceilinged hall.

'I was just going to say can you not smoke ... ?' My irritation was quickly subsiding into embarrassment.

'DON'T YOU TOUCH ME!!'

'I didn't ... I ...'

'DON'T TOUCH WOMEN!'

People were standing up to see what was going on, there were enough rape alarms and mace sprays in that place to dispel a riot, or start one. I turned back to my food, blushing. She smoked more fags.

New approaches to conversation with women, unheard of where I grew up, had to be developed, without the subject of football as an ice-breaker. Some of these people were livid. Which was a good lesson to learn.

When rehearsals for the play began, I became accustomed to the women's tracky bottoms and loose fitting T-shirts, and developed a crush on all of them collectively. Every now and then a baggy, inside-out sweat shirt would slip, revealing a bare shoulder and, like the Victorians fixated by a flash of ankle, a boy could be momentarily grateful for small pleasures. Provided he wasn't caught staring.

Being part of a cast especially appeals to the dysfunctional, providing, albeit temporarily, a new surrogate family. This family can absorb almost any eccentricity or idiosyncrasy since it is a temporary collective for the needy. Problems are now shared, and tackled, with mutual support. There is common anxiety and laughter, and the same unifying objective: avoiding humiliation in front of your peers.

The Boer believed he was successfully concealing his accent, thereby giving his golliwog with fine Received Pronunciation, but I told him that someone had asked me where he was from since his voice was so strange. He was very serious and had taken up rehearsal time with his golliwog-angst so I was slyly digging at him without the nerve to say it directly. Carol, our chirpy, and very funny, stage manager gave me a look and observed, with her customary perspicacity (and to let me know that she'd clocked what I was doing):

'That's a nice thing to repeat.'

My own performance was crippled by nervous inhibitions. Our director encouraged me to express myself more. I blushed whenever she spoke to me. She set up an improvisation where I was to come home and find my girlfriend with another man. I began quietly as ever but then flew into a rage in my role as the wronged man. When I'd finished I turned to the director who seemed taken aback but impressed. With all these emotions churning around, real or imagined, the rehearsal room was becoming my favourite place.

I was able to speak less and less frequently to Justine as I was rehearsing in the evening and she was at college during the day. She had been down to visit me but our summer together seemed a long time ago as my fixation on the women I was working with worsened. I spoke to my old friend from Loughton College, Gill, who told me that if nothing had happened with anyone, then I absolutely must not say anything to Justine, it would upset her and the play would be over soon. I said it was too late and I'd confessed to Justine that I fancied half the cast and especially the director. There was a silence on the other end of the phone.

Justine was prescribed anti-depressants and began seeing someone else. The play ended with a cast party in Whitstable. My crushes expired with no outcome, apart from the director snogging me briefly at the party, before laughing heartily and going to find the punch. Carol consoled me:

'She probably enjoys the thrill of the chase.'

My principal tactic for winning Justine back was to stand, unseen, in her parents' back garden, staring up at her bedroom window. It didn't work.

Carol lived in Hackney, not that far from Loughton, and

that summer we met up to see the National Theatre's Mystery Plays at the Lyceum, which now was staging theatre for the first time in thirty years. *The Mysteries*, adapted from the Wakefield Cycle of medieval plays by Tony Harrison, were traditionally performed on the backs of carts by trades-men, but were now thrillingly revived in a promenade production directed by Bill Bryden.

The move to the Lyceum came as the National Theatre's Cottesloe was closed down due to underfunding. Only a special grant from the Ken Livingstone-led, soon-to-be-abolished GLC allowed it to reopen later that year, since the private funding the government insisted the National should find could not meet the shortfall.

During a House of Commons debate on the issue of arts funding, Michael Foot said:

'What is the point of having a great and adventurous National Theatre and a cabinet of barbarians?'

The Mysteries were in three parts: *Nativity, The Passion* and *Doomsday,* telling the story of the Bible in three epic per-formances. Carol and I opted for seeing all three in one day, starting at 11 a.m.

I've never seen anything so memorable or remarkable in a theatre before or since. My personal highlight was Brian Glover as God, raised on a forklift, telling Noah to build an ark. Noah is resistant and God descends. When he stepped out of the forklift we could see he was wearing carpet slippers, as well as braces and a flat cap.

'Who are you?' he is asked and he answers softly, a little hurt, with a thick Yorkshire accent:

'I am God.'

With actors amongst us and the action unfolding next to, behind, above, or all around, the experience was funny, moving and inspiring.

The National Theatre was a centre of theatrical excellence to aspire to. It staged David Mamet's *Glengarry Glen Ross* in a scintillating, emotionally charged evening (apart from anything I was astonished the cast were English, so convincing were their American accents). Rik Mayall dazzled hilariously in Gogol's *The Government Inspector* and Anthony Hopkins terrorized menacingly in Howard Brenton and David Hare's satire of the press, *Pravda*.

The following year, Hopkins was a potent and agonized King Lear. The blinding of Gloucester drew gasps from the audience as blood squirted across the stage. Even from the very back row it was a shock, especially to those, like me, who didn't know the play (my Uncle George, who used to cheerfully recite Shakespeare's sonnets to me, could never understand how I could be studying theatre and not Shakespeare).

On the same day I saw *Lear*, by contrast, I also saw an engrossing production of Bertolt Brecht's *The Mother*.

Having witnessed all this excellence, finding something within our students' scope was daunting but Brecht offered a solution. His *Fear and Misery of the Third Reich* was a series of scenes encapsulating life at home in the Germany of the 1930s. It was written specifically to provide material for amateur German theatre groups in exile, as Brecht himself was from 1933.

One of the fourth-year directing students at Kent was staging some of the scenes as his final degree project at the Gulbenkian Theatre on campus. This was a 350-seat auditorium popular with the best touring companies, like Cheek by Jowl, Howard Barker's The Wrestling School and Red Ladder.

I was cast in a couple of small roles and appreciated the clarity and simplicity of the writing, though in one scene

I had to clean a pair of shoes that were plainly spotless when I picked them up. I must have looked like the most fastidious shoe cleaner in the Reich.

This time, when I developed a crush on one of the cast, Jill, I was not tortured with guilt. I bonded with her as we painted bedsheets bright red to make giant swastika banners. We went out together for two years after that initial *tête-à-tête* over the supreme symbol of evil.

I'd been in two plays, one with a white South African golliwog and another where I had to paint swastikas. Political correctness came in many forms.

My dad and stepmum came, which signalled a softening of his opposition to my studying drama in the first place:

'What sort of job is that going to get you?'

Drama students were second only to philosophy students in the ranks of graduate unemployment. I took a philosophy course that year, as part of Kent's cross-faculty approach to first years. My highlight was a balding, angry mature student (who brought to mind the picture of Brecht on the back of my copy of *The Mother*) shouting at me:

'Is it *ever* right to kill, *yes or no*?'

'Well . . .'

'It's a *simple question*!'

'What's the situation?'

'YES OR NO!'

The teacher was smiling. I enjoyed philosophy. I could have studied that instead and then acted in plays in the evening. Brecht's plays preferably, since they had a bomb-proof political message (social justice coupled with anti-fascism), and were written for amateurs. Perfect.

John Peel

Radio in the '80s was unimaginably terrible. With the exception of Steve Wright, who hired comedians, like the brilliant Phil Cornwell, to generate funny original characters, Radio One employed a litany of unlistenable halfwits whose unremitting delight in the sound of their own torturous voices kept them blathering away in an apparent self-parody of disc jockey jocularity. Everyone was their 'mate' and everyone was a 'great guy actually' or a 'really super lady'. Paul Whitehouse and Harry Enfield's hilarious portrayal of spoof disc jockeys Smashie and Nicey is a work of acerbic observational comedy rather than cartoonish outlandishness, though it is that as well.

Everyone has their own worst Radio One DJ. For many it's Noel Edmonds, but I didn't know about him until I had to endure *Swap Shop* on BBC1 on Saturday mornings, because my sister liked it. Only if she was out could I watch *Tiswas* on ITV with Sally James showing off the garter of the week and Bob Carolgees with Spit the Dog.

Others will cite Dave Lee Travis or 'DLT', the self-styled Hairy Cornflake, but the most unpardonable villain of the ruinous '80s radio landscape was Simon Bates and his intolerable 'Our Tune' slot, for which people would send in sob stories and Bates would read them out over a syrupy backing track. It's only because I was a skint student that I didn't hurl my radio out of the window every time that came on. It was an over-egged pudding of *faux*-emotion, oiled with false humility on Bates's part, which usually culminated in a tiresome, sentimental power ballad, to remind the day's subject of the time her two-timing boyfriend's Doberman bit a leg off her long-haired Persian, or something similar.

The choice of listening was severely limited as there were so few commercial stations.

Radio Three was out because that played classical music which I'd had no introduction to and was left cold by.

Radio Four was absent at home so I never learned to listen to it. As with a foreign language, it's important to be exposed to it at a young age or it becomes hard to pick up. Like cryptic crosswords and multi-syllable Scrabble play, it's an acquired skill to enjoy Radio Four and it must be absorbed in the formative years. Try as I might to immerse myself in its improving tones late in life, I would soon tune out and start to wonder what Bruno Brookes was playing.

Radio Two was for old folks with its Terry Wogan and Jimmy Young double bill. There was no Radio Five or Six or Seven or XFM, Smooth, Heart, Kiss etc etc.

In London the best bet was LBC with its joyous phone-ins, or Capital Radio.

Capital was a relatively new station whose profile was raised by the distribution of car stickers, window stickers, stickers of all kinds to the general population. If you went along to Euston Tower, from where they broadcast for years, it was possible to see actual DJs emerging and to ask them for autographs as well as collect stickers from reception. I waited there for a couple of hours one day in about 1979 and came back with Dave 'COD! Cash on Delivery' Cash's autograph as well as Desmond Hamil's, who was an ITN reporter. He said: 'You don't want mine.' I said: 'Yes I do.'

The only place to turn, to avoid a world of grim commercial pop and egotistical loons burbling away, was Radio

One between eight and midnight during the week when the Rhythm Pals would deliver two hours each of an eclectic mix of mainly new music that was superior to, and absent from, the hateful Radio One daytime playlist.

First of the Rhythm Pals up, at eight o'clock, was David 'Kid' Jensen, who had been a big-name young DJ, with an inspirational centre parting, on daytime radio. Now his true musical taste had made him surprisingly perfect for the evening listener. He was also allowed to be called David, since he was not a Kid any more.

Following Jensen was the greatest broadcaster that Radio One has had since its inception in 1967. One of the greatest broadcasters in the history of radio in Britain, perhaps anywhere.

John Peel, Peely or plain old Peel (as in 'Did you listen to Peel last night?') knew his musical trends and broke more bands than any other DJ. You heard it on Peel's show before you heard it anywhere else. Sometimes it seemed as though he liked every single thing that was ever recorded. He certainly seemed to have heard it all. He received demo tapes by the sackful and reputedly listened to every one.

It's difficult not to portray him as an obsessive enthusiast and perhaps he was, in the same way that John Motson is about football, but that would give an incomplete impression. His unruffled style and mellow warm delivery in his unhurried, restrained scouse tones were uniquely engaging. No one said they didn't like him and he always seemed to have a good word for every track, even the oddest and most impenetrable stuff. He was broadcasting to the hippest, trendiest, too-cool-for-skool audience but never appeared to succumb, on air at least, to the ready cynicism so common in the lives of tens of thousands of everyday students and schoolkids.

1978. Mucking about in a photo booth. The bottom picture is me trying an alluring half-smile which I'd decided to adopt, probably in an effort to be like David Starsky.

1978. On holiday aged twelve. I framed this photo and cut the word 'SUPERSTAR' from a newspaper to stick underneath it.

Skaters want run for their money

1978. I'm second from the left at the front. The tallest kid at the back became my stepbrother, Tony, four years later. They never built a skate park.

1978. Barry Sheene. Look at that smile, he was irresistible, everyone loved him.

1979. Liam Brady, like Bjorn Borg, had eyes that were close together, which some people in the 70s believed was a boon to sportsmen. He was my idol and was regarded as Arsenal's greatest ever player.

1980. John McEnroe flies in to another volley with his headband straining against the force of his frizz

1981. A campaigning postcard from Chickens' Lib.

1981. On holiday at Universal Studios. She's not with me.

1981. Blondie's lead singer strikes a pose which featured in my treasured 1981 Debbie Harry calendar.

1981. The late great John Belushi. I
watched his films endlessly.

1982. A gig I have no memory of. One
of the six times I saw The Jam, though
I only remember three of them.

1982. Paul Weller sporting the CND
badge so many of us wore and a belt
that no one did.

1982. Rik Mayall and co were the
funniest thing on television for
teenagers in 1982.

1983. Charlie Nicholas makes his debut v. Luton, August 1983. I went to the front with a camera. This, unbelievably, is the best photo I took.

1983. Four of us went to Devon in Danny McCarthy's Herald. Much scrumpy is being loaded in the background.

Hammersmith Palais	Hammersmith Palais
242 Shepherds Bush Road, W6	Box office open 12-6 Mon- Sat Telephone: 748 2812
MONDAY 21st FEBRUARY	MONDAY **21** 83 FEBRUARY
at 8.00p.m.	at 8.00p.m.
ADMISSION £4.00 Inc. V.A.T.	HEAD MUSIC presents **Fun Boy Three**
N⁰ 775	N⁰ 775
TO BE GIVEN UP	THIS PORTION TO BE RETAINED (PTO)

1983. Another gig I have no memory of attending. I loved the Fun Boy Three, though. They had noticed that the lunatics had taken over the asylum.

Student demo' closes canteen

★ Demonstrating students at the college this week. (Y531)

1983. Back in the *Gazette*. I'm at the top right of our 'placard'. We wanted a common room. They didn't give us one.

Look we're on TV

Loughton College Television in action. Clair Jones and Allan Davis put on the style for the cameras.

1983. Open day at Loughton College as reported in the free *Yellow Advertiser*. Me and Claire James act out a scene of domestic drudgery. They spelled my name Allan Davis, which was a disappointment.

1983. Loughton College Media Studies group decamp to Thaxted for a study of 'Culture'. The prat in the middle thinks that's a funny face. It means he's happy. Gill Bucknall is on the left at the front and Jamie the squat finder is on the far left.

1983. My drama teacher, Piers Gladhill, and me at Greenham Common.

1984. Champagne Charlie Nicholas, realizing my fifteen-year-old sister is too young, reaches out to cop a feel of my seventeen-year-old girlfriend instead. This was in the crowd at Crystal Palace Athletics Stadium.

1984. In France with my beloved Mini 1275GT. I have never had a clue about clothes.

1984. My eighteenth birthday party at Epping Forest Country Club with school friend Jeremy (aka Ji). I had been given five blue amphetamine pills by a friend from college. They had a powerful effect on me but fortunately it didn't show.

1985. Me and Steve about to play rounders at the kids' camp. Shorts like those were normal in the 80s. This picture has been described by my wife as: 'The gayest photo I've ever seen', which I consider to be an exaggeration.

1985. I ordered this copy of Neil Kinnock's brilliant speech. It cost 35p.

Neil Kinnock's Speech to Labour Party Conference, Bournemouth, 1985

'It **can** be done, it **must** be done'

1986. The cast of *The Empire Builders, 1986*. In the background is the set I knocked over during the play.

1986. On the terraces for Sweden 1, England 0. That is my 'James Dean' jacket. There was hooliganism in Stockholm that night.

1986. Ian Botham shows his true colours: red, gold and green.

1988. Me and my mum's mum, Dolly Price, in Adelaide.

Above all else he combined an absence of egotism with a sense of humour. His dry, self-deprecating remarks and his respect for his audience, who he allowed to think were as knowledgeable as he was by adding 'of course' at the end of each piece of factual information about an obscure guitarist's band history, all these things set him apart. He was greatly loved by the listening public for whom he was a lighthouse in a sea of sad broadcasting.

As passionate as he was about music so he was about Liverpool FC. On a wonderful compilation CD he made for Fabric Records (FABRICLIVE. 07: *John Peel*) in 2002, he opened with the great Peter Jones on BBC radio, commentating on Alan Kennedy's winning goal for Liverpool v Real Madrid in the 1981 European Cup Final before mixing commentary on Kenny Dalglish's winner in the 1978 European Cup Final into 'Love Will Tear Us Apart' by Joy Division. Liverpool were again European Cup holders in my first year at university, having beaten Roma, in Rome, on penalties in 1984. They reached the European Cup Final yet again in 1985 for the fifth time in nine seasons. Peely was delighted.

Students on campus at Kent in 1985 listened to a fair bit of radio since virtually no one had TVs in their rooms and there was only one TV room in each college. I was going back to Loughton and would have watched the final there but left it too late to leave and went to the packed TV room instead. I arrived at kick-off time only to find there hadn't been one.

Liverpool and Juventus supporters were involved in the kind of terrace-clearing skirmishes that had become familiar to anyone who attended football over the previous decade. When the terraces are cleared as they were in this instance, at the Heysel stadium in Brussels, a large majority of the fans, who are trying to escape, have to head somewhere. Ideally, as at Highbury in 1982, when a combination of a smoke-bomb, fighting and the police led to a clearing of large areas of terrace, the fans spill on to the pitch.

At Heysel this couldn't happen. There was no access to safe areas alongside the pitch either. The fans were squashed, trapped, many of them up against a wall.

A friend of mine, Keith, who I've been going to football with for over twenty years, was at the Heysel stadium when Arsenal played there in the Cup Winners' Cup Final of 1980. He later told me that the stadium had been 'falling down' even then.

Five years later a wall collapsed at Heysel and thirty-nine terrified Juventus supporters died screaming.

Something like it was bound to happen. Stadia everywhere were old. Policing was disorganized and football fans, who were routinely herded like animals into pens, could always turn very nasty, very quickly, particularly when provoked.

From the Juventus side stories emerged of right-wing 'ultras' with links to Italian fascist organizations wanting to attack Liverpool fans because the city itself was famously socialist, in their eyes a red city. Certainly, Italian fans played a full part: they could be seen on television, wearing masks over their faces and goading Liverpool supporters. It was Italians who died though, and it is Italians who mourn their loss on the anniversary each year.

For English football, already notorious for its hooligan problem, it was a catastrophic night of shame and disgrace. All English clubs were banned from playing in European competition and the ban was not lifted for five years. The first club denied an opportunity to compete for the European Cup, the greatest prize of all, decided by games between all the champions of the European leagues, were Liverpool's great rivals Everton.

On television, there was little information about what was going to happen next, or whether the rioting was out of control. Was the game even going to go ahead? Presenter and ex-footballer, Jimmy Hill, was now in the unfortunate position of running a lengthy live football show with no football. He filled in anxiously as his studio full of bemused football pundits brought their extensive knowledge of the offside law to bear on a heated debate (actually only Jimmy Hill was heated) about the return of National Service. Jimmy was adamant it was the answer and with the fervour of a barrack room bully tried to make his fence-sitting panellists agree with him.

Eventually the match started, ostensibly to quell the possibility of further rioting. It should never have taken place but, at least, while the memory of their dead was instantly disrespected by the decision to play, Juventus won.

By chance, later that summer, I would be in Liverpool for their first game after Heysel.

I had been working on a children's summer camp. It was non-residential so each day dozens of kids would be dropped off for a full programme of 'events'. I was the 'drama and video' person. When they came to me we would have an hour to devise a story, which I'd then video them acting out, using a camera the size of a microwave oven.

There were various different age groups and they cooked up some funny stories. The group of six- to seven-year-olds contained a skinhead who was so hyperactive, and frightening to the other kids, that I had little choice other than to make him the star of the video. He had a nine-year-old brother who looked identical with shaven head and green bomber jacket. He had told me his younger sibling would 'fight nine-year-olds'. That afternoon I waited to see who would pick them up. When their dad appeared it was no surprise to see he was shaven headed with a green bomber jacket on. He swept his youngest up in one arm and, without irony, said: 'That's my boy.'

One of my fellow camp staff, Steve, was from Merseyside. He had pitched a tent, without permission, in Epping Forest, where he was fending off hundreds of mosquitoes every night. I invited him to stay at our house. My dad was predictably annoyed:

'I can't *believe* you,' I said.

'*I* can't believe *you*,' he said.

Steve helped him with a bonfire in the garden and told him about the architecture course he was on at Huddersfield Polytechnic.

'Nice chap. He's studying architecture, you know,' said Dad.

'I know,' I said, swallowing his intimation that architecture was preferable to drama.

In August, Arsenal were due to play their first game of the 1985–86 season at Anfield. Steve was a big Liverpool fan. I went up to stay with him at Hoylake, on the Wirral, and he took me on to the famous Kop end amongst the Liverpool fans, where I kept my southern mouth shut, as Liverpool began another triumphant season with a 2–0 win.

The sun was out and the atmosphere was happy and good-natured. Everyone there loved standing on the Kop and being part of something bigger than the sum of its parts. There was one idiot though, poisoning it. Every time Arsenal's black full back, Viv Anderson, attacked down the right, this one individual would concoct some abusive diatribe finishing each time with the word nigger.

He knew he could take the opportunity to stand on the

terrace and vent his spleen in anonymity as long as no one dared to question him. A few people were tiring of his ugly voice, and uglier sentiments, until eventually, from a few steps up the terrace behind him, a voice with a calm scouse brogue said:

'My dad's a nigger.'

We all waited to see if the racist would spin around, looking to see who'd dared say that, but he didn't. He never said another word. He looked straight ahead while we all looked at him. Me and Steve grinned at each other and I looked round to see who'd produced this pearl of scouse wit. He was a middle-aged man, slightly overweight, with a twinkle in his eye and a half-smile playing under his grey beard. He didn't want the racist to turn round and clock him, not least because he wasn't black.

He did look like he'd enjoyed shutting the bloke up though, and he looked a lot like John Peel.

Neil Kinnock

Neil Kinnock's speech to the Labour Party conference in Bournemouth was a thrilling spectacle. The most passionate and lyrical evocation of what it meant to be a Labour supporter, and what the values of the Labour movement are, that I had ever heard. I sent off for a copy of the text of the speech, so excited was I by its sentiments, its vigour and its emotive truth.

This was what I had always wanted, someone to say how I felt. If I were asked why I supported the Labour Party I may have cited an opposition to privilege and a desire for social justice but little more. Kinnock described with real feeling just what the Labour movement had achieved for him and others like him. Actual achievements in improving the lives of the disadvantaged. It was compelling and appeared unanswerable. A plea to remember that good can only really be done in power and the unelectable are of no use to anyone.

After this speech the Labour Party will never be the same again. It is indeed a watershed. It may launch the bitterest quarrel in even Labour's turbulent history but Neil Kinnock judged that his party was going nowhere politically unless he confronted the people in his own ranks who are driving disillusioned Conservative voters into the arms of the [SDP–Liberal] Alliance. Disunity usually damages a party but this may be the split that many potential Labour voters have been longing for. If he wins them over, Neil Kinnock's 1985 Bournemouth speech will be a landmark in British political history.

John Cole, BBC Political Correspondent, at the Labour Conference 1985

Labour supporters everywhere were galvanized. It had been depressing for years to see the party tearing itself apart, more concerned with in-fighting and factional scrapping than with uniting to take on and defeat an unpopular Tory government.

The real damage had been done in 1981 with the establishment of the Social Democratic Party, the SDP, by four former Labour ministers, David Owen, Shirley Williams, Bill Rodgers and Roy Jenkins.

Labour, from then on, appeared left to the left. The party was seemingly unbalanced and unelectable. The former Labour ministers in the SDP attracted mainly former Labour voters and nowhere near enough of the disillusioned Conservatives John Cole referred to, leaving the vote split and the Tories comfortably in power with a huge majority, despite only three out of ten of those on the electoral roll voting for them.

The 1983 election defeat had been shattering and humiliating for Labour. The subsequent miners' strike, led by the hard-left militant Arthur Scargill, had left Kinnock virtually wasting a year on internal battles rather than taking on the government. The Labour leadership was at constant odds with the NUM leadership over the legality of the actions taken in support of the strike. Aware that public sympathy for the miners was strong, and the son of a miner himself, Kinnock was frustrated to see that sympathy being strained by mass confrontations with the police.

The refusal of the NUM leadership to accept the consequences of the breaking of the new Tory labour laws, and the persistence with mass picketing leading to criminal cases, resulting in huge fines for the union and its members, had angered the leadership of the Labour Party. The insistence of Scargill on leading his men into a class war led to greater hardship than was deemed necessary. Kinnock's refusal to promise reimbursement of the fines served on miners under the Tory legislation was to come to a head at the Labour conference. This was indicative of the kind of self-destructive internal warfare that was splitting the party and leaving an election win seemingly a million miles away. Kinnock decided he'd had enough and turned on the Militant Tendency.

This hard-left section of the party, epitomized by Liverpool's City Council led by Derek Hatton, was tackled head on amid stormy scenes in the Bournemouth Conference Hall. Kinnock launched into a passionate tirade against Hatton and his council:

I'll tell you what happens with impossible promises. You start with far-fetched resolutions. They are then pickled into a rigid dogma, a code, and you go through the years sticking to that, outdated, misplaced, irrelevant to the real needs, and you end in the grotesque chaos of a Labour council – a Labour council – hiring taxis to scuttle round a city handing out redundancy notices to its own workers … I'm telling you, and you'll listen, I'm telling you, you can't play politics with people's jobs, and with people's services and with people's lives

This was the vanquishing of the hard left. Expulsions from the party would follow and the ground was being laid for a modernizing of the party that would ultimately see it electable again.

Kinnock had previously always been on the left, which made his rounding on them personally significant to him. He was accused of hypocrisy as he undertook changes in policy to move the party to the centre in the hope of winning power.

He had been a popular figure amongst supporters of CND, a unilateralist and regular attender, with his wife Glenys and his good friend and political ally Michael Foot, at rallies. Later, though, he conceded unilateralism, so unpopular was it with the electorate.

As a young man in the House of Commons he had stayed put, with fellow left-winger Dennis Skinner, as the rest of the house trooped through to the Lords to hear the Queen's speech, so staunch was he in his opposition to an unelected second house. Nearly three decades later he accepted a seat in the House of Lords as a baron in order to continue real, practical work on causes he believed to be right.

In a lifetime in politics, idealism and realism can sometimes mix with and strengthen each other; at other times they are like oil and water.

Losing to John Major in the 1992 general election led to Kinnock resigning as leader, absolutely certain that a vicious personal campaign against him, led by the *Sun* and the *Daily Mail*, had caused enough wavering voters not to put their trust in him. He was very close to becoming prime minister but he undoubtedly paved the way for Labour's subsequent victory in 1997.

In 1985, though, he was a vibrant and exciting orator, whose performance at the conference was welcomed excitedly by party activists and ordinary labour voters alike.

The watching David Owen realized that now Labour might return to their previous strength and that would be at the expense of the SDP. That experiment, with its disastrous splitting of the vote, was over. The SDP Gang of Four should have stayed within the Labour Party.

For me it was less the bashing of Militant that was significant and more Kinnock's statement of values. I was profoundly opposed by now to all privilege. The Tories and their supporters plainly benefited most from entrenched privilege in British society and only the Labour Party wanted to tackle it. My life experience consisted of a catastrophic spell at a grim public school full of Tories, and a life-changing, life-saving even, spell at a council-run and council-funded further education college. On that basis alone I was convinced of the value of the Labour Party.

Furthermore, the notion of self-interest governing an individual's actions in relation to others and society as a whole seemed wrong. Margaret Thatcher said in 1987, 'There's no such thing as society', letting slip her true view of the world as a rat race, a survival-of-the-fittest battle where only the idle would be disadvantaged. This absurd notion, that if you work jolly hard the rewards of life would inevitably follow, was repellent.

At university there was a student who owned a cigarette lighter that cost £85. To the rest of us this was a small fortune. It was operated by passing your thumb over a beam causing it to ignite. Me and my friend Huw (with whom I went in for much late-night theorizing, which he termed 'perusing the mysteries of Fabianism', before driving the Mini that my chartered accountant father had bought for me up the A2 for breakfast at the twenty-four-hour services) asked him how he felt about such extravagance when there were better things he could do with his riches (give it away to the poor was our considered alternative).

'Survival of the fittest, innit?' he said.

Later that night we discussed how we should have

thrown his lighter in the duck pond outside Keynes College but we just sneered at him and sloped off.

He was wealthy, he was privileged and he was convinced that all of it was an entitlement. That only the lazy or stupid couldn't have it all. It was a popular philosophy that flourished under Thatcher.

The Labour party was committed to offer disadvantaged people the opportunity to progress. It was the following passage from Kinnock's speech that generated real emotion in the conference hall and for many of the watching millions on television:

I owe this party every life chance I've had from the time I was a child. The life chance of a comfortable home with working parents, people who had *jobs*. A life chance of moving out of a pest- and damp-infested set of rooms in to a decent home built by a *Labour* council under a *Labour* government. The life chance of an education that went on for as long as *I* wanted to take it. Me and *millions* of others of my generation got *all* their chances from this movement.

It was a theme he returned to at the Welsh Labour Party Conference in 1987:

Why am I the first Kinnock in a thousand generations to be able to get to university? Why is Glenys the first woman in her family in a thousand generations to be able to get to university? Was it because our predecessors were thick? Does anybody really think that they didn't get what we had because they didn't have the talent or the strength or the endurance or the commitment? Of course not. It was because there was no platform upon which they could stand.

This passage of his speech was used throughout the 1987 general election campaign. It's this quote that was used by Barack Obama's running mate Senator Joe Biden, leading to accusations of plagiarism (Biden had used the line, without crediting Kinnock, in 1987, and been forced out of an election campaign as a consequence). The renewal of complaints about it caused an awkward moment in an ultimately successful campaign for the White House in 2008. He actually used the line many times and usually credited Kinnock. I expect he changed the name when he used it, because that would give the game away.

In much the same way as I'd bought a Kinks album because Paul Weller said he liked them, so I bought Aneurin Bevan's *In Place of Fear* because Neil Kinnock had written the foreword. I didn't find the time to read it, though; nor did I manage to finish my copy of *Marx for Beginners*.

Kinnock caught the ear with his punchy eloquence as a young MP, and tried to maintain that spirit through nine difficult years as leader of the opposition, but he was never more passionate or articulate than at that conference in 1985, when everything he said, and the way that he said it, was heartfelt, courageous and inspirational.

1986

Sophocles

By the start of my second year at Kent things were not going well. Not since the dark days of the Minor Public School had I endured so much tutting and eye-rolling. Often we were dismissed as naïve, which seemed a bit of a cheap shot at a room full of teenagers.

In the first year my best experiences had been on courses in other subjects in the humanities faculty we were obliged to take. I loved the philosophy course, found a film studies course incomprehensible and enjoyed a course in contemporary European issues, which sounded unpromising but was very interesting. I wrote a long essay about the crisis in Cyprus. You could have asked me anything about the late Archbishop Makarios in 1985.

Drama in the first year had consisted of a 'performance' course on which the students were irked by teachers who were in turn aloof, mocking and overly tactile with the prettier girls. Were they not aware of the no-touching rules? I started to see why it must be a pain in the neck to be the recipient of unsolicited feeling, squeezing and patting. I sympathized with the girls who were irritated by it, and also a little with the paunchy middle-aged teacher who couldn't resist copping a feel of the occasional bare arm. The students did little but complain about it, and everything else.

After a few weeks I'd had enough and looked into transferring elsewhere. Drama didn't feel like a subject with enough to sustain it as a single honours degree. I was close to transferring to Middlesex Poly but stuck it out because I wanted to go to a university, not a polytechnic. Feeble reasoning but there was a distinction drawn between the two in those days.

In our second year I was the student representative at drama board meetings. The various lecturers appeared contemptuous of one another. Laughter was out of the question. One of them appealed to me, a grey-haired dishevelled academic, who suggested (apparently not for the first time) that the drama department ought to be studying television, since theatre was an increasingly outmoded form of expression. I liked the idea of a cultural studies approach, with drama a part of the whole, and looked around expectantly. One of the others appeared to hate him and waited until he'd had to leave the meeting early before pushing though a string of decisions he would have queried.

Fortunately, one of the lecturers was to take a sabbatical, leaving us in the hands of Shirley Barlow, the esteemed Master of Eliot College and distinguished classicist, for a term.

Shirley Barlow was the best teacher I had at Kent. Granted, this was a small and heavily handicapped field, but she was engaging and knowledgeable and inspired commitment to her subject, classical drama, from everyone in the group. At each seminar she sat before the dozen or so second years on the course, without notes or photocopied hand-outs, and began to talk about the plays, by Aeschylus, Sophocles or Euripides, we'd had to read that week.

Asking simple questions, she tested our understanding until she had a sense of how thick we were. From then on the conversation was pitched at a level that we could join in and be stretched by. If you hadn't read that week's plays you would feel that you had missed out. By running fascinating seminars in her calm, good-natured fashion she generated a desire in the students to do the work required to ensure they could be as engaged the following week. It was a treat and a privilege.

Half my problem, of course, was that once I'd made my conceited mind up that the teachers were crap, I went back to the mode of study I'd perfected at school. That is to say, I did none. No teacher there could say I was anything but a lazy, antagonistic, grown-out adolescent with time-keeping issues. No teacher, that is, apart from Shirley Barlow.

Sophocles' *Philoctetes* was my favourite play. I liked the story, about a man banished to the remote island of Lemnos because he has such a bad infection from a serpent bite to the foot that he both smells terribly rancid and wails in agony day and night. He is left by his colleagues with an invincible bow and arrow given to him by Heracles at his death. The arrows never miss. Years later it became clear to the Greeks that Troy would never be taken without this weapon. Odysseus and Neoptolemus, son of Achilles, go to Lemnos to try and wrest the bow and arrow, by subterfuge, from the abandoned Philoctetes.

To sympathize with lonely Philoctetes is a requirement of the drama but to empathize with him takes some doing. I was uniquely able to do so, having spent part of the previous four years in preparation, determinedly empathizing with the caged animals, under experimentation, depicted on Animal Aid posters.

Philoctetes had some similarities with the self-pitying Masha in *The Seagull* too, though, unlike her, he had sound reason. Chekhov had his characters moan like Philoctetes but with no good reason, which is where the comedy always came for me.

For Masha's: 'I'm in mourning for my life', take this lament of Philoctetes:

'Oh my country and you unsleeping Gods, if you have any pity still bring vengeance, vengeance, late though it be, on all my persecutors! Misery is my life, yet if I might live but to see them perish, I could believe my torture ended.'

That would make an amusing epitaph on a gravestone.

The pain that Philoctetes feels is of abandonment and loss. His terrible, oozing, unhealing sore comes to represent his inner torture as it becomes clear that the agony of his fate, alone on an island with only the hills and the rocks to talk to, is far worse to him than the physical injury that brought him there.

Which is harder to bear, a life of constant pain, or abandonment by friends and family? Sophocles poses the question and grants Philoctetes wonderful poetic speeches of anger to express his torment. The playwright dispenses with any other inhabitants on Lemnos, present in other versions of the tale, in order to emphasize the plight of Philoctetes.

If everyone bore their unseen emotional injuries physic-ally, for the world to see, then many would wail and scream like Philoctetes, and be treated differently, perhaps worse, by those who knew them.

I made an effort to please Shirley Barlow by working hard on essays, even achieving a B++ for one which was good for me. The last essay I wrote for her I spent all night on (I imagined that I worked better at night), consequently sleeping in and, to my lasting regret, missing her final seminar.

When I told my tutor about how good Shirley Barlow had been, he told me to tell her, as she would appreciate that. I hadn't thought of teachers being interested in the views of their students until then.

As dissatisfying to me as the course itself was the state of student drama, which had a deserved reputation for staging bad productions of well-known plays. No one was doing any writing of their own. There was no cabaret or revue. I wrote to the UKC Dramatics committee and suggested that we ought to be creating our own shows. They didn't reply so I put some posters up saying that a new theatre company was to be formed and anyone interested should come to a meeting. Half a dozen curious drama students turned up and we found an empty seminar room to try and work in.

Clutching a copy of Keith Johnstone's book *Impro*, I set about ineptly trying to run a 'workshop'. After a while we were put out of our misery by the college porter, who threw us out of the room since we hadn't booked it. UKC Dramatics had booked all the rooms in college that were available, for their rehearsals.

By now I was crosser and frowning more than ever. Undeterred, we decided to carry on by using whichever room we could until we were moved on.

I wanted to call the group Theatre Device, inspired as I was by The Stranglers' song 'Nuclear Device'. A couple of the others didn't think much of that idea and proffered Ad-Lib Theatre Company. I had my own way in the end through the time-honoured tactic of the Sulky Huff, also known as the Huffy Sulk.

Theatre Device decided to devise a play to take to schools. We sat down to discuss a topic. Only one issue was ever on the agenda at the time and it was immediately decided that we should do a show about violence against women, principally the always thorny subject of rape. I approached a well-known campus feminist who I'd met in the first year to see if the university Women's Group would help with any reasearch. After a day or two word came back that they would not talk to a man about rape and that they didn't think any men should be involved with a show about rape. I suspected they subscribed to the All Men Are Rapists school of thought. We decided not to do a show about rape.

Settling on a show about racism, we then had to deal with the problem that we were all white Home Counties types. Could we have a white person pretending to be a black or Asian person enduring persecution?

This seemed out of the question so we came up with the idea of depicting a couple with an Eastern European surname being victimized during the McCarthy era witch-hunts in America. None of us had any knowledge of the extent to which people were unfairly hounded as suspected Communists at that time.

We wrote to schools in the East Kent area and were invited to take our show to one in Canterbury and one in Folkestone.

Copying Snap Theatre's approach, as seen at Loughton College, we arranged the kids on four sides of a rectangle with entrances in the corners. The highlight of the show was the moment a brick comes through a window at the home of the couple with the surname that sounds like a Communist sympathizer's. Crouching out of a sight with a pane of unwanted glass, donated by a Kentish glazer, concealed in a box, at the appropriate moment I'd drop half a brick on it. The kids loved that. It made them jump.

After they'd watched our short play about bigotry and victimization we sat down with them and conducted a debate about racism.

This was a struggle. Faced with a bunch of cocksure kids I heard a familiar question from my school days:

'Why don't they all go home?'

We spent some time bringing their own bigotry into the open, failed to give them answers that satisfied them, and left.

A few days later I received a letter, on Kent County Council Education Committee notepaper, which read:

20th June, 1986.

Mr. A. Davies,
Theatre Devices,
29 Grimshill Road,
Whitstable,
Kent.

Dear Mr. Davies,

    I would like to thank you most sincerely for working with the 3rd Year classes on Monday afternoon. From conversations I have had with them today they all enjoyed themselves and certainly benefited from your approach and the subject matter has certainly given them a talking point.

    Should you wish to come back to the Frank Montgomery School again we should be delighted to have you in school.

Yours sincerely,

M. Askew,
(Head of 4th Year).

It hadn't occurred to me that the teachers would follow up with the kids the next day. Theatre Device had done something worthwhile. Whilst we were pleased with the response we immediately disbanded, due to artistic differences (the rest of them thought I was a control freak).

Diego Maradona

Watching the 1986 World Cup was going to be tricky.

Our damp and grimy student house in Whitstable, with its ice on the inside of the windows through the winter and its year round slug-farm kitchen, was equipped only with a tiny black-and-white portable telly that I'd brought from home.

Buying a colour TV licence was out of the question. Any spare cash we had (none) was converted to fifty-pence pieces for the electricity meter. Besides, my housemates (a couple, which makes for a horrible state of affairs for The Third Man in the house) were television snobs. If my girlfriend Jill had come over and we were watching TV they'd remark that we were 'tellyheads' as if we were missing the world around us which they, naturally, with their joss-sticks, ethnic fabrics and supercilious *faux*-casual manner, were at one with. If Jill went to make a pot of tea, the girl would mutter to the boy: 'well-trained', as if Jill was conditioned into servility by my caveman insistency. She wasn't, she was from Yorkshire, where they love a cup of tea.

Despite the sneering hippies, I brought another portable down, from my bedroom in Loughton. The fine for not paying the licence fee was beyond our means, so the colour telly was used for England matches, with the proviso that I'd pay the fine if we were uncovered by the supposedly ubiquitous TV detector vans no one had ever seen. This never came up thankfully and the hippies, predictably, watched the games.

The 'Mexico 86' tournament was intended to be held in Colombia but that turned out to be a disastrous idea and it was switched late in the day. England, managed by Bobby Robson, were to play their first match against Portugal.

Still thriving in England at that time was the unshakeable certainty that the English were the best at everything. Our television was the best in the world. Our police force was the best in the world. Our army was the best in the world. As was our legal system, our parliament, our chips, our beer and all of our goalkeepers! 'Best in the world' was a very popular phrase, often heard. The Portuguese were small fry and we would brush them aside.

3 June 1986 Portugal 1 England 0.

Doubtless they were up all night in Lisbon but in England the disappointment was tangible. Fortunately, the next match offered a perfect chance to make amends. Morocco had drawn 0–0 with Poland but would surely be 'put to the sword' to set England on their way.

6 June 1986 England 0 Morocco 0.

Bryan Robson, England's glass-jawed Captain Marvel, fell over and dislocated his shoulder. Ray Wilkins, Robbo's smooth-talking running mate with his perma-tan and apparent ability to play without perspiring, was sent off for chucking the ball at the ref. Now England would have to play Poland in their final group match with a hole in the heart of the team. Bobby Robson was forced into changes.

Trevor Steven and Steve Hodge played on the flanks. Peter Reid tackled everything in midfield and Glenn Hoddle was given a spot in the middle of the team at last, instead of being wasted on the wing. Hoddle was a cissy with vanity issues but his passes appeared to be guided by lasers. The manager's beloved big number nine, Hateley, was dropped, as was the winger, Waddle, who was supposed to cross for the big number nine to head it in, as part of England's 1930s tactical masterplan. Also picked, at last, was the best player England had found for years, Newcastle's Peter Beardsley.

11 June 1986 England 3 Poland 0.

England were better balanced, with the ball on the ground more. Beardsley linked well with Gary Lineker, who scored a hat-trick by half-time. Our lads were sweltering but, against a Polish team reared on pig fat sandwiches and acid rain, the Mexican climate was not an issue, even though players lost pounds of fluid every game, as we were continually reminded.

The newspapers, who had wanted Robson quartered in Trafalgar Square, now hailed England as potential winners of the tournament, as the knock-out rounds began.

18 June 1986 England 3 Paraguay 0.

Lineker, who'd already scored once, was elbowed in the throat, off the ball. This confirmed everything we knew about South Americans (particularly those of us who had never been to South America or met any of its inhabitants), that they were dirty, cheating bastards.

'Unquestionably deliberate,' said Jimmy Hill on the BBC. 'Lineker abused. Brutally, deliberately and cynically, by the South Americans.'

All South Americans, not just the one Paraguyan, the lot of them.

Beardsley scored while Lineker was off the field and then Goalden Gary scored again, putting England through to a quarter-final with some other South Americans.

Argentina had won the World Cup in 1978, playing in Buenos Aires. Just missing out on a place in their squad that year was a teenage wonder-kid who they had high hopes for. By the 1982 World Cup, Diego Maradona was twenty-one and part of their team. He had speed, close control, shooting power and a much-discussed low centre of gravity. His disadvantage was that he was about three feet high. He also had, as we found out in 1982, a blue touch paper personality, with a sense of injustice that probably kept him awake at night. He would go off at the slightest provocation. In a game against Brazil, having been denied a clear penalty and with Brazil winning comfortably, he planted his studs with maximum force into the crotch of Batista, who had just accidentally connected with another Argentinian's head.

As he left the field following his sending off, he struck a defiant pose that told onlookers he would kill any man who pointed out he was about to cry.

England had not been drawn against Argentina in the 1982 World Cup, fortunately, with that tournament coming a few weeks after the Falklands conflict. Football had been affected, with Tottenham's Argentine midfielder, Ossie Ardiles – who I had once collared for an autograph in a Loughton newsagent – having to buy sweets for his children in Paris for a few months as he was loaned to a French team out of harm's way.

By 1986, those Malvinas/Falklands scars were not completely healed. England and Argentina fans mingled in Mexico with one much repeated sequence on television showing two rival fans at first guarded and then embracing each other. Off the field things were tense, with trouble in the stands; on it there was one question only, could England handle Maradona? Now his country's talisman, he was the best player in the world, the captain of his team, its heartbeat and inspiration, a scorer and maker of goals, the player they would always look to. The match was played in front of 114,000 people in the heat of the day, at altitude, in Mexico City.

22 June 1986 Argentina 2 England 1.

It was 0–0 at half-time and looked too hot to bear. England had barely mustered a shot and looked to be evaporating on the pitch as a heat haze gave the pictures an otherworldly glare.

Watching with the scowling hippies and assorted other students, who were either indifferent, or who found the nationalistic tub-thumping of the pre-match build-up distasteful, I was finding it hard to concentrate.

Early in the second half, Maradona beat three men and tried a one-two. Fenwick intervened but sliced the ball back towards his own goal. Shilton came out but was beaten by a leaping Maradona, who had continued his run and adjusted to the trajectory quickest. He headed into the net. One nil.

Then we could see Butcher slapping the front of his wrist with his hand. Shilton was waving frantically at the ref. Fenwick too was protesting. They were all signalling handball.

'Handball!' I shouted.

The hippies had no idea what this meant.

'It was handball.' I said it as if I'd spotted it at the time, with my special football-eyes.

The referee gave the goal. The commentators began to question the selection of a Tunisian referee. How could he be *au fait* with the dirty tricks of the South Americans? Someone wiser to their ways should have been appointed, from a major footballing nation.

A few minutes later, Maradona, marked by Beardsley, received the ball in midfield, with Peter Reid, melting though he was, valiantly snapping after him. Maradona spun and twisted, sliding the ball away from Reid and past Beardsley before setting himself to face the England goal sixty yards away. He knocked the ball forwards with apparent violence but it stopped a few feet in front of him as he commanded it to. His method of control was unique, a range of chopping, cutting, jabbing moves, with his feet like the hands of a martial arts expert, only leather-clad and studded. The ball would spin and bounce around him, bemusing everyone else.

He accelerated as if powered by an inboard motor. First Butcher, then Fenwick put themselves between him and the goal but he slanted past them as if they were trees. Approaching Shilton, he feinted left, went right, and scored.

'You have to say that's magnificent,' said Barry Davies disconsolately, as the little cheat ran and jumped and bounded away. He celebrated as if all the world would thank him for taking these English down a peg or two. Perhaps it would.

I grumbled about the handball goal. One of the hippies pointed out it was 2–0 now.

'He'd never have scored the second without the first,' I said.

There was no logic to that but it felt true somehow. It was as if Maradona was now motivated to do something stunning, by the change in atmosphere, by a guilty conscience, by the sheer releasing joy of taking the lead for Argentina. Something seemed to power him on that amazing run to score the best goal anyone had ever seen.

Two years previously, Watford's John Barnes had scored a similar solo goal for England in a 2–0 friendly win at the Maracana in Brazil. Now Barnes was brought on and with ten minutes left he beat his man and chipped a cross on to Lineker's head for England to score. Just before the end he did it again but this time Lineker was flattened by an Argentinian and there was no goal and no penalty.

Argentina won their semi-final against Belgium with two

more goals from Maradona and then beat Germany in the final. No one has ever seemed more elated to hold a trophy than Maradona was. After being left out in '78, and sent off in '82, he was victorious. Asked about punching the ball into the net against England, he said it was: 'The Hand of God'. The colour telly was switched off for the last time.

That summer, me and Jill went InterRailing across Europe. I persuaded her that we should start by going to Stockholm to watch Sweden play England. At the game one of the rogues' gallery among England's away support asked me where I was from.

'London,' I said, in my best mockney. Loughton had an 01 phone number and it was on the Central Line but it certainly wasn't London.

'Lunnun?' he mimicked. I smiled weakly.

'Where'd you come from?' I asked.

'Harwich,' he said.

It took me months to realize that he'd boarded the ferry at Harwich and was mocking me.

England lost 1–0 and there was fighting in the town that night. We saw windows smashed at the railway station and heard the booming echo of hooliganism amplified by the cavernous terminal. I took a photo of a Swedish newspaper board the next day that mentioned English hooligans.

A year later Maradona turned out at Wembley stadium, playing for a Rest of the World team against a Football League XI. The League won 3–0, with two goals from the now repaired Bryan Robson and one from Norman Whiteside. The RoW team featured Michel Platini and Liam Brady but the focus was on Maradona. The Wembley crowd booed him throughout. It was merciless. His unique skill and talent was barely visible on a grey afternoon as the abuse weighed him down. An Italian, next to me in the stand, couldn't understand the chants being directed at Maradona.

'What is "wanker"?' he said.

I did a little mime.

Rory Bremner

Pete Nettell was a graduate of Kent University's drama department who stayed on for a further year to form the NATC. The New Adaptations Theatre Company. Clever and artistic, with flair and talent, Pete was also ambitious and planned to use our small drama studio to stage a promenade production of Ibsen's *Peer Gynt*, with a company of four men and four women. I volunteered, as did my good friend, the very handsome Andy Robinson. We were to rehearse for ten weeks, every night, in order to tackle the three hours of material. Pete wanted an athletic company so we had half an hour of aerobics each night. On all fours, waving my leg out behind me with a fellow student shouting, 'Five, six, seven, eight!' was the least appealing part of my day. After a few weeks, discipline slackened off. Jason Blake, who had become a good mate too, brought some cans of lager to a rehearsal and cracked a couple open. Pete was not best pleased.

Come the performances though, we thought Pete had pulled off something amazing. The best thing any of us had been involved in. Jason peeling away the layers of an onion as the elderly Peer was moving and the use of the studio to transport the audience around the world, following Peer's adventures, was ingenious and showed remarkable invention on virtually no budget. We were hopeful that the invited selectors from the National Student Drama Festival would be impressed enough to invite us to take part in their annual event. We had a clue it may not have been as good as we'd hoped when a Radical Feminist lecturer damned us with the faintest praise:

'You must have all worked very hard.'

We were turned down for the NSDF but Pete decided instead to go for the Edinburgh Fringe Festival that summer. We would all have to think of ways to raise money if we wanted to go, which we did.

There was to be a half-marathon held in Canterbury on 18 May and I entered. I went out training by myself. Running along the beach up to Tankerton slopes. I went five times and had managed nine miles on my last run. Having secured the life-altering sum of £70-worth of sponsorship, I set off in a hideous pale-blue and white candy-striped matching vest and shorts, with yellow-striped electric blue Adidas trainers.

It was a hot day. Starting near the back of the field I had a scare early on when the police, who had been holding traffic on the ring road for the runners, decided everyone had gone through and released some cars. Canterbury's ring road can be hairy enough in a car but in a pastel jogging suit it was hazardous in the extreme.

'Hey!' I shouted, while sprinting across a roundabout, dodging irate drivers. I made it through unscathed and was coping until I reached nine miles when I hit 'the wall' at Iffin Lane. The dire warnings issued by Scottish Claire, from the theatre company (that made her sound like Fraser from *Dad's Army* saying I was 'doomed'), came back to haunt me:

'People train for *weeks* for those things!'

'I've been running a few times.'

'How many times?'

'Five.'

'*Five!* You're mad.'

I jogged at walking pace for the last four miles. Despite

being only twenty, and looking the part in my outfit, in truth I was an undernourished smoker whose idea of complex carbohydrates was a packet of seafood Nik Naks. I was being passed by the elderly and the infirm.

The thirteen miles began and finished at the St Lawrence Cricket Ground. Jill met me, with Pete's trusted stage manager John. It took me two and a half hours. Fortunately, Jill had a way of laughing at me without it feeling unkind. Poor John had obviously been waiting for ages.

'Are you all right?' he smiled.

'Just about,' I said.

'We thought you'd died.'

Pete managed to persuade the student union to part with £2,000 to fund our Edinburgh trip. My £70 was also very useful, he assured me.

Edinburgh wasn't until August though; before that we all had to be involved in productions at the Gulbenkian Theatre, staged by the fourth years specializing in directing. I played the father in Boris Vian's *The Empire Builders*, in which a family flee a terrible noise by running upstairs. Each time they go up, they leave someone behind. In the corner of the room all the time is a *schmurz*, which the family assault when they can't express their frustrations adequately to each other. I can't remember who played the *schmurz*; he was mummified in bandages throughout. What a part.

I had to shoot him at the end. The *schmurz*, not the actor.

A few days later I went to a doctor, complaining of a loss of hearing. I told him all about the ear trouble I used to have as a boy, and how my dad had had the same thing, and how it felt like it used to back then but much worse. He examined me seriously for some time but couldn't find anything and began to look quite concerned.

'Have you been exposed to any loud bangs?'

'I did have to fire a gun in a play,' I said.

He looked at me across his desk.

'Was it loud?' he said.

'Very,' I said.

There was a silence as he wrote something on a pad.

'Do you think that's what caused it?' I said.

He raised his eyes to mine and then looked down again. More silence followed. He carried on scribbling. I left feeling like I might be in trouble. My hearing came back soon afterwards.

My dad and stepmum came to see the play. As usual, when confronted with a character in middle age, I just did an impression of my dad. He didn't seem to notice and they were kind enough not to mention my pulling the set over. To create the impression of rooms becoming smaller, the set was made with cardboard boxes which were pushed inwards each time the family went 'upstairs'. The cast had to wear cardboard clothes too. As I bent down to crawl through the hole in to the smallest room, prior to my epic act three monologue, I snagged my cardboard costume on the wall of the cardboard box set, bringing boxes crashing down behind me. I was oblivious and carried on acting away, while student stage hands, all in black, were suddenly revealed, slouching, bored, and staring into space. The glare of the lights fell on them and they froze before hurriedly trying to build the boxes back up.

'What a lot of lines you had,' said my dad.

Now we could look forward to Edinburgh. Pete wanted to put on a musical version of an ancient Greek comedy, Aristophanes' *Lysistrata*, and call it *Lysistrata!* as in *Oklahoma!*

Lysistrata is the famous tale in which the eponymous heroine persuades the women of Athens to deprive their men of their conjugal rights until they make peace not war. Early in the play she sums up her plan:

If Aphrodite of Cyprus and her sweet son Eros still breathe hot desire into our bosoms and our thighs, and if they still, as of old, afflict our men with that distressing ailment, club-prick – then I prophecy that before long we women will be known as the Peacemakers of Greece.

The thought of singing was appalling but it seemed there might be a chance for me and Andy to be funny. Andy made me laugh, usually with impressions. Walking down Whitstable High Street one day he waited for a car to go past before launching into motor racing commentator Murray Walker. Holding his nose he whined at high volume: '*Annnddd therrreee is . . .*' I countered with what I thought was a decent David Coleman. Scanning through the Edinburgh Fringe programme, we saw Rory Bremner was on and decided that we'd go and see his show before trying to meet him afterwards to share our impressions with him.

For most of *Lysistrata!* all of the men in the company wore concealed false erections. We had wire coat hangers around our waists with a piece of wire protruding quite a long way forward. This was then wrapped in fabric and tape before being covered with a stocking. We should all have had tetanus jabs as a precaution.

Wielding these members, the men are tormented by the women. In one scene Pete had the four men in the cast sit down while the four women came up behind them and suggestively rubbed up against them whilst unbuttoning the men's shirts and putting their hands inside. Eventually they retreat back into their barricaded haven, leaving the men at bursting point.

Rubbing up against me was the big-haired and big-breasted Sexiest Girl in the Company, who had allowed radical feminism to pass her by in favour of a first-class degree in 'Flirtation and if-you've-got-it-flaunt-it-ness'.

As I was being molested by her, the other three boys were all writhing in pleasure as they were being teased to a near-climax so I sat still, looked terrified and kept my shirt done all the way up to the top. As those magnificent mammaries bounced around behind me and a spectacular mane of hair was tossed about my face, the little audience in the Old St Paul's Church and Hall howled with laughter. Success! Laughs! From actual paying punters for the first time in my life! The scene ended and Andy winked at me as we went back to the wings. 'Well done,' he said conspiratorially.

Some of the cast weren't happy, feeling upstaged. Pete told me they'd been asking what I was doing.

'Nothing,' said Pete. 'It's just funny.'

He had wanted me to open up my shirt and writhe like the others but he let me have my funny moment. He also gave me the chance to rewrite part of the play into a more contemporary monologue. Creating a character called 'Gary Bailiff', I would enter to the strains of 'ooh Gary Bailiff' which we'd pinched from Radio One's *Gary Davies Show*. The monologue, attempting to persuade the women to come out and relieve the men, wasn't funny, but it was nice of Pete to let me try. He also allowed me and Andy to write a 'funny' blurb for the programme, which we ended with the line:

'Pete Nettell is 97.'

This joke, lifted from *Private Eye,* was hilarious to us but no one else. All our attempts at humour were exciting for us, no matter how hopeless. We sold some tickets after a reasonable review in *The Scotsman* and everything was going well, though me and Andy hated being out every day singing songs and trying to give out flyers. We would skulk at the back while our female company members worked the crowd. We loved the city though, the Royal Mile, Princes Street Gardens, up Calton Hill to Edinburgh's Disgrace. We climbed the Scott Monument from where you can see the Forth Bridge and staggered around The Meadows one night after too many pints of heavy. I've loved Edinburgh and the festival ever since and sometimes wish that I could experience it all again for the first time.

Some of the company were staying at Scottish Claire's parents' house. The rest of us had to share a tiny flat. Me, Andy, Pete and John shared a room with one double bed. We were there for two weeks so Pete and John had the bed for one week and me and Andy for the other. Lying on the floor one night, we struggled not to laugh as Pete and John bickered above us about whose toenails needed cutting.

Earlier that week we'd been north of Edinburgh to visit the family of the Sexiest Girl in the Company. We'd had a great time there and they'd shown us a video of *An Audience with Billy Connolly*. Me and Andy had never seen anything funnier. It was a packed hour of hilarious material, joyously delivered in front of a showbiz audience, many of whom were weeping with laughter throughout. We really wanted to see more comedy. One day at our venue, our song-writing pianist Kate arrived in a flush of excitement.

'Oh my god,' she gasped, 'I have just seen the *best thing ever*, you *have* to go and see the Joan Collins Fan Club.'

Regretfully, me and Andy missed out on Julian Clary but we did manage to see Rory Bremner. My face was aching from laughing so much by the end. He was brilliant, his impressions of the sporting commentators I'd heard all my life, like Bill McLaren and Richie Benaud, were hilarious. Towards the end, his comedy partner joined him on stage and they held a conversation as Roger Moore talking to Sean Connery. The audience were overjoyed and both Bremner and his confrere corpsed throughout. It was the funniest show I'd ever seen and, like the Billy Connolly video we watched, the performers were enjoying it too.

We went into the foyer afterwards and saw Bremner smiling and chatting to people. He was tall and seemed to shine with some aura of comic brilliance still around him. Our plan to share our impressions with him seemed less of a good idea and we went quietly away, rubbing our aching faces.

Dennis Potter

The board game Trivial Pursuit was launched in the UK in the mid-'80s and quickly reached such a degree of popularity it could have been classed as an epidemic. A medical epidemic, in which the psychological health of the nation was at stake. The national love of the quiz, evident in the lasting popularity of television shows such as *University Challenge, Mastermind* and *Ask the Family,* was being exacerbated amongst fledgling quiz-heads by the success of *Blockbusters,* which gave school-age family members their own Q&A at 5.15 each afternoon with 'Can-I-have-a-P-please-Bob' Holness.

Trivial Pursuit gave us the chance for a quiz at home, with the opportunity to choose your area of expertise, or at least preference, since the board was divided up into subjects such as 'History' or 'Science and Nature'.

In our house, playing the game at Christmas gave rise to an obsession with Sports and Leisure, since we were all comfortable with that area. However, a cultural desert was revealed and a collective groan would go up whenever Art and Literature was an option. 'Boring!' my dad would cry. Each roll of the dice afforded two squares to pick from so it was possible to avoid Art and Literature altogether, which was something we were generally well practised at. There were Entertainment squares and each time someone landed on one of these I would be summoned: 'Come on, Alan!' Studying for a degree in drama was perceived to give me the inside track on the work of Doris Day or Edward G. Robinson.

Trivial Pursuit rewarded those with a breadth of general knowledge and a good memory. Playing amongst students, however, it became a substitute for actual learning or ideas, a test of ego and intellectual vanity, since we had no other barometer by which to measure ourselves. Consequently it was no fun, since you only needed a couple of players who were convinced that winning at this board game denoted actual levels of intelligence, for the atmosphere to become so heightened that any enjoyment would evaporate, particularly if those people were losing.

This notion of the quick intellectual fix, giving a hint of what is possible in the world of knowledge, but in a palatable board game form that does not require any effort of learning, was a masterstroke.

Television audiences had a similar experience when watching the popular soap operas. An illusion of drama, an emotional fix, but without any need for effort on the part of the viewer with scripts that were anything but elusive or demanding, that required no knowledge beyond that which could be accrued from watching the programme itself. A pacifying, mollifying journey from nowhere, to somewhere next to nowhere.

These soaps, such as *Crossroads*, *Emmerdale Farm*, and the comedically superior *Coronation Street*, were the preserve of ITV, fulfilling its remit to provide accessible popular entertainment for a returning audience that advertisers wanted to pitch products to.

It was a cosy relationship that changed dramatically when the BBC decided it would enter the soap opera market, having had huge success with the weekly American soap *Dallas*.

Despite the classic American sitcom *Soap* brilliantly lampooning the whole genre only a few years previously (with an exceptionally talented cast of comic actors including a young Billy Crystal), the public appetite for soaps was perceived to be limitless. In 1985 *EastEnders* was launched in the UK and was immediately a huge success. Throughout 1986 the domestic warfare at the Queen Vic, between Den and Angie Watts, gripped the television audience and was a ratings triumph.

At the same time as *EastEnders* was being conceived and launched, the BBC was in the midst of an exceptional period of television drama. Yorkshire TV had made Willy Russell's *One Summer* about two lads from Liverpool who go on the run to Wales, which touchingly portrayed the humour and hopelessness preoccupying school-leavers in England in 1983, but there were three BBC serials in particular that are commonly regarded as perhaps the three best in the history of British television. Alan Bleasdale's *Boys from the Blackstuff*, Troy Kennedy Martin's *Edge of Darkness*, and Dennis Potter's *The Singing Detective*.

Boys from the Blackstuff came first. Bleasdale's tale of a gang of Tarmac (the blackstuff) layers who lose their jobs was originally a single play but was well received on transmission so further programmes were made, each featuring a different character from the gang. In between the shooting of the first episode and the eventual transmission of the rest, unemployment in Britain had dramatically risen and the relevance of Bleasdale's work was greatly magnified.

Its depiction of life on the dole struck a chord with an audience delighted to see warm characters (played by much loved comic actors like Michael Angelis from *The Liver Birds* and Julie Walters) facing hardship, reflecting so well the lives of millions at that time. *Yosser's Story* featuring Bernard Hill's

Yosser Hughes character, who undergoes a nervous break-down as he tries to prevent his children being taken into care, was the most talked-about television programme of the year. Hill's depiction of a man on, and then over, the edge is menacing, sad, harrowing and distressing. This was acting of the highest calibre, portraying an emotional journey with little respite for the viewer other than the un-witting humour of Yosser's staccato speech and Bleasdale's black (as the blackstuff) comedy. Yosser goes to see a priest and tells him he is desperate. The priest asks Yosser to call him by his first name, Dan. 'I'm desperate, Dan,' says Yosser. There is a memorable scene in which Yosser tells real-life Liverpool football player Graeme Souness that he looks like him. Yosser then moves in closer to tell him he looks like Magnum as well.

The show's impact was enormous. Within a few weeks of it appearing on BBC2 it had earned a primetime repeat on BBC1.

With comedy and pathos blending, there was to be no quick emotional fix for an audience who would have to endure the suffering of entirely credible characters they'd grown to love. It was a drama that required you to meet it halfway and rewarded you with an emotional truth and a comment on the world you lived in that would resonate for years afterwards. Importantly for me it offered no succour to supporters of Margaret Thatcher and a great deal of irreverent humour. I loved it.

Meeting the writer halfway, by committing to giving the same attention to a television drama as you would a play in the theatre, finds its reward when a complex story demands the full attention of the viewer. *Edge of Darkness* was a compelling political thriller built around a bereaved father's quest for the truth concerning his daughter's murder. Bob

Peck played Ronald Craven and his daughter was played by Joanne Whalley. After her death Craven discovers that some of his daughter's belongings are radioactive and that she is involved with an anti-nuclear group who have been dying, one by one, in suspicious circumstances. As he probes further into her story, the frightening world of covert and international government operations is partially revealed. Throughout, the vision of his daughter returns to him, both tormenting and spurring him on.

There is no humorous element here, other than Joe Don Baker's CIA good guy, whose robust manner contrasts so well with the stiff English establishment figures that Craven has to contend with. Very little relieves the tension and grief in Bob Peck's exceptional portrayal of the bereaved, determined father whose world view is shaken by every new thing thing he learns. The show was watched by huge audiences and won six BAFTA awards. As with *Boys from the Blackstuff*, it was so well received that it was repeated within a few weeks, in early 1986.

This exceptionally high standard of television drama was maintained later that year when Dennis Potter's *The Singing Detective* was shown over six Sunday nights leading up to Christmas.

While *Boys from the Blackstuff* had its roots in gritty kitchen sink dramas of the '50s and '60s, with its single-play format fusing with dialogue reminiscent of the best sitcoms, and while *Edge of Darkness* drew on dramas, more common in the American cinema but familiar none the less, about high-level corruption, with a principled man facing the might of the state alone, *The Singing Detective* ploughed a new furrow.

Dennis Potter's grim depiction of a psoriasis patient, torn from his profession as a writer of detective novels by a spell in hospital, while all the time wrestling with hallucinations about characters in his books and flashbacks to his troubled childhood, set a new standard in invention and originality, the like of which is so rarely even attempted, it is likely never to be bettered.

Multiple narratives fall over one another to absorb and divert the viewer, with actors playing several characters as figures from the past merge with those both in the present and in the imagination of the main character, Philip E. Marlow, played by Michael Gambon. Marlow undergoes what amounts to an investigation of his life, both in his own mind, and in the presence of a psychoanalyst. Throughout, characters burst into song and perform elaborate dance routines, as his hallucinatory imagination takes hold. Gambon's perfect take on the embittered humour of a highly intelligent man, talked to as if he were an infant because he is perceived as helpless by the medical staff, is both funny and brittle. Marlow's childhood traumas, involving seeing his mother with a man, and the violent mistreatment of another boy, unfold before the audience as a series of overlapping narratives with jumps in time and place. There is no hope for a viewer who is not prepared to meet Potter halfway, to commit to understanding what is presented to them, and the rewards, in gymnastic story-telling, fine acting and suspenseful drama, are very great

Glued to the tiny portable telly in the front room of our grimy student house in Whitstable, I was prepared to listen to and imbibe every last syllable, to see every nuanced look and glance, to relish every exchange between analyst and patient. Nothing like this had ever come our way before. I bought the soundtrack album and Jill gave me a copy of the scripts as a present the following year when I'd finished my third-year finals. It was my favourite show. I became determined to see all of Potter's work and never missed an episode of anything he produced from then on. Much of it was obtuse or disturbing, and struggled to meet the strict criteria for sexual politics that I had been indoctrinated with at Kent, but equally much of it reached the highest standards and none of it detracted from the memory of *The Singing Detective*, possibly the finest television drama ever made.

Of all those dramas from the 1980s though, it is *EastEnders* that survives, planted in the schedules like a tumour that has grown and grown over the subsequent decades, demanding attention with its insistent promise that nothing in the show will be beyond your comprehension, so long as you agree to watch every episode, in the expectation of some greater climax that may come tomorrow but will actually never arrive.

1987

Nigel Mansell

John Watson led the British Grand Prix in 1981. Alan Jones, the reigning world champion, had crashed into Gilles Villeneuve; Nelson Piquet, who would be champion that year, had blown a tyre; and Alain Prost's Renault had broken down. Watson overtook three cars and was running in second place to the delight of the crowd, when the fastest car in the race, René Arnoux's Renault, began to falter. Watson overtook him with eight laps left. Sitting high up in the stands on a family outing, complete with ham sandwiches and warm orange squash, it was difficult to keep up with what was going on, but the crowd around me knew Watson was in front and cheered the Belfast driver all the way around Silverstone. Ten of the first twelve cars on the starting grid had retired, leaving the Argentinian, Carlos Reutemann, the only one of the eight remaining racers on the same lap as Watson, but nearly a mile behind. Watson had started fifth on the grid in his McLaren, he wasn't expected to win, having won only one Grand Prix five years previously. Would he make it? Or break down? Would he spin off? Or be taken out as he lapped the back markers? It felt set up for glorious failure. He'd never have a better chance to win his home race. All he had to do was keep it on the road for eight laps, and not, please not, run out of petrol...

He won. We stood and cheered as he whizzed past the chequered flag. My first and only Grand Prix and a British winner! Very exciting it was too, sustaining us for the two hours it took to escape the car park, which must have been designed to prevent thousands of people trying to re-enact what they'd just seen by stalling them in a holding pattern.

Among those who narrowly failed to qualify for the race were a couple of British drivers. The first, future World Sportscar Champion Derek Warwick, features in my favourite 'if only this happened every day' anecdote, in which a friend of mine was hitchhiking and Derek Warwick offered him a lift. The other Brit who missed out was Nigel Mansell.

By 1986 it had been ten years since James Hunt had been Britain's last World Champion, but now the blazingly fast and madly competitive Mansell was set to triumph. He only had to keep his position on the track, for the last twenty laps of the final race in Adelaide, to win the championship. Like Watson in 1981 he just had to stay on the road, not crash, or run out of petrol, or suffer a puncture.

When his left rear tyre blew out he was travelling at 200 mph. Sheets of hot rubber flew around the track. Sparks burst from the rear of the Williams car as it dragged along the road. Only one front wheel was touching the ground. The car kicked and squirmed as it hurtled towards the television cameras at the end of the straight. Mansell wrestled with it as it snaked along, slowing it down before bumping into a wall at the end of the straight's run-off area.

Murray Walker was frantically yelling in the commentary box: '*And look at that! Ow! That's a collos— That's Mansell! That's Nigel Mansell! – and the car absolutely shattered!*'

'What an absolute tragedy for Mansell,' said James Hunt.

Mansell's Williams team-mate Piquet was pulled into the pits to change tyres in case he too had a blowout, leaving Alain Prost free to win the race and the championship.

Sitting at home watching, we were all terribly disappointed. It's just possible to imagine millions of oblivious

Britons, going about their business, neither knowing nor caring what the outcome of the Australian Grand Prix was, but they hadn't grown up in our house. My dad bought (or possibly leased, from Granada or Radio Rentals) a colour television when they first became available, mainly because it would make it easier to identify the cars when the Grand Prix was on. The first time (and every subsequent time for several years) a race was broadcast on the new colour set, Dad would stand in front of it saying:

'Look at the colours! Crystal clear, absolutely crystal.'

Our interest in the sport had been nurtured years before. My dad's enthusiasm for rallying, and participation in rallying events as a navigator for many years, meant that he would say, 'This would be a good rallying road,' every time we hurtled down a country lane. Each time we passed a sign with the white circle and diagonal black stripe denoting that national speed limits apply he would call out: 'Fast as you like!' and gun his Cortina/Morris 1800/Austin Princess forwards with a quick downshift.

1981 was our first trip to Silverstone but we'd been to Brand's Hatch to watch Barry Sheene racing and to the Isle of Man TT, where the distinctive castor oil smell of Castrol racing oil hung deliciously in the air. Dad would sniff deeply:

'What a marvellous smell!'

It was inevitable that we would have motorbikes at sixteen and cars at seventeen but not necessarily inevitable that I would want to motor around Essex like, first, Sheene and then Mansell. I did though. Having fantasized about racing as an eleven-year-old on a pushbike I was no different as a teenager on a fizzy or driving a Mini. A favourite game was to speed through Buckhurst Hill, up to the top of the hill itself, which runs steeply down for a mile into Loughton, then shove the Mini into neutral and coast, in the dead of night with Epping Forest whistling past on both sides, before screeching (I *loved* that) right and coasting up Spring Grove to the hill halfway down, just over the brow of which was our house. I never made it over the top; gravity would beat the Mini every time.

Hand-brake turns were another favourite. Dangerous ones, between parked cars outside the Burgess sisters' house, which would bring Melanie running out, shouting:

'*Bilbo Baggins!*'

This was her name for her pet cat, not her pet name for me. She lived in constant fear of his being run over by a teenager.

On one occasion, racing someone up Buckhurst Hill, with friends in the car, my unknown rival pulled alongside and his passenger showed me his constable's helmet. The police would ask you your age, and whether you wanted to see eighteen, and then would issue you with a 'five-day wonder' instructing you to 'produce your documents' at your local police station.

Fortunately, I never hit anything in the Mini (other than the back of the Co-op) though I did once hit a child on the motorbike. He was about eleven and standing in the road outside the Minor Public School when I came round a corner. I hit his foot and flew off the bike. He was still standing as I bounced down the road. That could have been worse.

I had always wanted to go fast. My dad raced, and men do like to compete with one another. When leaving a plane after a flight, I can't resist trying to beat my fellow passengers to passport control. It's nice not to have to queue for long, but I have been in foot races with men, all of us pretending that we always walk at that speed, even when the immigration desks in the distance are completely clear.

Some of this is genetic evolution in action, thousands of years of hunting a limited supply of food, that lingers on in the species. It's this, plus testosterone and adrenaline, which makes men speed through airports while women struggle behind in wedged espadrilles shouting:

'Where's the fire?'

Partly it's anger, though. Why some of us are afflicted with the capacity for road rage, and others are not, must go beyond genetics. Something has gone on in our lives that predisposes us to turn everyday situations into conflicts.

For me, I had to compete with my older brother all my life with all pleasantries abandoned very early in the piece. Trying to prove yourself day after day, for year after form-ative year, in angry contest after angry contest, leaves deep-seated behavioural patterns that can be quickly, and not always consciously, triggered.

In early 1987, as I drove my second-hand Vauxhall Cavalier round the M25 back to Kent, I found myself in a race with a small red sports car that kept tail-gating me. I decided to floor it (the Cavalier could go from eighty to a hundred in under five minutes) but then noticed a police car in my mirror. The police went off at an exit and I immediately put my foot down. They pulled me over a few miles later, having gone off the motorway to allow me to accelerate, and then enjoyed themselves chasing me down.

It went to court in Brentwood. I drove there and parked outside the court, which was adjacent to a police station.

The court heard that I was doing:

'Between a hundred and six and a hundred and eight miles an hour.'

I'd have said: 'That'll be a hundred and seven then,' had I had the nerve, or thought of it at the time and not later.

The magistrates banned me from driving for fourteen days and fined me £95.

'How am I going to get home?'

'That's your problem.'

'No one said I'd be banned.'

I was told to go next door to the police station and ask them how I could find my way to Loughton. A police-woman gestured vaguely:

'There are buses up there.'

In the car park a feeling of injustice took over. I was being hard done by and it wasn't fair. I decided to drive. If the police stopped me I'd say I was going to a phone box to call someone to pick me up. Foolproof.

About fifty yards down the road the blue lights came and I was arrested for driving while disqualified, which meant being uninsured too. Fool.

'You'll get eighteen months for this,' said the arresting officer gleefully. For a moment I thought he meant in prison, but he was referring to a driving ban.

There were an astonishing number of cigarette burns on the floor of the room I was locked up in and much graffiti on the walls. Rather than write AL of AFC everywhere, I sat and anxiously scribbled my 'mitigating circumstances'. These were never heard, which was a shame, because they were unintentionally hilarious.

After a couple of hours I was humiliatingly taken back into the court that had just banned me, and seated, at first, in the public gallery. The man next to me, enjoying a day's spectating, said:

'You should have parked in the hospital over the road, they catch about three people a week like that.'

A few weeks later I had to go back. This time my dad came with me and we had a solicitor on legal aid. I was banned again, this time for twenty-eight days, and fined £125 at £5 a week. My dad was almost sympathetic when he'd heard I'd been doing a hundred on an empty motorway. He'd always thought seventy was too slow and was a fan of the German autobahns with their limitless freedom.

That summer, we watched on TV as Nigel Mansell pursued Nelson Piquet, in an identical Williams, at Silverstone in the British Grand Prix. He made up twenty seconds in twenty laps, before passing with a spectacular feinting, swerving manoeuvre. He won the race and was then unable to finish his parade lap as thousands of celebrating fans covered the track. Murray Walker was jubilant:

'Amazing! What an absolutely incredible drive! We've always known that Nigel Mansell had enough guts, grit and determination for any ten men. He has shown that more than ever before!'

In qualifying for the penultimate round in Japan, Mansell crashed badly, missing both that and the last race through injury, handing the 1987 title to Piquet despite winning six races to the Brazilian's three. Five years later he became World Champion, having cut out the crashes. He'd learnt his lesson. I learnt mine too. I haven't been to Brentwood since.

David Rocastle

Tony Adams destroyed my dreams of playing for Arsenal. Never mind that I hadn't been good enough for Loughton Boys, I still fantasized about Highbury as I dribbled a tennis ball around our Alsatian in the garden and fired it between two trees. All hope was gone though, when the scrawny seventeen-year-old Adams ran out against Sunderland at Highbury in November 1983. He was six months younger than me. The first boy to play for Arsenal who was born after I was. The dream was over for me.

Early in the game Adams tried to control a high ball and Sunderland's centre forward pounced to smash it into the net. It was an inauspicious start for a player who was to become a great captain for Arsenal and England.

Some debutants become exhausted by the pace after ten minutes, recover enough to join in the game, and are considered a success if they make no big mistakes, remain unambitious in their passing, and leave the field to encouraging applause when substituted after an hour.

Occasionally a debutant shines, terrorizing the opposition defence, showing apparently limitless running power, dribbling past defenders with the crowd roaring him on, before coming off at full time frustrated he was unable to do enough to force a win, dissatisfied with a goalless draw with Newcastle. That was how David Rocastle's debut in September 1985 went anyway.

Rocastle was powerful, not lean like a conventional winger, but he played on the right with commitment and excellence in every touch. By the end of the 1985–86 season he was a regular, as was Tony Adams. The manager, Arsenal legend Don Howe, had resigned, having heard that the club was involved in clandestine approaches to Terry Venables, who was managing Barcelona. Arsenal also approached Aberdeen's Alex Ferguson, before settling on an ex-player, the Millwall manager George Graham, to take over in the summer of 1986.

Rocastle became emblematic of a new young Arsenal team that was motivated, energized and unrecognizable from the mediocre side that had underachieved for several seasons. Many fans were still bemoaning the sales of Liam Brady and Frank Stapleton in 1980 and 1981. The new young players rejuvenated the team and when the opportunity arose, halfway through the 1986–87 season, to re-sign Liam Brady from Ascoli in Italy, George Graham passed it up. He was building his own team, players who all owed him something. Brady joined the Arsenal Retirement Home at West Ham. I was disappointed by Graham's decision, especially when I saw Brady score a spectacular goal against Arsenal, in a 3–1 win for West Ham at Upton Park in April 1987.

Graham's team was improving though and had been on a then club record, twenty-two-game unbeaten run that took them to the top of Division One and into the semi-finals of the Littlewood's Cup (as the League Cup was known).

The run came to an end in a violent January encounter against Manchester United at Old Trafford. Many years later Sir Alex Ferguson (who had taken over at United two months previously) acknowledged that Norman Whiteside 'committed about forty-five fouls that day'. After Whiteside had kicked Rocastle again, the nineteen-year-old South Londoner turned to confront him. Following a brief fight with the much bigger Ulsterman, Rocastle was sent off, while

Whiteside retained his impunity. It is very difficult for a
United player to be sent off at Old Trafford, short of breaking a linesman's leg, they can do what they like. Rocastle was
in tears in the dressing room afterwards. Arsenal lost 2–0
and went another eight league games before winning again,
forfeiting their place at the top of the league.

I hadn't been up to Manchester for that game; instead I'd
gone with Jill to Selhurst Park, to watch her team, Barnsley,
win 1–0 away at Crystal Palace. Seven months later, in
August 1987, I was on the terraces at Old Trafford waiting
for the game between United and Arsenal to start. Beneath
my feet was a newspaper, which I picked up. On the front
was a headline about the Hungerford massacre in which
a lone gunman had committed matricide, slaughtered fifteen more people and finally shot himself. All this in a town
that hadn't seen a murder in over a hundred years. It was
horrifying and shocking. My dad said:

'Why on earth would he kill all those people? I can understand him killing his mother, perhaps she was nagging him
or something, but why all those strangers?'

Usually, if Arsenal weren't playing at home, I'd drive to
Gillingham, twenty-five miles up the A2 from Whitstable.
The Priestfield stadium had an open terrace, at the Gillingham End, where it was easy to find a barrier to lean on one
minute before kick-off. Crowds were rarely above 3,500 and
most of those would pack into the noisy Rainham End.

My old mentor from the Bobby Moore Soccer School,
Harry Redknapp (who received a princely £1,000 as Bell's
Manager of the Year), was in charge of Bournemouth, who
were running away at the top of Division Three, being
chased by Bruce Rioch's Middlesbrough. 1986–87 was to be
the first season in which play-offs were used to decide the
last promotion place. The fifth team in Division Three had

to play the fourth-bottom side from Division Two over two legs. If they won they played the winners of a tie between the third- and fourth-placed sides. The intention was to have fewer dead fixtures, as there would be the chance for teams to make the play-offs. It was perfect for Keith Peacock's Gillingham, who had a habit of finishing fourth or fifth.

Well over 5,000 people crammed in to the Priestfield to see the last two home games, against Wigan and Bolton. Tony Cascarino, the Gills' young, tall, thickset centre forward, scored the only goal of the game against Bolton to put Gillingham into the play-offs by a point (Bolton went in to the play-offs at the other end and were relegated to Division Four).

The Gills were to play Sunderland, from Division Two. The first leg was at the Priestfield and 14,000 people turned up. It was as if half the population of the Medway towns was trying to find a way in. Much of the Gillingham End had been given over to the travelling support from Sunderland. I squeezed into the Rainham End, near the corner flag.

Early in the game a Sunderland shot was goalbound when Gills' Paul Haylock threw himself across and just reached it with his right fingertips, diverting the ball on to the crossbar. A brilliant save. Unfortunately, Haylock was the right back, not the goalkeeper. There was no mandatory red card for handling on the line then (players were very rarely sent off) but Sunderland scored from the penalty and were one up at half time.

During the second half, the player nearest to our corner was the Sunderland left back Alan Kennedy, who three years previously had won a second European Cup with Liverpool, in Rome. He received no end of stick from the Kent football public. Sunderland had never played outside the top two divisions and the Priestfield was not what

Kennedy had in mind when he signed for them. Kicking towards the Rainham End, Gillingham pushed Sunderland back and Cascarino equalized with a looping overhead kick. The ground erupted into manic, chaotic, screaming bedlam.

TO-NY! *CAS* – CARINO! TO-NY! *CAS* – CARINO!

Cascarino headed a second and then slid in for his hat trick, to give the Gills a 3–1 lead. Delirious uproar! The game finished 3–2. It was the third most exciting night I'd ever experienced in a football stadium.

In the second leg, played in front of 25,000 people at Roker Park, Gillingham scored first but then Alan Kennedy put former England international Eric Gates through to equalize. Gates then headed in his second and the aggregate scores were level at four all. Paul Haylock made another save on the line, and again escaped a sending off, but Mark Proctor's penalty was saved. Eventually, two more goals from Tony Cascarino, including one in extra time, meant the game finished 4–3 to Sunderland for an aggregate score of six all.

The Football League, in their wisdom, had decided that away goals would count double and Gillingham were through by virtue of scoring three away goals to Sunderland's two.

Arsenal's Littlewood's Cup semi-final was against Spurs, who won the first leg at Highbury, with a goal from the expert goal-poacher that Arsenal had swapped for Kenny Sansom in 1980, Clive Allen.

Spurs had Hoddle and Waddle to run the show. They were quite the double act as they were soon to demonstrate, hilariously, on *Top of the Pops* as Glenn and Chris. Hoddle's extraordinary counter-soprano murdered the chorus of an already awful song called 'Diamond Lights', while Waddle murmured into a microphone like the embarrassed Geordie he was, having possibly agreed to the whole thing when he was drunk. For Arsenal fans it was the funniest moment of television from 1987, regardless of Victoria Wood pipping *Spitting Image* at the BAFTAs.

The second leg at White Hart Lane saw Arsenal cast as underdogs. Spurs were on their way both to third, one place above Arsenal, in the league, and to an FA Cup Final. Clive Allen scored again to put them two up on aggregate. At half-time, whoever was in charge of the Tottenham public address system played 'Spurs Are on Their Way to Wembley' by Chas and Dave. They also made a euphoric announcement about ticketing arrangements for Spurs fans for Wembley. All around me, on the terrace behind the goal, Arsenal fans were furious.

The Arsenal players, in particular the big Irish centre forward Niall Quinn, were incensed in the dressing room. They could hear the tannoy. In the second half, Quinn and Viv Anderson scored to give Arsenal a 2–1 win. There was pandemonium in the Arsenal end. It was the second most exciting night I'd experienced in a football stadium.

The Football League, in their wisdom, had decided that away goals would *not* count double in the Littlewood's Cup semi-final. George Graham and the Spurs manager David Pleat came out on to the pitch to toss a coin to decide the venue for a replay. The coin stuck on its side in the mud so they tried again. David Pleat stepped out and, with a dramatic sweeping gesture using both hands, indicated that the game would be on Spurs' pitch. A huge cheer went up from the home fans.

The replay was three days later. I went with my dad since I missed out on tickets for the Arsenal end. He managed to pick up two for the terrace under The Shelf. Surrounded by Spurs fans I was in agony as Clive Allen scored again.

With eight minutes left, Ian Allinson squeezed a shot in at the near post to equalize. Extra time was looming when Allinson fired a ball low into the Spurs penalty area, it ricocheted and fell to David Rocastle who controlled it instantly before squeezing it under Ray Clemence with his, usually dormant, left foot. I controlled the urge to jump, flinching and jerking slightly as I tried to stay still. Arsenal won. My dad went home. I stood there in ecstatic silence, unsmiling, with litres of adrenaline circulating through me. Two lads came up as the terrace was emptying and said:

'Are you Arsenal?'

Perhaps I wasn't as unsmiling as I'd hoped. I weighed up the risks and said, 'Yes.'

'So are we! *Great,* isn't it?'

It was the greatest night I've ever had in a football stadium. I went back to Whitstable after the game and was still on a high two days later when I had a party for my twenty-first birthday.

Gillingham's play-off final was to be over two legs against Lou Macari's Swindon. Jill came with me to the Priestfield. When we arrived we found that the match was all-ticket. We bought a spare from someone and, just before kick-off, came across a drunk Gills fan slumped in an alleyway. Holding his ticket out to us he slurred:

'Have it. I'll never make it.'

'Do you want any money?'

'No. You go. Go in. Come on, you *Blues* . . .'

Our two tickets were for different sections of the ground but the woman on the turnstile, with much encouragement from all the lads behind us, let us in together. Gillingham won 1–0.

They lost the second leg 2–1, conceding a goal a few minutes from the end. The Football League, in their wisdom, had decided that away goals would not count double in the play-off final so, while away goals were good enough to relegate Sunderland, they were not good enough to promote Gillingham. I went up to Selhurst Park to watch the Gills lose the replay 2–0 with Swindon's star player Dave Bamber in form. It was a huge disappointment made worse because, bizarrely and against any geographical logic, Swindon and Gillingham were fierce and hated rivals. The Gills stayed in Division Three where they would play against Sunderland, who won the championship at the first attempt.

Arsenal won the Littlewood's Cup against Liverpool with two goals from Charlie Nicholas and in so doing became the first team to beat Liverpool when Ian Rush had scored. Kenny Sansom held up the first trophy I'd seen them win. Rocky Rocastle played superbly down the right.

Where I stood at Highbury, on the open northwest corner of the North Bank, there was a group who would break into the *Rocky* theme whenever Rocastle began to dribble. He won two league championships with Arsenal before Graham sold him to Leeds. He was in tears when he left.

Several years later I saw Rocky at an awards do. I went over to tell him he'd always be a legend at Arsenal. He said that meant a lot and thanked me. In 2001, aged thirty-three, he died after a short illness.

The fans still sing his name at every match.

Ian Botham

When England played Pakistan in the Fifth Test at The Oval in the summer of 1987, they were one down in the series and had to win to tie. Pakistan batted for two and a half days. Javed Miandad scored 260 over ten hours and they were finally all out for 708. England made 232 and were asked to bat again. By the end of the fourth day England had lost three second innings wickets. When Chris Broad was out on the fifth and final day, Mike Gatting, the England Captain, was at the crease and needed someone with dogged determination to drop anchor, bat all day for the team, not do anything flash, self-indulgent or reckless and forego personal glory to save his country. Next man in? Ian Botham.

I. T. Botham, the free spirit of the England game, easily bored, a tempest rarely becalmed, virulent scourge of opponents for over a decade, responsible for a series of sustained down-the-order shot-fests of towering power and ferocity. Gatting was a fine stroke player but had to restrain himself as, with no chance of winning the match, they boarded up for the draw. At the other end was the brilliant Pakistani wrist-spinner, Abdul Qadir, who had already taken ten of the fourteen England wickets to fall.

At close of play Gatting was 150 not out and I. T. Botham was still there after well over four hours with fifty-one to his name. Reining in all his instincts, he'd proved again that his reputation for selfish indiscipline was unfair. Yet, the previous summer it appeared that Botham, England's greatest ever player, might never play for his country again.

Beefy, it turned out, in the summer of 1986, liked a spliff, a bifter, a reefer, a joint. His friendship, born of many years playing together for Somerset, with West Indies batting legend Viv Richards possibly went beyond cricket and into other Caribbean pastimes.

Botham acquired the habit of wearing a red, gold and green wristband perhaps from Richards, an Antiguan with a keen interest in his African heritage. The red, representing the blood shed on African soil, the gold, symbolizing the riches plundered from Africa by imperialists, and the green, for the lush fertility of the African land, is the most important symbol of Rastafarian culture and the three colours make up the flag of Ethiopia as well as being used in many African and West Indian flags. Richards had to deny that he was a Black Power advocate when he displayed the colours.

Botham wore them too, not just on his wristband, but also on a jumper playing golf, or in blazers worn by him and Richards at a special cricket match organized by his then manager. The man portrayed as a hard-drinking, womanizing, angry bruiser had brushed up close to the easy-going reggae culture of the man he regarded as his older brother, Richards, but it only led to more trouble for him when it came out that he'd made acquaintance with cannabis.

He revealed his love of a toke in an article in the *Mail on Sunday*, which seems an astonishing misreading of the possible consequences. The readership of the *Mail on Sunday* had, at that time, voted *en masse* for Margaret Thatcher and would do so again in 1987. They had previously shown little interest in a liberal attitude to drug use and didn't care to be reminded that the world beyond their net curtains was not as they would wish it to be.

Botham triggered an immediate 'disgusted of Tunbridge Wells' backlash, coupled with moralistic attacks in all the other newspapers (whose noses may have been put out of joint by Beefy's exclusive deal with the *Mail on Sunday*). There was more to the story than met the eye, inevitably. Botham was forced to settle with the *Mail on Sunday*, having previously tried to sue them and did so by providing them with a confession, of sorts.

All Botham's chickens came home to roost and he was banned for nine weeks over the summer, which would mean missing several England Test matches. Plenty of time for barbecues and big fat joints in the garden then.

Botham's rubbishing of the establishment figures that ran the game led to trouble within cricket and his news-worthy exploits outside cricket sold newspapers. When he lost his place in the England team it was the first time he'd been dropped since he made his debut in 1977. That had also been the year of John McEnroe's breakthrough at Wimbledon, and, like McEnroe, by the time Botham finished his playing career he would be unarguably among the best of all time, and would upset the entire establish-ment running the game in England on the way. He would also become the most popular sportsman in the country. There will never be any cricket team, never mind just an England side, that would not be improved by the inclusion of Botham.

The spirit of rebellion was in the air in 1977 as the Sex Pistols were barred from BBC radio and prevented from reaching number one in the charts with their contribution to the Queen's Silver Jubilee, 'God Save the Queen'. Botham was not channelling Johnny Rotten though, as he bashed his way around England's cricket fields. His rebellious-ness didn't appear to be a calculated thing. He seemed to have more energy, vitality and gusto than anyone else. The relatively sedate pastime of cricket was too frail to hold him.

There is just too much time, with too little to do, at a cricket ground. Too much time for Botham's inner rubber band to wind and wind itself taut, before spinning him into a confrontation, a row, or a boozy release.

In 1977, my dad sometimes put my brother and me on a train to Southend to watch Essex play cricket. We were also taken to Lord's to see England. We had been taught to score, in little cricket scorebooks, while sitting at the boundary line at Woodford Wells CC. None of the club players were known to us so my dad would give them nicknames based on their appearance.

Black Hair, c Baldy b wrong foot 18

Long drives on summer holidays were made to the accompaniment of Brian Johnston on BBC Radio's *Test Match Special*. We were also taught a solitary cricket game, known as 'Dob Cricket'. Using a pin, the player sticks it into a page of newsprint where the lettering is densely packed (the *Daily Telegraph* obituary section was best), each letter of the alphabet was equivalent to some action in cricket. If the pin landed in space it was a dot ball (the dot referring to the cricket scorer's notation of a ball from which no run is scored and no wicket taken). A variation of this game can be played with dice. Using a cricket scorebook filled with made-up teams and made-up games, hours of time alone can be filled. These carefully devised games successfully re-created the to and fro of a cricket match. Scores were realistic, even though it was not possible for the pin or the dice to differentiate between a batsman who was a clueless number eleven and the great Viv Richards. The game was good enough for a schoolboy anyway and fostered a love of cricket.

No game devised though could have incorporated the

talents of Botham, who changed the parameters of what is possible on the field of play. It was 1981 when Botham redefined cricket excellence and set a standard by which every hapless English cricketer has been judged ever since, casting a shadow over the sport in his country in the same way that Don Bradman had in Australia and Gary Sobers had in the West Indies.

Botham was leading England in the Ashes against Australia. He was playing poorly and England were one down in the six-match series when Botham quit as captain after the Second Test.

His natural talent and restlessness made him an inappropriate choice for captain, traditionally the role given to the most mature, clear-thinking player in the team. Those who had appointed him were quick to announce that they were about to sack him anyway, which seemed unhelpful. He was by far England's best player and his confidence was shot but they still felt inclined to humiliate him. It was by no means certain he'd be selected for the next match. His failure as captain appeared to delight those who thought him fortunate to be blessed with talent but without the intelligence to make the most of it. Others sympathized with the plight of a man cast as the scapegoat.

The Australians held Botham in high regard and wouldn't have minded too much if he'd been dropped from the England team altogether. A few years later Botham is reported to have told the Australian batsman Allan Border that he was contemplating emigrating to Australia. Border allegedly told him he'd receive a passport quicker than Zola Budd (the South African distance runner who was shamelessly fast-tracked into the British Olympic team as a medal hope in 1984 while her home nation was banned due to apartheid).

Fortunately, Botham was selected and took six wickets in

the first innings of the Third Test, held at Headingley. He then scored fifty but England were skittled out and forced to follow on. With five wickets down in the second innings and close to defeat, Botham said to his partner, the young fast bowler Graham Dilley, 'Let's have some fun.' He smashed the ball to all corners and amassed 149 not out. England had seemed so certain to lose that bookmakers were offering 500–1 against them winning. The Australians Dennis Lillee and Rod Marsh had a bet on England since the odds were so crazy (and seemed indicative of the English need to kick their own men when they're down). Botham's remarkable, thumping, swinging, battering innings, combining the power of a heavyweight boxer with the hand-to-eye co-ordination of a concert pianist, thrilled the television audience. It was easy to be lifted out of your seat in excitement. It became necessary to watch standing up, because his best blows would cause you to jump and shout out:

'YES! GO ON, BOTH! WHERE'S THAT ONE GONE? LOOK! IT'S GONE MILES! *MILES!*'

The next day, England bowled out Australia, with eight wickets going to Bob Willis, and the series was tied.

In the Fourth Test Australia were back on top and needed forty-five to win with five wickets standing. An easy target, a foregone conclusion. Botham came on to bowl. He took all five wickets in twenty-eight deliveries, conceding only one run. It was the single greatest spell of bowling in living memory. He charged in and hurled the ball down and through Australians who were flattened as if he'd bowled a wardrobe at them. The Birmingham crowd roared their approval. England were now ahead 2–1 in a series that, without Botham, they would have been losing 3–0.

In the Fifth Test at Old Trafford, England were five down in the second innings for 104, and in danger of not setting the Australians a high enough target. Botham came in and assaulted the ball and the Australians simultaneously. One of his sixes appeared to be aimed at his good mate Lillee, who was far more used to playing the fearsomely intimidating aggressor. He had to take evasive action.

Botham scored 118, set a record for sixes in an innings against Australia, and helped England post 404, which was enough to win and clinch the series 3–1 with one to play. The last match was drawn with Botham taking ten wickets. It's highly likely that, had he been dropped after the Second Test, England would have lost the series 5–0. It became known as 'Botham's Ashes'.

Living up to those standards for the rest of his career weighed heavily but his achievements were still remarkable. In 1986 he was recalled to the team, after his marijuana suspension, needing one wicket against New Zealand to equal Dennis Lillee's world record number of Test victims. With the crowd roaring him in once again he managed it with only his second ball and within twelve balls had broken the record. He then picked up his bat and smashed fifty in no time.

That winter England went down to Australia with Botham back in harness and retained the Ashes. His 138 in 174 balls in the First Test in Brisbane set the tone. It was his fourteenth and last Test hundred. He finished his test career with over 5,000 runs and a record haul of 383 wickets.

Following his retirement from cricket, he continued to inspire with remarkable feats of distance walking, all to raise money for leukaemia research. The pace of his walks was extraordinary as he ignored pain and left would-be accomplices by the roadside. News crews would struggle to film him as puny local reporters were forced to run alongside the striding, unsmiling giant, hoping for a comment.

The millions he has raised will have contributed enormously to developments in the treatment of leukaemia patients, perhaps prolonging the life of some mother's son. Or some son's mother.

Ian McKellen

The hurricane of 1987 blew across Kent, knocking down six of the seven oaks of Sevenoaks. It woke me up by blowing next door's chimney stack into their backyard and blocked the back road from Whitstable to Canterbury with fallen trees.

Other than that meteorological intrusion, the campus felt cut off from reality, perched on a hilltop overlooking the town. It began to feel necessary to connect with the rest of the world. The previous summer, many of us had travelled out to Folkestone every day to teach English as a foreign language, to teenagers from Germany (generally diligent) and Switzerland (generally struggling to establish an identity to the point where one of them insisted on being called Vladimir).

This was good fun. A couple of the Swiss kids were into bike racing and wanted to go to the Grand Prix because a Swiss rider called Jacques Cornu was racing in the 250 cc class. I said if they wanted we could go to watch speedway. So we did. It was a four-team tournament, hosted by the Canterbury Crusaders, which included the Hackney Kestrels, who I saw win the British Cup in 1984. The Swiss kids loved it, as did I.

In the classroom, I found it difficult to keep control unless I was talking, so I told them stories to entertain them. They said they loved my funny stories. Of course they did, while I was talking, they weren't having to write or speak any English. Furthermore, while they were in the classroom they weren't being chased all over Folkestone by local youths, who could easily identify them, since they all had the same bright blue EFL bag.

During term-time by far the best way I found to remove myself from the university life I was beginning to hate was to go on demonstrations and the late '80s were full of them.

An anti-nuclear rally was held in Hyde Park to commemorate the first anniversary of the Chernobyl nuclear reactor disaster in Ukraine. At the time of the accident, Ukrainians were not told about it, since there was only one week to go until the May Day celebrations and to cancel those would have been an indicator that something serious was happening. Which it was. The heat of the meltdown was detectable by satellite and radioactivity was picked up in Sweden, which was how the West became alerted. After the May Day parades Ukrainians were told to go inside and shut their windows. Hundreds of firefighters lost their lives at the plant but more cataclysmic loss of life was averted by the wind taking the cloud of radioactive material away from Kiev, which is only sixty-five miles from Chernobyl.

Since Arsenal were playing away on the day of the anniversary rally, I went on the march from the Embankment to Hyde Park. Later I made a note in my diary for 25 April:

CND march
Billy Bragg – ace
Style Council – naff.

Another demonstration was held in opposition to what became known as the Alton Bill. This was Liberal MP David Alton's Private Member's Bill introduced in an attempt to reduce the number of weeks into a pregnancy a woman could legally terminate. For the left, the matter was simple, the woman's right to choose was being attacked and mass demonstrations against this retrograde step were organized.

We boarded coaches outside the recently renamed Nelson Mandela Building on campus and some hours later were sitting down on Westminster Bridge, with mounted police looming over us.

'What do we want?' someone yelled.

'ABORTION RIGHTS!' we yelled back.

'When do we want em ?'

'NOW!'

It may have been more effective had we chanted:

'What do we want?'

'ABORTIONS!'

'When do we want them?'

'NOW!'

We didn't think of that, though, and given the majority of those blockading Westminster Bridge were young men it would have been an un-serious choice.

That evening the women on the demonstration held a women-only candlelit vigil on the Embankment, while all the men went to the pub until they were done. Reconvening later we asked how it had gone. The women all agreed that it had been moving and peaceful. They looked tearful.

'What did you do?' asked one of the men.

They said they'd sung some songs and were, frankly, vague about their oh-so-special candlelit carry-on, which, frankly, sounded a bit feeble and hardly likely to break down the barricades and persuade the powers that be to *change!* The coach journey back was a little quiet. It seemed odd that men should be campaigning for abortion rights and absurd that other men had a say in making laws about it.

Other demonstrations were easier to join in. Such as the one held when Margaret Thatcher came to Canterbury

Cathedral to meet President Mitterrand of France in order to sign the Channel Tunnel accord.

The posters went up all round campus:

THATCHER IN CANTERBURY

That was it. Nuff said. Anyone who didn't want to go down into town, find her, and string her up, clearly hadn't been *listening* these last few years *to the arguments!*

Of course, not everyone on campus was on the left. The Kent University Conservative Association were as far from the left as it was possible to be, without reporting for duty with the National Front. KUCA had been formed after the student Tories had been thrown out of the Young Conservatives for behaving over-exuberantly at a Tory ball in London. At least that was what we on the left had heard. It seemed impossible that a Tory could be thrown out of the Young Conservatives for having too much shampoo at a do, but there it was. I hoped they'd actually been thrown out for wearing their 'Hang Nelson Mandela' T-shirts.

Many of the university's young Tories were enthusiastic participants in Thatcher's great public utilities sell-off. If you befriended one, he or she would lend you the money to make a share application, as Thatcher's dream of making everyone shareholders was brought to life. Once you had received your shares they would immediately buy them from you. I wrote an irate letter to the brilliant campaigning journalist Paul Foot (nephew of Michael Foot), whose columns in the *Daily Mirror* were consistently excellent. I was excited when he wrote back immediately, thanking me for writing to him and urging me to find some written proof, but there was none. It was an easy scam to pull off. That was the point.

Thatcher swept through Canterbury in a black limousine

and we caught only a glimpse of her, which was disappointing as we'd waited half the day. How much of 'Maggie, Maggie, Maggie! Out, out, out!' she heard, behind her bullet-proof glass, is questionable.

The biggest campaign across the country at the time though concerned section 28 of the proposed new Local Government Act. Clause 28, as it became known, was intended to prevent the 'promotion of homosexuality' in local authority schools. In response, Labour councils began campaigning to oppose discrimination on the basis of sexual orientation.

The battle lines were drawn, between the liberal left and the conservative right, over whether or not, fundamentally, homosexuality was contagious. A new book, *Jenny Lives with Eric and Martin,* depicting home life for a child with a gay couple as perfectly normal, had been made available in London schools by the Labour-run Inner London Education Authority (ILEA). The *Daily Mail* was incensed and determined that its readers should be too. In fact, it was knowing that their readers would be incensed that possibly motivated them to create a fuss in the first place.

The issue of AIDS had been hugely prominent in the news since 1981, when what was to become an epidemic began to take hold. While some people's understanding of gay culture had been enhanced by the subsequent publicity, others had hardened their anti-gay prejudice, as what was perceived by many as a 'gay plague' impinged on sexual practices amongst straight people.

At the Royal Court in 1986, Martin Sheen gave a re-markable performance in Larry Kramer's funny, defiant and profoundly moving play about the effects of AIDS, *The Normal Heart.* Sitting by myself in the pub across Sloane Square from the theatre after the show, I became aware of many small groups of people who were quietly holding hands, some weeping, others just staring outwards. I'd been moved by the play but these people had clearly lost someone to this frightening new disease.

Gay people were being portrayed as abnormal, undesirable and a menace to children. The next week a large meeting was being held in the Cornwallis Lecture Theatre, the biggest on campus, as part of the campaign against Clause 28. The guest speaker was to be the Shakesperean actor Ian McKellen. Badges with a pink triangle, the symbol given by the Nazis to identify homosexuals, were distributed.

McKellen had come out as gay, largely in response to Clause 28. He campaigned widely even though to come out as homosexual was really seen to be sounding the death knell for a career in Hollywood. The drama teacher who had invited him was so excited to receive McKellen's call on his answerphone, accepting the invitation to speak, that he vowed never to erase the tape.

The lecture theatre was packed to the rafters. McKellen was charming and funny. He began to speak about Shakespeare and in particular the sonnets that famously have given rise to speculation about the bard's sexuality. All of this was eloquent, witty and received in good humour by an audience who had come to praise McKellen, not to bury him.

We were all quietened though, when he began to deliver Shakespeare's verse. As soon as the first line he had chosen left his lips, the room fell to pin-drop silence. He held us transfixed as his sonorous voice, slightly amplified, seemed to flow towards us as if around our feet at first, before rising up through our motionless bodies, through the heart, before delivering its message to the last organ, the brain. He was entrancing.

We were asked if anyone had any questions and I asked

331

what I should have said to the angry gay boy in Whitstable who had demanded that I take off my pink triangle since I'd never shown any interest in gay rights before. McKellen asked us all to be undeterred and to wear our badges. Later one of the gay kids in the drama department said he was surprised I'd asked a question since he didn't think I'd be interested. When I asked him why not, he said:

'Well, you go to football and stuff, don't you?'

Later still, the angry gay boy collared me again. He'd heard about my speaking at the meeting.

'That was a lame question, wasn't it?'

Billy Bragg singing 'Which Side Are You On?' came to mind.

Shortly before Christmas, for reasons long forgotten, some of the campus lefties decided that the university registry building should be occupied. Having recently become single again, I spent long hours lying under a desk trying to persuade a beautiful radical leftie girl to maybe go to the Neptune with me, obviously only once our demands, whatever they were, had been met. Some time later, she told me that she had decided against going out with me because of my trainers:

'I couldn't go out with someone wearing trainers like that.'

'I'd have changed trainers for you,' I told her, but she knew I'd never be cool enough for her. White trainers with velcro straps were fine in Essex, but only in Essex. Fortunately, I did not write a love letter to her on the wall of any of Canterbury's numerous subways.

The week before Christmas a minibus was organized to go down to Deal where Billy Bragg was going to play at the Deal Miners' Welfare Club. All three of the Kent pits had been closed with thousands of jobs lost. Although the strike had finished in 1985, continuing efforts were made to provide for the families of ex-miners who were out of work, especially at Christmas. Bragg was on good form, making light of the tiny stage he was standing on by saying they'd asked Paul Weller to come but there wasn't enough room 'for all his suits'. He played all his best and most rousing songs and then broke off to pay tribute to those comrades present who were engaged in ongoing struggles. These included some local nurses involved in a dispute, plus one or two other groups, and then a mention was given to students at Kent university:

'... who are occupying their registry build – is that right? Yeah? Yes, occupying their registry building!'

We all cheered and smiled at each other. Later the Deal miners presented Bragg with a commemorative brass miner's lamp as a token of their appreciation. They expressed regret that they could offer no more. There was barely a dry eye in the house and the seriousness of the situation for the families was brought home to the bunch of tipsy students at the back, whose 'occupation' seemed less important somehow.

Bragg then sang 'Which Side Are You On?' which fortunately ended to rapturous applause, allowing those of us who had been welling up to hide our emotions in a flurry of clapping and cheering.

It was good to leave campus sometimes.

1988

Kylie Minogue

This year saw the beginning of the end for me and Kylie Minogue. The pint-sized star of addictive Australian soap *Neighbours* had branched out into pop music and in the three short minutes of her number one single, 'I Should Be So Lucky', lost her devoted student fanbase.

It's one thing to watch a soap knowingly and ironically, but music, that was beyond a joke. I was still of the opinion that if you hadn't written the song you had no right to be singing it, though this was not a hard and fast rule, since my love for The Velvelettes singing 'Needle in a Haystack' knew no bounds. Most of that year though I was listening to 'George Best' by The Wedding Present.

Neighbours was on twice a day on BBC1, at lunchtime and teatime. If you missed the new episode they repeated it the following day. It meant it was difficult to fall behind and easy to catch up. Besides, characters were forever finding excuses to recap the plot, by going to the coffee shop and finding a character who hadn't heard the latest on Ramsay Street. We knew what we were watching was so bad it was beyond parody, since it was eerily reminiscent of Victoria Wood's spoof soap opera *Acorn Antiques*, with Julie Walters as Mrs Overall.

Ramsay Street was named after a family who were in a long-running feud with the neighbouring Robinson family. The family elders took it all very seriously. It was joyously absurd nonsense and quickly became an established favourite amongst the student population of Whitstable. It's fair to say that *Neighbours* episodes comprised at last half of the drama I watched in the final year of my degree.

For that final year I was sharing a flat with the super-bright Frances, who could be found re-reading *Jane Eyre* for pleasure in her spare time. A clean two-bed flat with central heating, a witty flatmate, with none of the pretentious excesses of opinion that some were capable of, I'd fallen on my feet. Across Canterbury Road from us, living in a shop window, was our mutual friend Richard, and elsewhere on those premises, in a more conventional room, his cohort Gary. They were both devotees of *Neighbours*, their pub-singer version of the theme tune putting the original to shame.

When Kylie joined the cast as firecracker tomboy Charlene, it was unforeseen that she would rise to stardom and blossom into a sex symbol. In the early episodes the cameramen, working on a tight schedule, would often miss her as she passed beneath the lens, out of shot. For the first two months they could only pick her up on the low level camera used for Bouncer the dog's close-ups.

Not really. When Kylie was on-screen the viewer's eye was drawn to her tiny, scrawny frame.

Charlene was always under cars, fixing oil leaks and flying off the handle in grubby dungarees. Kids loved her and identified with her, largely because she was the size of the average ten-year-old.

I was taking a course in radio drama, with Gary and Richard, on which we quickly established that the majority of radio plays were not just written to be listened to while doing the washing-up, but were also, quite possibly, written while doing the washing-up.

Gary and Richard had aspirations to write comedy and Gary's success in being given a First for an essay on his

English course in which he argued that Shakespeare had written *Macbeth* as a comedy suggested he had an eye for humour.

While our love of *Neighbours* was all very ironic and considered, we did actually like the soap. Had we known how soaps were going to proliferate across the TV schedules over the next two decades, eliminating comedy slot after comedy slot, we may have been less enthusiastic, over pints of Flowers in the Neptune, about our daily fix of Aussie melodrama.

It was like a fix too. We hardly watched any other television and reverted to serious artsy undergraduates as soon as the theme tune died down, straight off to the Marlowe Theatre to see a touring version of Ibsen's *Rosmersholm*.

It was also possible to read plenty of books despite being skint; they were quite easy to steal from the campus bookshop. By now I was a devotee of Saul Bellow since I'd read the hilarious *Herzog* as well as *Seize the Day*, *Henderson the Rain King* and *The Dean's December*. Even though most of his books were about middle-aged men in the throes of mid-life crises, battered by relationships, disillusioned by the workplace, and not content to stay put any longer, there was enough humour and outlandish behaviour to appeal to an undergraduate too young to identify with the protagonist.

When up in London for demos, I would try to enhance my left-wing credentials by visiting leftie bookshops, like the now extinct Collets on Charing Cross Road, and the still-soldiering-on Housmans on Caledonian Road. I'd usually buy political postcards and a copy of *Searchlight*. The only book from those stores I read from cover to cover was Robert Tressell's *The Ragged Trousered Philanthropists*, which I loved. I tried to read about Karl Marx, and had a go at *The*

Communist Manifesto, but there weren't many jokes in there and, as it was humour that was my primary interest, I reverted to Groucho.

By now, I'd been in a production of Steven Berkoff's two-hander *Decadence* with the only really talented student in the department, Jackie Clune. Our director robbed all his ideas from a recent revival of the play, starring Berkoff and Linda Marlowe, a brilliant production I'd seen at the Arts Theatre four years previously. It was fantastically good fun to perform. A series of rhyming monologues delivered alternately by two upper-class and two working-class characters. This meant breaking out the impression of my dad once again, alongside my best mockney, as used on the football terraces. We were well received. Even a drama lecturer was sincerely complimentary, and that never happened. Our friends loved it and it was very rewarding, with the packed drama studio rocking with laughter. A fix of that sort of adrenaline rush could become as addictive as *Neighbours*.

Soon after that, some comedians were booked to put on a show in the junior common room. There were about two hundred people in there on the night. It was all going well up until the last act, who took the whole gig up a level. His exhilarating, high-octane anecdotal rant, mainly about his schooldays in Liverpool, was perfectly pitched for students, whose memories of chopper bikes and the like were very recent, and who were wiping their eyes in recovery from their own laughter.

Considering myself, by now, a comedy aficionado (I had seen Richard Pryor and Eddie Murphy videos after all), I approached him after the gig and asked him his name:

'Simon, Simon Bligh.'

I told him that he was hilarious and should be on television. I said this seriously, as if I knew what I was talking about. He looked as though he'd heard it before but was good-natured and grateful for the compliments. If I hadn't seen Simon Bligh I might never have thought it possible to try stand-up comedy.

Andy, who I'd been in several plays with, wanted to try some comedy, as did I, after seeing Rory Bremner and Simon Bligh and having the experience of *Decadence*. It was difficult to persuade Gary and Richard to put together some kind of revue though. Their stated aim was to write the new *Hitchhiker's Guide to the Galaxy*, without going to the trouble of working their way up to it, with some half-good, half-awful, comedy shows on campus. After three years or more of acting badly in student productions, I'd overcome the fear of being thought no good.

Most of my time was taken up rehearsing plays as I was now a fourth year specializing in directing. I'd chosen one of Barrie Keefe's *Barbarians* trilogy, *Abide With Me*, about Manchester United fans outside Wembley, without tickets, at the 1976 FA Cup Final. One of the characters was black and since there were no black people in the drama department we decided to put, in small print at the bottom of the notices announcing auditions, the ugly phrase:

BLACK ACTORS NEEDED

Passing out these notices in the student bars, I was castigated, by white people, and accused of racism.

In the event two black students turned up who had never auditioned for a play before, and I ended up feeling bad about having to tell one of them he hadn't made it. Then I had to negotiate with another director on the course (there were six of us), who insisted that if he wanted to use the two black men in *his* play then he should be allowed to, since it was racist to suggest that black men should only play black parts. He was directing a play with no specifically black characters. Eventually I was able to cast the one I wanted. I was looking forward to leaving that university.

I took my three cast members to Chelsea, because they were playing Man United. As we went into the away end, I was stopped by a constable to be searched. I looked at his smiling face and realized it was an old friend from school. We'd once been in a fight with two lads in Essex, outside a pub. The landlord's son, who'd started it, slashed my mate with a chisel which cut his temple, missed his eye, and carried on across the bridge of his nose. We'd gone back to a girl's house and he'd had to chat to her mum, while remaining in profile to hide the blood. We had a chat about old times before I went in. I didn't bring up the time he'd asked my girlfriend whether she spat or swallowed.

My three student actors loved being on the terraces, and the experience helped them to act well in the play. I was proud of them.

After that I put on *Christie in Love* by Howard Brenton, a very dark tale about the real-life serial killer. I was bored in the rehearsal room now, so we played a fair bit of cricket with a stick and a juice carton. On the night they all did well, even the lad with the thankless task of portraying Christie himself. With my final year dissertation about Peter Brook finished, I was starting to wonder what I was going to do next when a friend of mine, Alistair, who was in a band, said that they were taking part in an Amnesty International benefit at the Whitstable Labour Club and would I like to MC the night. I could try some of the comedy I'd been talking about. I wasn't sure but he put my name on the poster anyway so I had to.

I roped in two friends of mine, Steph and Mandy, to help with a spoof of a Cadbury's Flake commercial on TV at the time. Set in the tropics, it featured a girl reclining in the heat, eating a Flake, while a lizard ran across a nearby telephone. We found an old phone and taped a toy lizard to a stick. One of them sang the Flake song about the crumbliest chocolate while the other one erotically rubbed the toy lizard over the phone. Meanwhile, I unwrapped a Flake, very obviously a phallus in the commercial, to reveal it was wrapped in a condom, as everything had to be in those AIDS-conscious times. Eating a condom full of chocolate was no fun for me, and watching me spit out a condom full of chocolate was no fun for the audience, but, thankfully, they were laughing.

Steph and Mandy then exited to applause and I began my stand-up routine, with Alistair poised to come on with his band at any second, in case I bailed out. Rooted anxiously to the spot I talked, at high speed, about Whitstable and the fact there was no cashpoint there, about the campus bookshop and how they must copy the student shoplifting techniques when they go to the wholesalers, in order to pick up their stock for nothing to break even. I talked about the Channel tunnel, I think, I don't remember clearly, it was an adrenaline-fuelled blur. I may have tried a David Coleman impression.

The audience members, standing in the dark, smoky back room of the Labour Club, which was under railway arches, were mostly students or people I'd seen in there every Saturday night. They were facing the right way and some of them were laughing. It seemed to be working. I finished what I'd prepared, introduced the band and came off. Everyone clapped, everyone was smiling, it was a thrill and an enormous relief, both for me and for my peers, who were terrified I would humiliate myself and they'd have to say something nice about it afterwards.

I had decided by the time I came offstage what I was going to pursue after graduation a few months later.

It was the support of friends like Alistair, Frances, Gary, Richard and Andy that gave me the confidence to have a go at stand-up. We laughed a lot together, often leaving the pub early to go back to watch *The Last Resort with Jonathan Ross*. That Christmas I'd had a dinner with Alistair and his housemates. Someone set light to the streamers they'd decorated the table with, and someone else threw a glass of brandy on it to try and put it out. Alistair put on 'Burning Down the House' by Talking Heads as we extinguished the flames in fits of laughter.

Laughing together was also the appeal of *Neighbours*. We were all young, with next to no life experience, no money and nothing in common other than having been seduced by the same university prospectus. It's the things that are shared together that create real bonds between people and sharing jokes about the Ramsays and the Robinsons was our private world of fun. Since then, Gary Howe and Richard Preddy have made careers in comedy writing, Alistair Friend is a professional musician and Kylie Minogue has done quite well too.

Dolly Price

Reaching the top of the escalator, a group of Singaporean schoolchildren in uniforms were huddled together waiting. They were young, maybe twelve years old, in dark jackets and white shirts with their ties loosely done up. A mixture of boys and girls, about six of them altogether, hanging around the shopping centre after school. One of the girls was cowering behind the biggest one, a lad who may have been a year or two older than the others. He approached me and said:

'You a boxer?'

I looked at my sister next to me, who didn't say anything.

'You a boxer? he repeated. The girl behind him was giggling now.

'Boxer? You a boxer!'

I was struggling with his accent.

'A boxer? No I'm not a boxer, I told him.

'No, not boxer. Popstar!' He laughed and turned to speak to his friends in their own language. They all laughed with him.

'Oh. Popstar.'

'Yes, you a popstar?'

'No, no, I'm not a popstar.'

'Yes, yes you lick ash tray.'

'What?'

'Lick ash tray! You lick ash tray!'

The accent was very strong but then the penny dropped.

'Oh! Rick Astley?'

'Yes, yes you lick ash tray!'

'No, I'm not. Sorry. I'm not Rick Astley.'

He turned to the girl and said something. He'd apparently been enquiring on her behalf. She now plucked up the courage to speak.

'You Rick Astley?' she almost pleaded.

I should have just said I was Rick Astley, the young singer responsible for the biggest selling record of 1987, 'Never Gonna Give You Up', a number one in the UK, the US and apparently Singapore too. Would it have done any harm to sign an autograph and give them a little Astley arm shimmy by way of an exit? No, it wouldn't, I could have made her happy but I trod on her dreams.

'No. I'm not,' I said. No one had ever remarked on any similarity between me and Rick before and no one has since.

Me and my sister went to the Raffles Hotel for a Singapore Sling. We had one night in Singapore but we really just wanted to head back to the airport and catch our onward flight to Adelaide. Still, the old colonial Raffles Hotel was very nice, much better than the seventy-storey modern monstrosity next door. Much of old Singapore had been flattened and replaced by gleaming new soulless buildings. Now tourists were turning up and asking for the old town, only to find it had largely gone. I asked the barman at the Raffles what was the greatest number of Singapore Slings he'd made in an evening? He said they once made 2,000 in one night when a US navy ship was in port.

The next day at Adelaide airport we looked out for our Auntie Hazel. We saw a white-haired lady who I thought must have been my gran but it turned out to be Hazel. I'd only met her once before, when she flew to England in 1972 after the death of her sister, my mum. She had darker hair then.

Emerging from behind Hazel was a little, round, sun-tanned older lady that I didn't recognize. I was looking for someone pale, thin, drawn and anxious, but this buoyant, welcoming, smiley imposter was pretending to be the same person who had emigrated, from England to Australia, in 1979, after suffering a nervous breakdown in the years following the death of her eldest daughter and her husband.

Hazel greeted us and we headed outside to find their car. As we walked, both Hazel and this old woman who was masquerading as our grandmother continually remarked on my sister's resemblance to her mother.

'Ooh, doesn't she look like Shirley?'

A few more steps and general chit-chat and then again:

'Doesn't she look like Shirley? Ever so. Ever so much.'

My sister, who had lost her mum at three years old and only had the one photo to remember her by, was smiling shyly. We hadn't seen our gran for nine years, and when she left my sister was only ten. Now grown up at nineteen, maybe she did look like Shirley. It hadn't come up before.

They took us to their house in Fullarton Road. We knew the address 'off by heart' since we used to write thank you letters every year for birthday and Christmas presents sent by Auntie Hazel.

Hazel asked whose idea had it been to finally come and visit after all these years? I told them it was mine. They were disbelieving and double-checked with my sister that I was telling the truth. My reputation, in my own family, was ruinously awful, even amongst people who didn't know me. Later on, talking to my gran, since this happy tanned, relaxed old lady was indeed my gran, she said to me:

'Ooh, you were a bugger.'

'Was I?' I said, a bit helplessly.

'Ooh, you were a *bugger*.'

Gran was born in 1905. Her mum, Fanny Binks, was her father's second wife. When Gran was five years old, she saw Fanny Binks looking through the railings at her, in the school playground. She never saw her mother again. From then my gran was raised by her half-sisters from her dad's first marriage. She described them as cruel. She married Fred, who worked in the post office; they did their courting in Walthamstow. Sometimes she'd catch the bus with Fred down to Finsbury Town Hall for afternoon tea dances. They moved to Chingford and had two children. Hazel, the youngest, was married first, to Geoff, and had a son, who was eighteen months old when the family boarded a ship to Australia in 1963. Hazel said she walked to Australia since her little boy wouldn't stay in one place for the entire six-week sailing. They settled in Mount Gambier and later moved to Adelaide. Soon after they emigrated, my mum and dad were married, having delayed so long that Hazel missed her sister's wedding, which was a terrible shame for her.

We spent ten days in Adelaide, getting to know the three of our four cousins who were living there at the time, and hearing stories from Hazel, Geoff and in particular my gran.

We heard how Hazel hadn't been told that her only sister was terminally ill. How a letter had arrived saying she was dead, and how Hazel had sat on the bench in the back garden crying for three days. My cousins were told to leave her alone while Geoff cooked for them and waited for her to come back inside.

We heard how my gran and granddad agreed to leave their retirement home in Blackpool and move down to a flat in Loughton to help look after us. Then my granddad died and Gran was on her own, with her youngest the other side of the world. Both my dad's parents passed away, leaving only my dad and my gran to look after us. Then she had a nervous breakdown, and then she was in Claybury, the mental hospital near where I grew up.

Claybury was an insult at primary school. 'You're from Claybury' meant you were stupid, simple, an idiot. It didn't mean you were ill, or desperate, lonely and sad beyond words. I went to Claybury with my dad but he didn't take me in to see Gran. He left me in the car and told me not to unlock the doors. In case there were any dangerous nutters in the grounds was the implication.

My gran had always suffered from depression and mental health problems. They called it 'milk madness' when she was raising children. It was as if the intolerable strain, inflicted on her by the events of her life, was solely her responsibility to cope with.

The medical profession, at the time of my mum's terminal illness, was divided on the issue of how much to tell the patient. She was not told how ill she was. She didn't have the chance to say goodbye to her children or her sister, and her children and her sister regretted that hugely.

Male doctors deciding what's good for the weak and vulnerable female patient. There's something patronizing about it. She'd better not be told, she has three young children, she won't be able to cope. She's only a feeble woman. Hazel would have flown to England to be with her, but she wasn't told either.

At Claybury my dad told my gran what the doctors had told him:

'Complete breakdown. Mental and physical.'

Gran said she felt as if it were her fault, her weakness.

When she left England we assumed we'd never see her again. She was so frail and beaten down. I thought she'd die within a year.

She revived, with her daughter and her Aussie grand-children, living in a granny-flat on the side of the house, feeding her cat, Fritz, on leftovers from her lunch (which was likely to be a saucer of cup-a-soup; no wonder Fritz was so grumpy all the time).

Me and my sister would go in to see her, sometimes together, or one at a time, and she would talk to us about our mum and anything else she could recall, until she was tired, or the memories became too much and the tears would come and she would then prefer to be on her own so as not to make it worse.

Many of the stories had her chuckling, though. A gentle chuckle and a hummed tune from the distant past, these were the sounds you heard before she came into view. Her warmest chuckle came when she described living in a flat as a younger woman. In the flat above lived two other young women. They had a lot of 'gentleman callers'. She was telling me about the time she lived beneath two hookers, 1930s hookers, with a quiet suburban residence and no one, other than my gran, any the wiser. She said they were nice girls, very funny, with a few tales to tell.

She told me she was surprised that it had been my idea to come to Australia, that I'd been a terrible handful as a boy but that she was so pleased that we'd come to see her, so pleased, and she missed us very much. She told me she wished she'd been allowed to tell us all about my mum at the time, but was told not to, that my other grandma had said, 'Least said, soonest mended.'

At teatime she'd come in and join the family. Sitting down, her back bent, so she was barely seeing over the table, she would witter and twitter away, saying: 'Wassat, dear?' in her still-Walthamstow accent, whenever anyone spoke to her. Every now and then she'd share the benefit of her

350

wisdom on some issue of the day, banging the palm of her hand down:

'It's the pill, that's the trouble, people can go around willy-nilly and it's all because of the pill.'

'What about all the unwanted pregnancies without it, though?' said Hazel. 'All those girls with babies on their own.'

'What about all the coat hangers up them in the back-streets, Gran?' said my cousin. Some Australians are quite frank.

'Yes, I suppose so,' said Gran, and winked at me.

After tea she'd go next door, have two paracetamol tablets for her back pain ('I'm only allowed eight of these a day. Not enough') and then have a Bailey's. She always wiped round the inside of the glass with her finger to reach the dregs.

In the evening, Geoff would pour me a 'black and tan' and tell me more stories about London in the '50s and about Hazel and Shirley. I tried to commit it all to memory.

After ten days we were to fly to Sydney and then on to Hong Kong. These sightseeing parts of the trip didn't interest us now and we wished we could have scrapped them for a few more days with our gran. Sitting on the plane at Adelaide airport, my sister was crying next to me.

'We'll never see her again.'

'Yes we will,' I said.

I wasn't sure though. My dad had bought these tickets for us, since we wanted to visit so much. We wouldn't be able to afford tickets of our own for years and gran was already eighty-two.

Three years later I managed to save up enough for another visit. I made a futher two trips after that, always with a bottle of duty-free Bailey's in hand. I cherished every minute and felt for my sister, who couldn't afford the flight. She never saw her gran again.

Dolly Price passed away in 1995 at the age of eighty-nine. She was doubtless relieved, since every time I went to see her, she'd pour a little finger of Bailey's, reach out to take my hand, and say:

'I want to be in my box, Alan, I want to be in my box.'

Steffi Graf

Epping High Street is quite pleasant on a nice day, a few old buildings and a market if you're lucky. Like any shopping street, though, it's less appealing when it's raining, and less appealing still when it was my job to walk up and down it, come rain or shine (or just rain, actually, lots of it), with two heavy, flat pieces of plywood banging into my legs and two lengths of gnarly, knotted, old string cutting into my shoulders. There was a girl working in a travel agent's who caught my eye, sitting there all day, meaning I could swing by for another look, and maybe catch *her* eye. I stopped outside the window and looked in at her. As I did so, I caught sight of my own reflection in the glass. She hadn't noticed me and I was glad. There was no way she would want to speak to this dripping, bedraggled, hopelessly optimistic, sandwich board man. I moved on before someone called the police.

I was peddling antiques and, with hindsight, perhaps the antique dealer who had advertised in the local paper for someone to carry a sandwich board for a full Saturday for fifteen quid, had acquired the board itself as an antique. Despite some nice calligraphy on the front (and back of course), it was yellowing, old and weather-beaten. As I ambled back up the High Street, past the branch of Curry's outside which I used to meet the rest of the Garnon Rangers under-15s every Sunday morning before we'd go and be soundly thrashed somewhere in Upminster, I was approached by a burly man. He wanted to hire me to promote the Epping Flea Market the following Saturday. I said I would, since I was desperate for money, having recently graduated with an overdraft. He also had a scheme to generate publicity by having customers at the flea market keep an eye out for a 'mystery man'. If they found him they would win a prize.

'You can be my mystery man,' he said.

The following Saturday I drove up to Epping from Loughton, having moved back home after graduation. My dad was still paying for the running of my car, and his question of four years previously, about what sort of job a drama degree would lead to, was coming back to haunt me.

As I approached Epping there were temporary signs on the lamp posts saying:

FIND THE
'MYSTERY MAN' !!
TODAY !
at the
FLEA
MARKET !!

I was found after less than five minutes. He'd told some of the stall holders what I'd be wearing, and as the place had only just opened, and there weren't many customers around, I was a sitting duck. I felt a failure, but my attempt at anonymity was crucially undermined by the marketing expert's decision to issue a *Crimewatch*-type description, right down to:

'He will have a blue jacket over his shoulder.'

The deal was that I would go on to sandwich board duties after I was discovered. I was hoping for a half-day of it but no such luck.

'Where's your sandwich board?' he asked.

'I don't have my own board,' I told him.

'But you're the sandwich board man!'

He was really grumpy now. He hurriedly made a sandwich board out of stiff card and string and I was sent out on to the High Road looking glum and, if anything, a deterrent to would-be customers. I looked even more ridiculous than the previous week and so avoided the travel agent's as, in my lonely imaginings, this sight could tarnish what me and the girl had built up the previous week.

I was not rehired as a sandwich board man and, with that avenue closed off, decided to fruitlessly apply for jobs from the *Guardian Media* section, along with thousands of other graduates, without usually receiving a reply, never mind an interview. I tried for BBC radio producer trainee but had no chance.

Then a fellow graduate said that a few Kent students were going down to the Wimbledon Tennis Championships on the first morning of the tournament, because if you went to gate four at 6 a.m. (or was it gate six at 4 a.m.?), the catering company would hire a few people. So we did, and we all were given jobs, starting work immediately. With no waiting or bar experience I was eventually assigned general dogsbody duties and given a white coat.

Walking through the grounds we could see players practising on the outside courts. A few courts away, a blonde ponytail was bobbing around in a blur of perpetual motion. She was eye-catching, even with Martina Navratilova, the most famous and greatest women's tennis player of them all, practising in the foreground with her entourage. Martina had a ghetto blaster the size of a Vespa and a couple of cool-looking friends with her, making encouraging noises over the music, as she hit back and forth with her coach. She was the reigning champion, having defeated the ponytail the year before, but the ponytail was on the march in 1988, winning the Australian Open (against Chris Evert in the first final not played on grass), and retaining the French title. Now Martina was in her teenage sights at Wimbledon. Beneath the ponytail, of course, was Steffi Graf.

Most boys only had eyes for Gabriela Sabatini, the raven-haired Argentinian beauty in the women's draw, but Steffi did it for me. Despite Adidas insisting on clothing her in T-shirts designed for junior boys, and netball skirts, her mile-long pins and flowing blonde tresses marked her out as a duckling heading swanwards.

Each morning, after a two-hour drive from Loughton, I'd keep an eye out for the tell-tale ponytail bouncing around as she rifled forehands low across the practice courts. She walked back to the baseline urgently, with short steps and no flighty tossing of the hair or look-at-me posturing. She was all business, all work, and apparently self-contained. Would she somehow find the time for a suitor from the catering company? Would she stop hitting and tell her coach to –

'Take five. There's a young man in a white coat who's caught my eye every time we've been out here in the morning. I simply have to talk to him.'

This was an even more unlikely scenario than an Epping travel agent coming out on to the High Street to say:

'I'm on my lunch break at one, why don't you ditch your board and come to Gregg's for a real sandwich. I like wet-look hair.'

I couldn't stand and watch Steffi for long; I had to head for the Food Village, which was a big marquee with various different stalls including a bar, a donut stand and a fish-and-chip counter. The staff swapped jobs each day. It was not too bad when the weather was good, because the Food Village was for ordinary punters, not corporate hospitality freeloaders. Real punters watch tennis and don't hang around marquees that smell of batter and donuts.

When it rained though, it was chaotic. Thousands of people would come in to take shelter. It could become a dispiriting place then. Fortunately, in our midst we had a handsome young Dubliner called Jim Byrne, who had an exceptional talent for making the most of each day, for sweeping you along on a tide of laughter, pranks, and banter. He liked everyone and everyone liked him. Every day, several times a day, he'd say:

'What's the crack?'

The crack, it turned out, was actually the craic. It meant the mischief, the fun, the scam at each moment. The craic with the refrigerated lorries at the back of the Food Village was to go inside and pinch a few donuts, without anyone noticing you do it, or spotting there were any missing. To do that, without being shut in the lorry and freezing to death, was the craic all one afternoon.

The craic with the bar was to disappear for ages collecting glasses. People would buy drinks from the bar and then wander off to the outside courts with them. Going out to find empties meant being out of sight, and if you were sly you could skive off and watch some tennis. Some of the forces personnel, on the entrances to the show courts, would turn a blind eye to catering staff in white coats sneaking into matches, while the hospitality tents were heaving with people stuffing their faces and not taking up their free tickets.

The craic with the free programmes dished out to corporate customers was to sneak into the tents, find unwanted programmes, then sell them to punters for 50p each. With a white coat you looked like a programme seller. Sell a few of those and you could up your take home pay, from £16 to as much as £20 a day.

The craic behind the refrigerated lorries was to climb up the tarpaulin fence concealing them from Court 14, which always had top matches on it, and peer over to watch. This was quite high up and precarious but the view was good. One day we were up there watching women's doubles. The fence was swaying a bit and me and Jim were giggling like schoolboys, though we didn't realize how loud we were because of the noise of the lorries. Then we realized that play had stopped on Court 14. All four players – Martina Navratilova, Chris Evert, Gabriela Sabatini and Steffi Graf – plus the umpire were staring up at us. Then Martina was pointing in our direction. Without so much as an 'I love you, Steffi' we dropped like stones on to the grass below and rolled around in hysterical laughter before quickly busying ourselves with some jobs while Jim worked out what the craic would be next.

When Wimbledon finished, a few of us signed up for the next event the company was doing, the Farnborough Air Show. Sadly Jim wasn't going to come. We swapped addresses and he smiled his big smile at us all as he left. He was off to Florida to train as a pilot with Aer Lingus.

I stayed in a tent at a campsite near to the airfield but there was no craic at Farnborough other than watching the Red Arrows every day. I was on washing-up duty and needed Jim to lighten the mood.

I never saw Steffi again. She went off to the Seoul Olympics, having bashed Martina in the final at Wimbledon, and Sabatini at the US Open, to achieve the coveted Grand Slam. She then converted that into a Golden Slam, by winning at the Olympics too. Her achievement, though, like everything else in Seoul, was overshadowed by the astonishing men's 100 metre final, which lifted the watching billions out of their seats, as Ben Jonson smashed the world record, only to be caught out by a drugs test. Flo-Jo Joyner was the Queen of Seoul, not Steffi, as she obliterated sprint records and won three golds, but she never raced again and died young with a cloud of suspicion hanging over her.

Some months after Wimbledon, a letter arrived for me. I didn't recognize the handwriting. It was from Jim's girlfriend. She said she was writing to all the people in his address book to let them know that he had been involved in a training accident. A plane had gone down with Jim, another learner, and an instructor onboard. All three had been killed.

Jim was an inspiring character and it still saddens me that he is gone, someone who could light up every day, with optimism, and humour, and a love of the craic.

John Hegley

Time Out magazine listed all the comedy clubs in London in its cabaret section in the 1980s. Their rival listings magazine, *City Limits*, also listed many of the same places. There were only about twenty-five venues in London running cabaret nights. After I graduated I wrote to all of them, asking for gigs, based on the strength of my scrap of material, road-tested only once at the Whitstable Labour Club. Only one of them replied, the Black Cat Cabaret in Stoke Newington. I didn't know it but this club was run by my old drama teacher, Piers Gladhill.

I hadn't seen Piers for four years so it was great to receive his letter, which began:

'Hello, it's me!'

He said he was running a heat for the 'Allcomers Talent Show' being staged by the Hackney Empire, in August, as part of the Hackney Performers Festival 1988. Theoretically, this was only open to people residing in the London Borough of Hackney, not at their dad's house in Loughton, but Piers turned a blind eye and encouraged me to enter. He ran the Black Cat once a week, in a room above the Rose and Crown on Stoke Newington Church Street.

I was as nervous before going down to Piers's gig as I had been the first time I'd done stand-up the previous March. The anxiety started early in the day and thickened as the event came closer. Standing in front of my bedroom mirror, with a broom handle stuck in the back of a chair to simulate a microphone stand, I practised my routine over and over again. All the way over to Stoke Newington in my car, I was running routines out loud, gibbering away at traffic lights, to the consternation of people in other cars.

I was profoundly anxious and it's difficult to understand why I put myself through it. The satisfaction and improved self-esteem I enjoyed after the gig in Whitstable made that worthwhile, but to do that again was unnecessary, surely? I had conquered the crippling fear and made some people laugh, so now I could go and find a job. Except I didn't want a job, I wanted to be onstage. One hit of appreciation wasn't enough. I needed more validation, more affirmation, more self-esteem. So I went down to the Black Cat with my new act, tweaked a bit to remove the more obscure Whitstable jokes.

It goes without saying that my act would have to be entirely self-penned, non-racist and non-sexist. This didn't mean anti-racist or anti-sexist. The choice was to omit cheap offensive references. I'd learnt well at the Reconstructive Cultural Training Camp that was the University of Kent, Humanities Faculty.

Piers asked how I was and I told him I was very nervous. He said, 'What's the worst that can happen? You'll have to walk from there' – he pointed at the stage – 'to there.' He pointed at the door at the back of the room and smiled broadly.

It was disappointing not to receive any replies to my letters to the clubs but it worked out well that my first gig was going to be at Piers's place. He filled me in on how to approach people about gigs. Don't write, since most clubs are only in the venue one day a week, so you can't be sure they will even receive letters. Instead, ring them repeatedly until they offer you an open spot and then do your best to be funny. At which point you may or may not be booked to do a twenty-minute set.

Twenty minutes seemed an eternity. Just preparing the few minutes I had was hard enough.

A few other nervous newcomers were also in need of kind words or possibly just oxygen. Fortunately the atmosphere, as created by Piers, was entirely supportive. Eventually it was my turn. From the low stage in the corner I could see the door at the back that Piers had pointed out in describing the worst-case scenario earlier.

It's important to know where the emergency exits are in planes and hotels, but there are two pastimes where the exit is really your friend, where an unobstructed route out could become more important than anything. One is shoplifting, the other is stand-up comedy.

The small crowd were in good spirits. They hadn't paid much to come in, some of them knew some of the other acts, and they knew it was an 'allcomers talent quest' so were prepared to cut some slack. I rattled through my act at breakneck speed and they liked it enough to pick me as one of the acts to go through to the final to be held at the Hackney Empire the following week. I was delighted and Piers was delighted for me. He said he'd book me for a proper gig at his club.

Going home afterwards I was euphoric. The adrenaline rush after a day of anticipation was such that I didn't recover for hours. It was exciting to have found something I wanted to do. I loved the atmosphere in the comedy club, the people, the attitude to life, the laughing. If I managed to pick up enough bookings, then I would be able to apply for an Equity card and maybe find some acting work too.

That weekend, I went to the Red Rose Club on Seven Sisters Road. Housed in a Labour Club, the Rose was packed with around 200 people and was altogether more intimidating than the little Black Cat. I was only there to watch though, and found a seat at one of the front tables, with their candles and red and white gingham paper table-cloths. The stage was in the middle of the long side of a rectangular room. At one end of the room was the exit, at the other end a raised area, which had once been used as a stage but was now filled with punters.

The Red Rose was just up the road from the Rainbow, where I'd come to see bands years before. Ivor Dembina, the genial host, went up and started proceedings before bringing on Andy Greenhalgh to open. Andy's gentle humour was a good solid start. Then Ivor introduced a newcomer who was going to try a ten-minute half-spot as he wasn't yet up to the full twenty minutes. A young man in his mid-twenties, with floppy blond hair, ambled on and began an off-the-wall monologue which left an audience, keyed up for political material, a little unsure. He hadn't quite sorted out his approach but he was different. He said, 'My dad served in Vietnam,' and the ears on a few of the older Red Rose lefties pricked up, until he said, 'He was a waiter there.' He was quite funny but ten minutes was enough; there was little sign of the boundless potential that Eddie Izzard was later to fulfil so spectacularly.

The next act really kicked things off though. A pair of monkey boots thudded up on to the stage. A hand grabbed the microphone stand as the comedienne opened with: 'I'd better move this or you won't be able to see me, will you?'

Twenty minutes later and a huge ovation was ringing around Finsbury Park as Jo Brand rejoined her friends in the audience and immediately sparked up a cigarette. It seemed so effortless for her, the audience eating out of her hand. She was droll, she was assured, she was saying things that no comic had ever said before, female or otherwise, she was cheeky, sharp, hilarious and a one-off.

Ivor kept the 'cornucopia of comedy' going and introduced Mark Thomas, whose punchy left-wing material, about the London everyone lived in, and the government everyone hated, was every bit as well received as Jo's act had been. He derided the muzak in supermarkets and wished they'd play The Clash instead. The laughter was cacophonous. Ivor called an interval. This had already been the best night out I'd had anywhere, anytime, ever, and there was still another act to go. How could the closing turn top the brilliant stand-ups that had gone before?

When Chris Lynam was standing a few feet away from me, stark naked, with his genitals out of sight between his thighs, those people in the audience who weren't laughing were sitting open-mouthed. This was an act you could not take your eyes off. He produced a roman candle, stuffed it between his buttocks and clenched it tightly, he was a strong-looking man, slight and lean but wiry with wild eyes and a mountain of black hair. He threatened to light the firework, but I didn't think he would, until the shower of sparks was landing all around us in the front row, burning tiny holes in the paper table cloth. The response for him was rapturous too.

It had been an amazing night. The London comedy circuit was the place to be and the Red Rose Club was at the heart of it all. I went up to Ivor and told him I'd love to go on there. He asked me about my stand-up experience and when I told him he advised me to go away for six months, play all the little rooms over pubs and the smaller clubs, and then come back to him, since it wasn't as easy as it looked up there. It was sound advice.

The next Monday I went to the Hackney Empire for my third ever stand-up gig. The theatre was, and remains, as beautiful and perfect an environment for performance as has ever been built. Designed by Frank Matcham and opened in 1901, it had become a bingo hall in the 1960s before eventually closing down altogether. Now Roland and Clare Muldoon had taken over and were determined to re-establish the theatre as the home of variety in London, as it had been when Marie Lloyd was the Queen of the Halls. Charlie Chaplin and Stan Laurel had performed at the Empire so to tread those boards was very exciting. At least it was until I arrived there and saw seventy-odd people scattered around the stalls. The theatre can hold 1500.

John Hegley was hosting with Otiz Cannelloni and I thought they were terrible. The atmosphere was flat, they weren't being funny, the acts were struggling and it was hopeless.

I went on, did my bit, and was declared the runner-up, receiving a trophy and two tickets to see John Hegley at the Hackney Empire the following Friday. I couldn't believe it, what a rubbish prize. I had nothing better to do so I went anyway; it was free after all.

That Friday the Empire was packed and the atmosphere was crackling. The bar was busy, the noise of expectation filled the auditorium. John Hegley came on and in no time had improved the mood of the audience immeasurably. He was to bring huge pleasure and joy over the next two hours as he and his band, The Popticians, played a set of hilarious poppy comedy songs, interspersed with beautiful comic poems from John, some of which I recognized from the previous Monday when the verse had reverberated around an empty theatre and died a death against hundreds of tipped-up seats. Monday had been an impossible gig and should really have been staged in the bar at the back of the stalls. Otiz Cannelloni, it turned out, was also a very funny comedian and a superb foil for Hegley as part of their double act, the Brown Paper Bag Brothers.

I saw many shows at the Empire after that and will never forget some of those nights. Lee Cornes and Steve Frost, as Dickie Valentino and Reg Prince, in particular brought the house down. Hegley himself proved to be an inspired and inspiring comic genius whose world view, through his favoured glasses, of dogs and passers-by, of unrequited love, belligerent in-laws, scoutmasters and furniture, is uniquely framed and heart-warmingly delivered. He was the most popular comedian in London by a mile in 1988 and he's still the best.

I went up to the Edinburgh Festival in August, travelling by coach and staying at a youth hostel, to try my act at the Fringe Club. The folk singer on before me had caused unease after one song, unrest after two, and unruliness after three. After her fourth song the entire audience was imploring her to eff off in unison. She did a fifth song, announced where and when she would be performing that night, and left the stage to riotous disapproval.

Then I was introduced. There was never any doubt that I would go on: I wanted to be a comedian now, nothing else, and I was going to take any gig I could. The audience talked all the way though my act but at least they weren't booing or demanding I leave forthwith.

Back in London, I booked myself in for open spots everywhere I could, and went along to the Black Cat Cabaret for my first paid gig in December. Piers divided up the takings and we all received £9. They were the rules, equal door spilt. Had Hegley been on, and the place packed out, we'd all have received more.

The main thing was, I was on the circuit now, and very happy times lay ahead.

Thank You

To Michael Foster for reading each chapter as I finished it and encouraging me throughout.

To Rowland White at Penguin for sound advice and discreet nudging towards a deadline.

To my wife, Katie, for giving me helpful notes on many of the chapters, for putting up with several one-sided conversations about my life long before we met, and for her support and kindness.

Sources

Websites

www.youtube.com
www.bbc.co.uk
www.cricinfo.com
www.motorcyclenews.com
www.motogp.com
www.football-england.com
www.newagebd.com
www.sportsillustrated.com
www.essentials99.com
www.suite101.com
www.unionhistory.info
www.strike84.co.uk
www.guardian.co.uk
www.comcast.net
www.aswa.org.uk
www.pure80spop.co.uk
www.answers.com
www.urbanimage.tv
www.comedy.org.uk
www.bfi.org.uk
www.wikipedia.org
www.geocities.com/paulwellerlive
www.1980sflashback.com
www.onlineweb.com/theones
www.all80s.co.uk
www.80scinema.com
www.football-england.com

www.newagebd.com
www.orangeamps.com/artists
www.thejam.org.uk
www.imdb.com

Film and Television

Together We Can Stop the Bomb (ACT Films for CND)
The Singing Detective (BBC Video)
Citizen Smith, series 1 & 2 (Universal)
Starsky & Hutch, the Complete Second Season (Sony)

Playscripts by Faber and Faber

Comedians –Trevor Griffiths
The Singing Detective – Dennis Potter

Playscripts by Methuen

The Empire Builders – Boris Vian
Fear and Misery of the Third Reich – Bertolt Brecht
The Mother – Bertolt Brecht
Peer Gynt – Henrik Ibsen
Barbarians – Barrie Keeffe
The Room and *The Dumb Waiter* – Harold Pinter
The Normal Heart – Larry Kramer (Methuen/Royal Court)

Plays in Penguin Classics

Plays – Anton Chekhov
Electra and Other Plays – Sophocles
Lysistrata and Other Plays – Aristophanes

Books

Collected Works, volume 4 – Antonin Artaud (Calder & Boyars)
The End of an Era: Diaries 1980–1990 – Tony Benn (Arrow)
The Making of Neil Kinnock – Robert Harris (Faber and Faber)
The Theory of the Modern Stage – Edited by Eric Bentley (Pelican)
Brecht on Theatre – Edited by John Willett (Eyre Methuen)
Brecht in Perspective – Edited by Graham Bartram & Anthony
    Waine (Longman)
Drama from Ibsen to Brecht – Raymond Williams (Pelican)
The Selected Letters of Anton Chekhov (Picador Classics)
The Theatre of Revolt – Robert Brustein
Chekhov: The Hidden Ground – Philip Callow (Constable)
On Being John McEnroe – Tim Adams (Yellow Jersey Press)
Serious – John McEnroe (Little, Brown)
Herzog – Saul Bellow (Penguin)
The Story So Far – Barry Sheene (Star)
Behind the White Ball – Jimmy White (Arrow)
News of the World Football Annual 1987–88 (Invincible Press)
Rothmans Football Year Book 1986–87 (Rothmans/Queen Anne
    Press)
James Dean: The Mutant King – David Dalton (Plexus)
British Hit Singles and Albums (Guinness World Records Ltd)

Records and CDs

Too many to mention, but in particular:

Snap! – The Jam (Polydor)
Café Bleu – The Style Council (Polydor)
Smile Jamaica – NME (Island Records)
John Peel (Fabriclive, 07, Fabric Records Ltd)
Brewing Up with Billy Bragg (GO! Discs)
Life in the European Theatre (WEA Records)
Live in Trouble (Part 1) – The Barron Knights (Epic)

Appendix

Sir John Biggs-Davison M.P.,
1 Whitehall Place,
London,
  SW1

12th May 1983

Dear Sir,

      Recently, I am sure you will have become aware of the controversy surrounding the construction of the latest nuclear power station. For the following reasons, I, as one of your constituents, urge you to support the proposed ban on such power stations in this country.

      Firstly, nuclear power stations are potentially very dangerous. The near meltdown at Three Mile Island in America endangered thousands of people. Such a catastrophe in such a densely populated country as ours could kill millions of people.

      Secondly, the C.E.G.B. has admitted that, for the amounts of money invested, the current nuclear power stations are producing very poor returns in terms of energy.

      Thirdly, the new Pressurized Water Reactors which your party are intending to build are even more dangerous than their predecessors. Some workers may be exposed to up to five times the radiation levels previously encountered in other nuclear power stations.

      Fourthly, investing in nuclear power inevitably leads to the development of nuclear arms, the biggest threat to civilisation as we know it of all time. Never before have we been on the verge of total destruction as we are today. "We are living on borrowed time" to quote Paul Weller, an idol of thousands of young people. The banning of nuclear power would be an excellent start in the struggle for nuclear disarmament.

375

Fifthly, the money spent on a PWR station could used to insulate hundreds of thousands of lofts, or to research into wind, solar, and wave power.

It is for these reasons I implore to grant your support for this campaign to ban nuclear power.

Yours faithfully,
Alan Davies.

An excellent well argued letter that I happen to agree with! Even if I did not, the letter would be impressive for the clear way in which you have presented your arguments in a logical sequence. You also urge the MP to act on your behalf.

20/25